The Charmed Door

Rod McBeth

The Charmed Door

Olympia Publishers
London

www.olympiapublishers.com
OLYMPIA PAPERBACK EDITION

A CIP catalogue record for this title is
available from the British Library.

ISBN: 978-1-83543-921-0

First Published in 2026

Olympia Publishers
Tallis House
2 Tallis Street
London
EC4Y 0AB

Printed in Great Britain

Contents

CHAPTER 1
THE SENARY DOOR

1. Vestige of the Machine

Rain falls. Down, down from the sky. It's time to take the motorbike to a parade of shops behind central, institutional buildings. These outlets spread into several back streets: a second-hand furniture repository happens to be just round the corner. Parking the machine, I walk down a wide pavement before the stores. They are due for demolition. Windows display phones, game consoles, "intelligent" televisions topped with faded price-cards. A stall aprons from a greengrocer's. Cauliflower heads with damp, rubbery stems squeak under the fingers of customers. A dog sits on a paving stone, facing the traffic.

After walking back to the bike, I rev it up and drive through wet streets to an arterial road. Central grass reservations contain shrubs, deserted amid the vehicles. There I pick up speed; the rain drills at my face, drains off the elliptic backs of petrol tankers. Widening borders hold fine transplanted cedars.

The machine thunders beneath me. It is a companion true, but impassive, committed in purpose. Only after a thorough drenching do I leave the arterial, cover a leafy residential access-road, take a passage intended for pedestrians. And eventually follow a minor, narrow road: it is surprisingly long, going far enough for a change of terrain if not of weather.

A metal gate in the road now marks the beginning of a concrete-paved avenue. After stopping, swinging the gate open, pushing the machine through, putting it on the stand, fastening the gate; I ride off over the wide slabs with feelings of privacy, seclusion. There's no litter no wear from tyres or tracks, I could be the first visitor for months. Driving further along only reinforces impressions of isolation and remoteness. The bike jumps on tufts of wet, grassy weeds between the blocks. It is necessary to slow down, some slabs are tilted, broken.

One wheel missing, a car rusts in the corner of a field. Any trivial such sighting is enough to uncatch rolls of tensed, trapped memories. Visual, auditory, sexual, secret, fleeting. Offices, bargains, a liquid oxygen transporter, vintage movies. Not-after-all-forgotten names zip through the head. Sentences, voices return sharp as bits of glass. Their remains flash purposelessly, randomly:

'sometimes he uses his finger'

'In the early, early days of space exploration'

'There's another do on the 19th!'

'...I overheard them saying...'

Shiver! Motor-cycling jacket and helmet are not enough to keep out the forceful, wet wind. But vegetation thrives brilliantly in this weather. Everywhere trees and shrubs display flushes of leaves, paler at the tips. Surely fast growth brought on by rain.

The avenue reaches a fork, marked by an old spreading conifer. My turn leads through a wood; the firs rise above because of a cutting through the underlying granite. Veins of quartz show, part covered by dark, sodden mosses. Rock-face and trees give way to a stretch of moorland. Treacherous with mud, the route winds and twists. There! Rising behind a clump of foxgloves appears a concrete structure, abandoned, overgrown. On one side trees cluster, beyond extends the desolate moorland. Toward this place the machine bears me, picking up speed.

The driveway leads to a wide access-yard, full of weeds. Drawing up but with the motor still running, after a brief pause at the bronze entrance I take the bike over to a nearby shed. Locking it there and stowing the cycling jacket, I walk up to the concrete emplacement. Turf squelches underfoot, long blades of grass lick at my feet. On approach, the overall shape becomes clearer: from the arrangement of windows or slots, there's evidently more than one floor. Yet the general impression is of a low building. Turning impulsively, I watch wisps of vapour moving away from the bike.

The strong, plain entrance is near a corner: the side of the trees. Steps apron out, leading to a dirty porch. For a minute water drips off, pooling around me.

The door is wide, its panelling discoloured by weathering. This entrance may not have been used for generations. Yet it is unlocked. With an effort against a spring closer it can be opened from outside.

Shaking rain back to the porch, I pass in. Almost noiselessly the door shuts, clamping darkness around me. None of the ground-floor windows is broken but there's a fusty smell, the air is damp, full of decay. Layers of chlorophyll lichens have filmed onto the reinforced panes:

they prevent seeing out over the moorland. After a while the eyes accommodate to dim, greenish light.

Empty! No sign of carpets, charts, office furniture, factory equipment. Flights of stairs, angled corridors and tunnels lead from the lobby; to the right the outline of another stairwell rises into gloom. But ahead the reception area continues as a passage along one side of the building. For some time I stand over a puddle of rain-water, looking at my faint reflection.

Light glimmers in the corridor ahead. This place is surprisingly large! From the floor faint reflections show through successive doorways: the passage is a series of doorless rooms. It appears to lead to a far opening or entrance, there's a small amount of daylight. In this direction I walk, subdued greenishness always to one side.

The reflections are dim because the corridor runs unexpectedly far back. But they begin to brighten, the passage leads to a final doorless entrance. And out to an extensive area paved with weed-infested, concrete blocks.

So the interior is exposed, vulnerable to the weather. During a storm such as this moisture gets into the passage, leaves and dead branches have blown in. But even after a brief poke around no rubbish, litter from bygone ages turns up. A curious medicine-chest catches my attention. Filled with grimy antique bottles, it is let into the wall.

Rain outside hits the concrete, fast-moving drops wrap its surfaces in a whitish fur. A tangled, grassy way leads into undergrowth. Filled with inscrutable clouds, the sky remains dark. Sitting on this final sill, I arrange a few miniature bottles. Refraction in the glass throws tinted cusps across the floor. Lightning strikes! There's immediate thunder, it has a definite smell. I take the darkness, the gap which leads in.

Almost empty, the passage has a few indistinct abandoned articles. Peeling cement just shows; without cornice the ceiling is of slab. But in the subdued light, so far I've encountered no further way in. What's that...? Facing the darkened windows! My position is halfway down, somewhere between the paved area and the front porch. No doubt about it. A door-frame can just be discerned in the shadows.

2. Senary, Charmed

Wide in proportion it is quite large, heavily coated in dust. The door itself is difficult to make out. Indeed while the frame can be seen quite plainly, there appear neither panelling nor handle. Probing where these might be causes the coating to fall. Underneath is a polished surface, hard and cold. My finger-tips produce a faint squeak: it is glass! The scored dust lets through light from beyond.

Repeatedly wiping at it reveals a dimly-lit hall. A filamentous, vertical channel appears along the frame edging. Thus it is possible on the in-side of this, to lean my weight. Dust almost rattles to the floor, the channel widens as the door slowly opens. It is easy to push it a metre or more forward: flooring inside is clean, free from all obstruction. The hinged barrier moves slowly, the glass as deep as a brick wall. Almost inaudibly it falls against receiving cushions then silently rebounds until coming to rest midway-open. I enter, walking through the space and into what may be described as a modern foyer.

Walls rise by several storeys, the staircase and landings have modular glass balustrade, stainless steel handrails. Raw concrete is visible in places, otherwise there are only opulent materials and contemporary styling. It's not easy at first to take in the faint scene. What illumination there is resembles daylight, yet as if arriving from a distance. Also it has a slight but definite colour.

This place could not be contained in the building outside! Its inertia impacts and receives me, informs me this is somewhere else, as different from past experience as from my own imagination. Perhaps there is no other life here!

Climbing the elegantly slung stair-treads, I pause once or twice just to perceive. On the in-facing side of the door is cut a fine hexagonal design. From a cloud somewhere, a word floats down. Senary. Wait! Is all truly still? Surely, there's been a shift, too slow to be picked up as movement. Some feature has altered.

Leading away from the first floor landing are wide passages. For most there's no illumination: one passage is filled with mirrors, even this soon gets

dark. But I steal in. Amongst the glass a right turn looms, it leads into another corridor in total blackness.

There is not a sound. Why not see how far it is possible to go? Becoming accustomed enough to see a short way down the turnoff, I notice a special door to one side. Yes, it's a mirror with a handle, the hinge is on the near side. Pulling it I swing the door open, blackness cuts along the other side. On feeling around, I discover the cabinet has a step. Stop! Was that a soft creak or footfall, down the passage on the away side? After squinting round, looking, listening there's no more, carefully I move forwards onto the step. About to put my full weight on it, the dry wood splits and cracks almost in two.

'Mind! It's deeper than you'd think!' Someone grabs me under the shoulders. One foot skids off the jagged step into space.

'Whoozzzat?' He drags me upwards.

'Careful! You'll pull me in too.' Finally he pulls his catch into the side passage, by the waist.

'Thanks, mate!' The operation makes a racket loud enough for three, for half a dozen people. Crashing, grunts seem to come from inside the hole, from the corridor as well. But the noise and echoes shrivel to nothing.

'It's worse than dark in there... never been touched by light. You OK?'

'Well, fine! Thanks a lot!' I give him a terrific shove, we play fight in the gloom, there are shouts. Someone tumbles against a wall. *Crack!*

'We've broken it!'

'No! It's just the frame complaining...' He gives it a comforting shove.

'...So. My name is Roland! And you are...' The stranger knows my name! He smiles, holding out a hand. We shake hands.

'What...! Howdy! Who are you? How come you turned up out of the blue like that?'

'Out of the *blue!* You can't be serious!'

'All right. Out of the black!'

'I'm your guide...' We walk back towards the staircase. '...Here to make sure you don't cause excessive damage!'

'Is this your home? Do you... own it?'

'Not at all. This place is as baffling to me as presumably to you...!' Indeed, despite encounter magnetism we're both compelled to look and gaze around.

The new fellow adds, '...You'll see what it is in a while.'

'The main door! Must shut the door!' Why am I suddenly concerned with this? Anyway, descending to ground level we stand behind the glass, its design on the side now before us. Snowflakes, honeycomb cells, the carbon ring. Everything in the etching is based on six. Both jamb and lintel are cut so as to let the door open only inwards. And once closed, there is no means of pulling at it from the inside. In fact once the cut-glass slab is back in contact with the frame, it'll scarcely be possible to even see a division from the inside.

'If you're wondering... it cannot be re-opened! But... you're right, now it must be closed.' With one foot he moves it slowly towards the wall.

'Wait a sec! Don't want to be thinking about going back at this early stage! But... stop!'

'It'll be all right,' he says, looking me directly in the eye, then suddenly giving the door a forceful push. I move violently for it.

'No! Wait!' However it is too late, he yells.

'Mind! You'll get hurt!' I spring back as my guide re-secures his position and pushes harder than ever.

At first considerable force hardly seems adequate. Then it picks up a certain speed, and finally, just before striking the frame, the whole door lifts up a very slight distance. With a crack it locks closed: the glass slams home with a dull thunder. Echoes boom and roll around the hall and through the tunnels for some time.

'I can see where you came from through the door!' We talk intensively, exchanging facts and information.

Mirrors carry further what light there is: a large one is fixed to the hall ceiling. Their reflections often include images of other mirrors. Occasionally, bevelling flashes with a faint, linear gleam.

'Why don't we look upstairs, explore there!'

'You bet...! Of course...!' He ascends the wide stairs, soon I follow. There are a few pictures which might be paintings, but direct light is needed to be sure. With the hovering of an edgeless shadow, the closer my approach the dimmer become the outlines.

'Look at this...!' One depicts a marsh with rushes growing out of it. The tall, indistinct shapes are familiar! '...Roland! I saw these earlier, just recently!'

'Quite possible...' His voice is getting further away. Where is he? '...Here!' Already halfway up. The man's a baritone, a tenor maybe. '...Come on! We've a long way to go!'

Two floors above, the stairs open to an upper landing. It passes all the way around the top of the well: there's just enough light to glimpse the central mirror. This unexplained world appears boundless. Yet it feels like only the outer layer, almost a deception, as if to be used to cushion my entrance to somewhere beyond.

His face is normal, average, no distinguishing marks at all, hard to describe. He asks whether anybody accompanied me. And I ask by assertion, 'There's no one else about. Here, I mean!'

'Nobody... where we are there's no one at all. But...'
Suddenly, he seems at a loss. '...Have to admit to you, I've
never been here before!' We lean on the balustrade, gazing
down, chatting... but even with the talk, hairs on my arm
rise... an attribute of this place haunts me. Sometimes it
feels no different from being here totally alone!

From nearby the top flight leads a bold, square-
sectioned passage. Another identical passage extends
immediately opposite, across the well of the entrance area.
And between these two is access to a third passage, also
leading directly away from the stair well. Against the wall
is a drinking-faucet.

'Yup. It works.' Straight away we are, shoving to get a
turn. The water is cold on the face, he flicks cupped
handfuls toward me.

All light here gives the impression of being second-
hand, the entrance is now at considerable depth. So the
weak, relative glare is enough to obscure details down in
the hall, including of course the picture of marsh rushes.

Briefly, I walk down the middle corridor. Here the light
progressively fails, gloom gives way to utter darkness. He
is behind, getting nearer. This far in we have scarcely
silhouettes to converse with, 'Er... to reach the weeds and
paved area at the back, had to pass the downstairs entrance.
I must have walked straight past it.'

'Uhhuh.'

'On the way in I scored patterns in the dust, on the
glass.' Now he seems to acknowledge.

'You mentioned finding concealed shapes in one of the
pictures. They appeared familiar?'

'So you do know what I'm talking about! Yes, downstairs. An image shows those very lines!'

'Coincidence.'

'Well, all right. But how did you just happen to be there by that ink-pit?' Arguments over this continue awhile.

Back on the landing we stand there, in the grip of true silence. Against it, every slight noise is sharply audible. Rapidly clasping my hands so as to strike the air smack-on makes a terrific noise. I shout aloud, do crazy things one after the other, the calls interweave with a series of echoes from ever greater distances. There's nothing here to stop me.

3. Life's Predicament

'Roland, ROW! *ROW!*' I shout his name louder and louder. But Row's riposte is to make a shocking, powerful noise. The screech, corncrake call is so much louder. Suddenly we pause, there is another noise: perhaps after all the din has disturbed someone. Now there is a muffled crash, like a building-sized object falling. But the sound is no more than a freak echo.

This man must be quite young, the clothes are easily described: fairly smart, casual, recent. But the physical appearance is very smart, especially the hair. It seems to have enjoyed years of careful, assiduous brushing, giving the demeanour of, say, the youngest ever Secretary of State for Foreign Affairs.

'What an atmosphere the place has! Do we rely on pure chance from here, Row?'

'No, shouldn't be quite that bad. I mugged up a few facts shortly before meeting you.'

'But this fine warren could be dangerous.'

'No again. Well, only if we ask for it!'

The man himself is something of a trap. Row catches meanings very quickly, seemingly before I have even spoken. Consonant but... extraordinary possibilities can now be taken for granted. Possibilities before ruled out for me, for everyone. So close and direct, he is the beginning of a world as different to me now as normality is to a baby.

The entrance area offers no clue as to where its passages may lead. By unspoken consensus we choose a route from this, the top floor. He glances upwards then gestures to a corridor.

'We should try to get to the other side of two or three rooms. They're in this direction.'

Taking the square-sectioned passage closest to hand, we walk away from the entrance. From floors below, glimmering very faintly via the outer passage, the massive glass door passes out of sight. Leaving this place, moving forward seems to bring a knowledge that we will not return. He looks around and at me.

'You may come to accept the natural world as more like a park, a wild tract contained within architectonic form.'

'Er, what's that?'

'Mountains supporting buildings... buildings containing mountains.' For a moment I have no reply. There's a hint of decor. The wide corridor and its turnoffs have pastel relief cornices, serrated stone reaches into the ceiling. The floor, the walls have a predominantly beige, yellow cast. We pass several recesses.

'An advanced civilisation?'

'Civilisation? Well, if you like. But as out of control as it is unlimited!' Striking, lucid designs fill the walls, the perceptions push aside thoughts.

'It goes on indefinitely! None of this corresponds with what I could see from the other side of the door!' Roland absorbs the comment, but carries on with more orientation for me.

'We have risen above, stepped forward from the level of your world reached further... into the unexpected, the uncharted.'

'That puts the best interpretation on everything so far.'

'I fear you underestimate the unknown.'

'That's an easy mistake to make of course...' He is keen to get certain ideas across.

'Life is incredibly, radically dishonest. But as well, the parts, the bits don't fit together properly. Here, where you have entered and where we, the two of us, are still entering, practical matters are liable to prove that life has set you up, and landed you with a problem... our problem...'

'Oh! Roland! Look at that!' The concrete is surfaced so that under a dominant motif, a raging river appears to crash out of the wall!

'...Are you listening?'

'Of course, I'm listening. Not only that. I'm wondering and... agreeing.'

There's a second drinking-fountain. Pausing by it, Row says, 'The basic alimentary functions can be taken care of by these tablets.' He reaches for a packet.

'Really?'

'There's a version with sparkly colours in the capsules that make you feel sexy! These are just to cover the primal needs…!' He smirks, handing me a couple of the large buff capsules.

'Great! Slurp!' Very cold water carries each down.

'Your ground-floor entry was only the preliminary…' he says, '…together we have to complete the process. This is because my task is to ferry you a chosen place. We've some way to go, obstacles to face. More really than a matter of covering distance.'

'Chosen place, did you say?'

'Very much so. In order to meet someone of outstanding distinction.'

'Well, very flattering. But why would this figure wish to meet me?

'From all the many billions who have walked your world, you alone are capable of doing what has to be done here.'

'Nonsense!'

'You'll just have to take my word for it. Not one of the others would be of any use.'

'Who is this person? May I ask, what is the distinction?'

'Her title is Directrix of the Presidium.'

'Directrix… Look at us! We're vagabonds, trespassers… we're not prepared!'

'There's no problem. Really, you mustn't think about things like that. It's true this is someone very highly regarded, an erudite statesperson, proficient in the four indestructible languages…'

'It'll be pleasure to accept the invitation.'

'I'd say you can hardly fail to find the encounter interesting. Her knowledge is unlimited; under the right hand the Lady controls an appalling instrument of destruction!'

'Does she? Well, you're right. Where exactly will the meeting occur?'

'Senator Aza will come in person, to a place accessible from here, to receive you.'

'Deeply flattering, great, but... here! Not actually in this place?'

'Further on, shall we say. Very little is known about this architectural labyrinth. But it is believed to give access to a place regarded as a safe option, acceptable to the highest levels of the Senate.'

'Safe from what? Are you serious?'

'By any standards the reception site is untouched, cut adrift... shockingly remote... security for such a meeting will not be a problem. The likelihood say of anyone barging in and committing an act of sabotage is just about zero.'

'And me? Does your government regard me as some kind of threat?' He does not smile.

'Not at the personal level.'

'What is the link between this meeting and what I have to do?'

'Lady Aza will tell you! But let me stress the Senator has a crushing, impossible schedule. Allocation of her time demands expert counselling.' To this I nod. Then:

'Hey, you were right!' Ahead in a straight line are two rooms. The first is coming into full view. It appears to be part-filled with cushions! Beyond its far wall, the passage continues.

'Yes, and we'll find another… Let me get back to this meeting: it's not yet in the bag. There is an element of uncertainty as to our completing the transit quickly enough. It'll be tricky, we'll have to be patient. But until it's accomplished Lady Aza may well have to divert for imperative business.'

While he's been talking a problem has appeared with the room now before us. Access is hindered by the floor, which is at least four metres below the doorways. Through the short continuation can be seen the second, seemingly smaller chamber.

But it is only a small problem: cushions inundate the room! The soft colours, striking designs form a deep crater which completely hides the floor. Heaped against the walls, in places they rise almost to the ceiling. Perhaps surprisingly no odour rises from the fabrics.

'Unless I'm mistaken…' He steps onto the nearest cushions. '…these should take us.'

'You'll drown!'

'They're OK, but you tend to sink in after a while!' I watch his progress for a while. Roland descends and covers the middle quickly, soon he'll be at the far side. Turning to look around the room, I notice two more doorways. But like some tunnels in the hall they lead into darkness.

Cushions reach to just below the floor; I step onto them. The yielding objects slide down the wall, exposing an undecorated, bevelled surface. Clambering in is easy; but gaps become unavoidable, soon I am buried to the waist. The lowest place of the room is reachable only by throwing myself forward.

Row has got out, using cushions that reach up towards the far entrance. He stands looking back, indeed appears to be looking past me and straight down the corridor we've just taken.

Once or twice the cushions reach up chest-high. Having assumed the shape of my body, they may as well embrace it with the grip of cast iron.

'It's not bad down here!' He nods without looking.

Unable to detect a lower floor, I grope towards the far entrance. Climbing up the pile, onto the threshold takes two or three minutes. Row has used the chance to go into the shorter passage; but by the time I get out and stand up, he has resumed gazing along the previous corridor.

'Stand here. No, over a pace, so you'll be able to see straight through the entrance hall. Yes...!' From this point it is possible to review the room of cushions, its etchings and mirrors, an onyx niche, its ledges.

'Now... do you notice anything?' I exclaim.

'You can see to any level of detail!'

'That is right. It's called unlimited visual acuity!'

Through the opening opposite I now study the yellowish passage. The ornamented walls lead to a gap, the entrance hall; and then into the continuation of the corridor beyond.

Surprisingly, my perception now reaches far into the remote corridor, where the cornices and skirtings converge to a distant vanishing-point. The more nearly does the gaze approach it, the more detail arrives of the many recesses and entrances along the way. However this exact point is elusive, to fix or hold it would take time.

4. Scale and the Metropolis

As we turn and make a move for the next room, he explains, 'The new acuity allows a glimpse at the vanishing-point itself. But then what you see is not located in the direction of the corridor. Far from it. You will see the place where we are aiming for.'

'Must try and hold it this time, Row.' I look back towards the stair-well.

'No need. Come on. You can try again from further down.'

There's an obstacle in the middle of the next room.

'Let's have a look at this well or depression!'

'Sure. Take care!' He follows as we pace the short passage.

Equal in width, this next room is shorter than the salon of cushions. Dominating the middle is the well: it is large but less than ten metres square. From the right wall, a deep slot opens into the side. And besides these rather daunting features, to the left of the far wall opens another entrance.

Closer by to the left is a smooth ledge, wide enough to walk around. It is the part of the floor not used up by the depression: The ledge leads to the only way out of the room. But to walk its length, it is necessary to negotiate a part sectioned off by two thin vertical marble blades or vanes. These rise into the ceiling; the bases extend to within almost a foot of the well. Moving inwards, we approach the drop.

'An empty shaft!' The vertical walls are metal-inlaid, golden or brassy in colour. Beginning at the mouth, the design snakes downward. Its development entices one's viewpoint ever nearer to the edge, in order to see further down.

Cautiously, we move still nearer. The mouth is finished in polished stone, to a depth of about one metre. Beyond the walls are highly burnished, their design is created by inlaid wire. The polishing is so complete that light entering the shaft is repeatedly reflected, illuminating it to any depth.

'Just a sec! I'm going to try something!' Lying very flat, while he watches I stick my head over the edge. Four perfect lines converge dizzyingly to a dot. It's impossible to tell whether light passes up the shaft, providing some slight illumination for us, perhaps even reaching the entrance-hall.

'A long way down!'

'Anyway the problem is getting past. The slot to the right...' He is looking into the well as he speaks, '...obstructs us!'

'What about the other side? There's no handrail of course. But surely we can go round past the narrow blades.'

'We can. We will... the depression could hardly have been full of cushions. But the slot might have been full. It would then have been possible to crawl over to the other side...' Now he glances upwards, appearing to be reading symbols from the cornice. '...This is a kind of apology for not offering you a choice, on account of the possibility of you rolling down the slope into the well!'

Gazing downward to maintain balance Roland walks fearlessly onto the wide, flawlessly horizontal ledge leading to the far doorway. He comments on the absoluteness of the drop as I carefully walk onto the ledge. After taking the corner we follow the wall to where it is necessary to negotiate two marble blades. Their bases approach the edge, but with ample clearance. Grabbing hold of one of the vanes I insinuate myself between; as he does.

The inside surfaces thus form a channel passing down to us. Row arches his hack then settles in a corner, hands behind the head. Leaning on the marble, I stare upwards. The cornice combines shading and relief otherwise the ceiling has no decoration.

'Uhhh…' he groans, now stretching out on the marble. '…That's better! It's quite possible to lie comfortably on a hard surface. Try it. Helps the frame.'

'OK. You know, I did try this one time…' For a while we study the ceiling. '…Yes, just like before it feels great, but it gets cold… Hey…! Row, was that… movement!'

'No! It wasn't. I know what you mean though.' Around edges and contrasts there appear changes in shadows, reflections.

'There appeared to be movement earlier, in the hall. Perhaps the shifts come from adjacent passages, from the depression.'

'I don't know the cause. Nor even where our supply of light comes from. But as I said, there's nobody else here who could have had a hand in it.'

Beyond the bottomless, unprotected shaft the facing wall consists entirely of mirror-glass, there's been no escape from its reflection. Row gives me a nod and gestures to the far wall.

Therefore leading our party, I get up, brush my front past the second blade, stepping gingerly, and move on towards the doorway which leads out. Joining me, Row glances into the unknown passage. The flat ceiling appears highly polished; further along another room can be seen. But he continues further round the depression, 'You see how from a certain point, the door where we came in and the two before are aligned? You can see right down the far corridor.'

'Unlimited detail! Startling effect... You said we'd give it another try?'

'Of course! OK. Let's go for the bullseye this time.'

After a few moments careful positioning, attempts begin to gaze further than ever beyond the entrance hall. Endless visual acuity soon arises.

'I'm getting there! You all right?'

'Sure!' Vision strikes through the room, the one before, across the foyer and straight into the remote tunnel. Again the square-sectioned walls appear to converge to a far-away vanishing-point. Attempting to fix this with the gaze is no easier than before, but I manage to look directly at it. There is a curious feeling, a knowledge that he is progressing just ahead of me.

A couple of times the objective jumps away from my gaze. But...! Done it! Before me opens an abyss run through with *enormous, really giant skyscrapers.* The viewpoint is far above the floor of a rule-straight canyon of vertical forms. From somewhere behind, near the horizon the Sun blazes, giving razor contrasts in illumination and shade. Slots of light, reflections from tiers of windows perhaps, sweep upward on either side. The shapes resemble no thing on a smaller scale. Above there is no wisp of cloud, the sky free of haze and dust.

'Where is this?' I exclaim and demand: but my words hit an invisible wall... it is a lot bigger than a city, way bigger. I did not know it was possible to look at anything so big. Yet it can only be described as a vast, modern city. 'Look how orange it is above, almost...' I grope for the chance to talk to Roland, he is surely less than a metre away; but we have had to climb separate pinnacles to gain our viewpoints. Each of us has become part of the brilliant, inert place.

Scarcely perceptible movement is enough to break the spell: standing again before me is one of the entrances, not so distant. And two paces away is Row!

'That... That is the very location where we have to enter!

'What! Never seen such large buildings! Were they buildings? There was something else...'

'Buildings. Er, yes, certainly, several things. And of course you won't have seen there's the foundations...' I move to speak but he carries on, '...They reach far enough down to form into a single labyrinth: further below ground level than the structures rise above.'

In a slightly raised voice, I assert, 'That place is dead!'

We return to the corner, pending his response. Those buildings could not fit into what is normally meant by a world. They rise above cloud level, into the stratosphere. I become tremendously inspired: fantastic ideas arise. There not only is scale different, there are no clouds anyway; nothing ever moves... not even the Sun.

'Dead? Yes, it is. Just a sec...' He peers upwards at designs on the walls and cornices, then points down the far passage. '...full penetrative access to that place should be possible from the room along here.' I grapple with the notion of actually visiting the super-city.

'To reach somewhere so remote? You said something about direction?'

'Distance, direction will mean little or nothing... because the vanishing-point is able to show you anything.'

With a brief upward glance, he adds, 'According to the cornice, we have no choice.'

Unsure what lies ahead we strike into the passage, away from the precision well. The area now behind provides some light, reflected by walls of polished stone.

5. To Ride over the Sun

'Hey, look... definitely brighter down there.' The passage runs into a half-panelled, untidy room.

'Well, if you say so.' The prospect is now so changed: perhaps we've taken a wrong turn.

'Uh... all right. Doesn't look particularly promising.'

He insists it is here we have to search. For a while forgotten items are surveyed in silence. A curious glass object rests in the corner of a sofa, some kind of mirror or prism. We pass amongst cased musical instruments, piles of photo albums. To get through! Like a railway station, the place becomes invested with departure.

Reaching a facing wall, I move very close to the oak wainscot. Without clearly-bounded shadows, its outermost surface becomes dark; light from deeper layers shines through a quasi-transparent veneer. My movements in front of the panel impose effects similar to those of intermittent daylight in a room. When darker clouds ride over the Sun, objects all around are seemingly caused to shift in one direction, and to turn slightly.

'Look! There!' Up on one side near the ceiling, is an escutcheon enclosing a small pair of doors. There would be room for either of us to crawl through. A chest underneath, large and very stout is obviously strong enough to give support.

'Who's it going to be?'

'You! You can use the shelves as a ladder to the top!'

'All right!' I open the chest. Climbing to the castellated rim is easy, if rather noisy. Further up it is necessary to crouch to avoid clouting the ceiling. The doors get within close reach. Its handles are knurled, to each I give a twist. There are unexplained restrictions.

'Hang on…! Something tricky with the handles…' Occasionally, it is possible to turn only one at a time. A metallic click!

He shouts, 'Mind!' The small doors open suddenly, to reveal an empty high-level closet.

'There's an inside door at the back, it's open!' To my surprise beyond this feature is a ceiling: detailed leitmotifs, touches of gold paint can just be seen in neat diagonals, some kind of circuit-board disappears into the shadows.

'Does it lead anywhere?'

'Might well do. But it's too small! No chance of getting through!' Reaching precariously, I am just able to close it. The inside walls are firm, they do not yield.

'Something's happened above the chest!' Shutting as well the pair of doors, I struggle round and look up. Along the ceiling just behind me runs a casing or conduit, perhaps for the sprinkler jets. From this a spring-loaded handle has silently lowered.

'Going to try it…!' Grasping the handle, I force downwards: with the lever comes a kind of skylight panel. Until opened the panel was easy to miss, being only one of many. Above now hovers a dark opening… lined with deep-pile velvet.

'Row! Where does this lead? Any idea?'

'No! Of course not. Not a clue. It'll be OK. You go first! Go ahead. I'll follow, we'll meet up.'

'Are you coming now?'

'Go on! Go on… I'm coming straight after you!'

I stand up into the space, feeling a vague rigidity beyond the soft lining. It's possible to get enough leverage to wriggle all the way through the skylight panel, but at the same time having to make a sharp turn. This is only possible by leaning heavily on a neck of the fulsome lining. The stuff gives a little, simultaneously, the skylight panel below me swings shut.

CHAPTER 2
THE COPPER PYRAMIDION

1. The Sofa

Total darkness. There is surely no possible return through the trap door, even if it could be found in the perfect blackness. Velvet absorption closes around me; the cloying fibres have an extraordinary feel. Odourless, they make a very faint sound when brushed: touch and hearing must be relied on to give a sense of progress. Shortly afterwards I hear the trap door again.

'It's me! Just here!' Faint sounds are accompanied by an assortment of grunts.

'We'll have to find somewhere better than this to pass the time.'

'Hang on. Going to sneeze... *Aghhh*!'

'This is no laughing matter!' Row's voice becomes muffled, I can hardly hear it. Alarmingly, we become separated. This is the opposite of being surrounded by brilliant light. But also an experience for the ensemble, the whole body; like plunging into a swimming-pool. No sign of him I just about manage to think, bedded in the silence.

Reverie is overridden by a vague, fitful awareness of moving along a particular path. Was that... ? A few more twists... There's the faintest light! Diffuse certainly... but most of it seems to be arriving from one direction, I try to move towards there. It is not always possible; at one turn I fall into a velvet crevasse. For a while, it cramps around me the oppressive blackness.

Grabbing handfuls of springy velvet, after several attempts on the cloud of light I reach a steep, pliant slope. Then, combining grip and propulsion edge my way up the surface. After what feels like much distance the slope eases, the billowing ceiling winds back and away. Slipping once or twice, I scramble upright and begin to walk forward. A glance to the front demands that I hold my head in both hands. It is not just the soft floor that sways the balance. Eyes shut! Look again... look down! I am now standing... on the padding of a *gigantic sofa.*

Steadying myself, I contemplate a whole scene, contained in a room or chamber of staggering vastness. Only by making successive forays into its reaches with my gaze can I grapple to comprehend the extent. The sofa rests on the upper crescent ledge of a tremendous amphitheatre-like structure. The couch is arranged beside many others, all unoccupied. Mammoth objects rest on the lower ledges too; the crescents are elliptical in form rather than semi-circular. Cutting down through the ledges are enormous flights of stairs or steps, they converge to a gleaming, patterned floor. One flight descends quite near; far beyond and very far above it rises an immense glassy niche, the colour of stainless steel. The sofa it seems lies nearest to the central flight, where the curvature is most gentle. Its L-shape confronts the scene, the corner therefore pointing back toward the steely glass. Reflections flash from the concave surface in vertical bars.

The air is odourless... so still it gives the impression of having never moved!

Nearby, is the rustle of satin.

'You're under arrest!'

'Roland...!' The joy of linking up, sharing an unknown adventure is soon sucked away, it lasts hardly an instant! The room appears as a terrifying wonder standing before me alone. By sheer will, I overcome the illusion by turning to him, saying something, '...Thought I'd lost you!' Row appears to have regained normality, but he hasn't. Trying to speak, his jaw stills, there's a gasp before getting out some observation.

'Ummph... Bigger than I expected. This must be...' There's a slightly smug smile. '...yes we've come out at the cushiest place, between the padding the back and the side.'

'*Ha, ha.* This isn't happening!'

'Wait a moment. Anything on this scale must be the stateroom of the whole tower... somewhere near the summit.'

Now we are part of the source of the mirage, far beyond the entrance-hall laughter explodes as conflicting perceptions knock one or the other off balance. Our sounds are at first absorbed, but then return as trembling, bending echoes.

'So... are you disappointed?'

'What? We've made it! Made it!'

'Shocking...' Unsettlingly, he goes on to say, '...It's a long time... a very long time... I've almost forgotten what it's like entering a high-scale interior.'

Starting at our level, the steel or mirror rises far higher than do the various flights descend. Indeed it rests on a platform, only a small part of which is removed to form the amphitheatre.

After a certain amount of fooling around, sobriety sets in. Jokes, we ourselves seem to disappear into a lost crevice of the vast space. Again it's necessary to clamber over and stare at him for several seconds; so forceful is the distraction all around. On turning away, there's the out-of-control feeling of being lost.

'Basically, we have to get across this room from A, here, to B, where the Lady is.'

'We'll never make it.'

'We will, we will. The two points have been plotted to be close as possible. Actually she won't be there yet.'

'Your leader will arrive by some type of aircraft?'

'Er, not quite. Look, I don't want to go into the technicalities now…'

'But I'd like to find out about…'

'Sure, sure you can quiz me later, there'll be time, but just now we should focus on getting over there, preparing and relaxing.'

Evidently square in plan, the chamber contains at its centre a copper-tipped pyramid, two visible faces rise high above all other architectural forms. The main structure is polished black granite, surmounted by a smaller pyramid of veined marble. And this is yet surmounted by the tip, a pyramidion of burnished copper. Just-perceptible details still arrive, surely… the pyramid twists gently as it rises. The edges are thus not quite straight. Indeed the faces are very slightly convex.

'This is a modern sofa, we're surrounded by contemporary artefacts, it's orderly, austere. But… surely everything should be in a state of collapse, run through with decay? Illuminated from outside, or in darkness?'

'Well… a dead city is not necessarily ruined!'

I nod slightly, but go on, 'The power's connected, there's water's falling, look… there are trees or cacti growing down there!' For a moment he is silent.

The steep-sided pyramid marks the exact centre of the appalling room. Everything arrayed around it can be seen, through air of perfect transparency, in unimpaired detail. The curved mirror behind us is one of four facing the geometric solid: over beyond the pyramid far indeed rises another, as to either side of all we see.

'Your senary door, the outer door… you were lucky to find it, seldom if ever has the cut glass entrance opened. That's why hasty decisions had to be taken: in the short while I've been guiding you, a safe location has been found, this building chosen… this room furbished.'

'Safe area, location… do you mean a safe country?'

'This site is secure, that was the priority. As to this tower, well what it contains has nothing to do with us. The room itself has been done up especially for you. Hope it meets with your approval, you can hardly find the scale less strange than I do.' Roland evidently expects me to swallow huge questions unanswered like how did they do it?

'It's an adventure! Tremendous.'

'I'd relax while you can. You won't be laughing for long.'

Obliques are pleasingly played off against the square. The room as a whole is symmetric: to every major form there is a symmetric reply. Yet everywhere are features which disturb this property.

2. Refractor

Gigantic seating-panels of the couch have scattered on them smaller cushions: as satin arrays, wide stripes in beige, ecru. Climbing past these, a mountainous side arm to the right, it is possible to see to very great distances.

'This room wouldn't fit into anything!'

'Admittedly, this is the main central chamber, but still just a room high up in a vast tower, itself no more than a sliver of frontage…'

I break in, 'You mean despite all this, we could be near the top of the city! Row, this is the future! We're in the future?'

'Well, something like that… the remote future, if you like. Look, if I were you I wouldn't place too much weight on the idea.'

We gaze far into the extraordinarily large room. There are several slender obelisks, altogether… of course… four. Surely, they are made from very light, high-strength building elements, maybe I've seen them used to support bridges in the most recent motorway construction.

The tapered shafts are equally spaced, each some distance inwards from a corner of the chamber. They are spanned by zig-zag girders so as to support a sky-sized, jagged square above us.

'Even ignoring the shapes, there is no way the hardest rock could provide enough strength, it would collapse under its own weight. The material must be very light. Buoyant! Why not?'

'Huh…!' Row draws in a breath. '…Look. Just where the square should rest on the uprights: there's a space!'

'There's nothing there at all! Just floating above!'

'But what holds it in place…?' The voice trails off, his mind on something else.

Offset, well offset, from the middle of these zig-zags rise smaller uprights. These support a smaller jagged square; thus the whole is repeated on a reduced scale. In the same way still lesser squares are supported, the process repeated indefinitely: the squares converge in spirals to the point directly above the copper apex of the pyramid.

'…If it makes any sense, this is just about the safest possible of all no-go areas.'

'Not your usual haunt?'

'On the nail. Explorers might get help from local people to climb an unconquered mountain… a totally new experience for both groups. Actually, this is a stillborn city, selected as a precaution.' As he speaks, four lesser pyramids become prominent. The farthest can be seen almost unobstructed, its left flank is occulted by sloping black granite. What did he just say?

'Pardon me… Really? Against what?' My guide gives me a glance.

'The alien child, surely through no fault of his own may have opened the door to ill-foundedness, retroactivity.'

'Disease? I'm some sort of carrier?'

'You are not. That capsule I gave you took care of such things. I was talking about blight, damage to reality.'

The elliptic marble recess is run through with convergent stairwells; these plunge straight down, reaching the vast floor at a corresponding curve. The nearest steps pass down out of sight, the walls are relatively close. This flight appears to be the central one; another can be seen descending, beyond a nearby sofa. Gradually, it sinks in that we are facing a challenge as he says, 'We have to make our way to the focal point of the room.'

'Have to get down first. Focal point? What is it? Where is it?'

'The key place. Not far. Where all the symmetries can be viewed to best effect. That'll be... Just a sec. Oh, yes' – he gestures – 'over there. It'll take an hour though.'

'Then let's go!'

'But you happen to be right, we've got a problem. Getting down!'

Clambering, the two of us make a diagonal across the satin material. Dirt, foreign matter is nowhere to be found; we aim for the opposite corner of the couch. Joins between the padding take some negotiating.

The furniture rests on a rug of its own, laid out on a larger carpet. At the far corner, a front sofa-leg runs down to the rug many yards below. In the motionless air we ourselves, sofa, carpeting, rest on the topmost of a series of ledges or terraces leading down to the vast optically-smooth floor.

The loose cushions are not so small: one of the silky haystacks has tumbled to the floor.

'What luck, we'll be able to get down!'

'Yes! You're right, it'll be OK to jump. So... you going first?'

'Come on! They may be decoys! Might be hard as rock!'

'Don't think so.'

'Well, let's check!' I rip off a shoe, and holding on to some trimming, hurl it forcefully at the middle of the cushion. It pushes in with a soft noise, springs out and to one side. Before there's time to comment, Row is already jumping down feet first, his hair rises. The whole cushion moves slightly as he lands, gets up and swings himself off one corner.

Get down! There's definite hesitation, I grab a hurried gaze out, out as far as possible across the abyss then whwwerrr...! I'm down with him. After rescuing the shoe, there's a comfortable drop into six-inch pile. Leaving the cushion, each of us strides through the dense mass of fibres. Again there is no odour, no trace of dirt, the long coils give way immediately.

The couch and its padding are now a multi-storey building above; but the loss of altitude makes little difference to the distant perspective. What lies in the near-to-middle-distance is obscured, nearly cut out completely. Still we spend time surveying and regarding the interior.

It takes will to gaze up at the ceiling: at first only a couple of impacts make sense. There's a middle, and a boundary. In these enormous curves gently screw round in opposing directions. The offset walls appear as immense pastel slivers, trapped between the grandest artefacts. Yellow, pink? The slight colour varies. Over to our right is another imposing mirror; on its far side a chink of faint blue can be seen. Similar hues appear on the canopy of squares, in places their floating shafts of stone can barely be seen.

The fabric of the carpet appears to stretch to the horizon.

'Somewhere in that direction will be the edge. Should give us a stunning view of the whole room.'

'Yes. But bear in mind the gravity here is normal.'

'I should hope so. That's just how it feels.'

'It is maintained that way…'

'Is it? Why would that be necessary?'

'…at all levels…' He gives me a look, letting the questions pass, gesturing to the edge. '…so take care, please!' Until now I'd not noticed that Row has a watch: glancing at it he says, '…Let's do some exploring!'

'Shouldn't we be steaming forward to this meeting?'

'There's no hurry. Something like this can't be a rushed job.'

'*Ha, ha!* Really? No, I suppose not.'

'Come on, I'll show you something.' No doubt about it, the two of us get on well. In a direction of away from the pyramid we pass round between the sofa and its companion. It stands to the left, I stare up at it.

'This piece…' Saw it already. '…back in the depository, remember? Piled high with cartons of detergent and water-softener!'

Passing through the wide gap, we continue… towards the immense niche. The curved surface rises far before and very far above us… no known vitreous material could withstand such weight. This is not quite pure mirror glass: fired into it is some kind of message or image. Our advance has nearly no impact on the apparent position. The sheer enormity of the reflections is becoming horrific!

'This is your civilisation, Row?'

'Ours? That's hardly fair. We do rather well… overwhelm and abolish the language barrier… travel beyond the stars. And then what? We find this!'

The carpet pattern is scarcely discernable. But in the midst of it the rests an object.

'Someone's just polished that!' Of all things, mounted on a tripod on the rug, is a sizeable refracting telescope, in full working order. Large, the instrument is to our scale, it's for us! Grabbing the barrel first, soon I have it pointing steeply upwards, the eyepiece adjusted.

'Only an antique! It's really powerful!' He comes over, has a quick glance and hands it back. Imaging on the vitreous envelope swims into view, upside down. Training the instrument on it, I obtain the maximum magnification. The work, which depicts the scene in another vast chamber such as this, contains detail within detail. Bringing a magnifying glass right up to the glazing would seem to reveal still more intricacies of the picture.

Besides the instrument, few objects are to be seen. Over to the left, on a scale noticeably greater than the sofa's stands a circular glass table. On tall legs, the cut disk gives an illusion of deep hexagons reaching down.

We push on towards the awesome metallic foundation of the mirror, but the deep pile proves too much. The halt is a chance to gaze up at the cylindrical recess. Its glassy-steel is three hundred or more metres wide, it soars almost a kilometre and a half to the dizzying cupola.

Attention now turns to getting access to the stairs.

'We have to reach the point where all the flights begin.'

'We've come the wrong way of course.'

Row agrees, 'Um. The only sure route involves reaching the edge and following it round.' There is little for it but to walk back over the carpet, the sofa now to the right. But as we pass the refractor he resumes gazing through it, 'Carry on! I'll catch up with you.' My guide crouches in a slightly awkward position, frowning into the eyepiece as if enjoying himself too much to let go of the image. After twenty paces or so I glance back: he moves, but only to get a better view.

3. The Future of the Pyramid

The vast room is modern contemporary, modernist. Ideas clash with cut-away ideas. The strikingly appointed interior is in clean lines, syrupy curves. There are tinted or transparent platforms which don't show any support. These do not move, they seem to have remained in place indefinitely. To one side is an alarming, witty artificial plant.

Where does the light it come from... the same which filtered into the velvet tunnel? The chamber is not in shadow, as it would be if light reached in from somewhere beyond. It does not appear as a negative, as it would if its objects were phosphorescent. Where is the orangey Sun? There are no windows.

Beneath there is no fluff, nothing but the material of the carpet. The textiles curl and flatten; following a rise at the hem the fibres shrink to nothing. Soon after the border Row catches up. He tells me, 'Swung the scope round this way. Had a look at the copper tip. Looks like the actual tip of the copper is made of gold.'

'What about the lighting, Row?'

'Puzzling, eh?' he gloats. 'Daylight panels. Incandescent. All around these panels give shadowless illumination, the output is low. Not just the walls, but the ceiling as well, even some of the objects.'

The marbly material of the floor is often laid in sharp contrasts. On this we pace, always in the direction of the centre of the awesome room. Moving on the flat, polished surface in so open a space takes getting used to. None of this is marble… none even is stone. No deposit could be found which could be cut to blocks large enough!

Unexpectedly, he stops. Feet wide apart, we stand facing one another. Quite clearly he is fighting back the joys of being in this crazy room. It's a moment before his smile fades, he draws a deep breath.

'There's a defect here, where you've arrived…'

'Oh, I'm sorry to hear that!'

'One which I'm sure you would wish to set right…' I gaze at him rather wide-eyed. '…It can only be got rid of through the application of your potential.'

'Surely not. There must be some mistake!' The smile returns.

'Let me reassure you: it will be a largely passive encounter, requiring hardly more than a willingness to give your assent.'

'Assent! To what…?' Speechless. With me too, even these revelations hardly shake awareness of being in the vast room. '…What kind of defect?'

'A serious one. We know what it is, what has to be done about it, all but all of this has already been done. The balance is now so fine as to be within a gestalt, so to speak. Fine enough to be tipped by your will alone. I'm not really authorised to go into more detail now…' I snatch in a breath. '…Shortly, you'll be free to question my superior.'

'Hold it… you mean you work for her? Directly under the Lady, er, Directrix?'

'Yes. And we expect that so will you, temporarily. The plan is to send you out to a unique processing site, to observe a confluence of events.'

As to this place I press him for information, we discuss it, but while Row is talking, I ask, 'Of course you'll be coming as well to this special place?' We move over flagstones of clashing textures.

'Er, no. The Senate will not agree. In theory I could possibly accompany you, but the Lady is advised by experts with technical knowledge far in advance of everybody else's. There's a chance, but it's highly unlikely they'll let me go in as well.'

'No... come on, this'll obviously be more than I can handle!'

'You won't have to handle anything. There's no need to go into what are abstruse matters now. You'll see why.'

'No, no. I'd rather you did.'

'We missed something earlier, at a more primitive stage of our development. An essential part of life is combing for errors and omissions...'

'What was it? Something in the past. Does it matter?'

'Even in an early, diminished setting this detail is very tiny, it is just a matter of dotting a letter i. Less than that even.'

'Well, can't you sort it out?'

'As I said the catch is: only you can do it.'

'Hmm. All right...' My attention re-fixes on the present. '...Let's, er, make the most of this room.'

Still acclimatising, we head towards the front of the massive ledge supporting the sofas. To the right is cut the stairwell: ahead objects resolve at extraordinary, far greater distance. While underfoot sweeping contrasts become replaced by text-patterns; these are on a scale small enough to read, together we peer at them.

'There's danger here...' I pronounce. '...The drop is enormous!'

'Well done again, you're a quick reader!'

'Whew...!' I look at him. 'You're right! I was reading the pattern, not looking ahead as I said that!'

We approach the drop. The sofas must be fifteen times, more than that, too big. Yet as we were saying, these are still small in comparison to objects further away. The scaling clearly increases with distance: objects before the amphitheatre look a hundred times bigger... for the remote architectural structures, for the vast room itself the factor must be more like a *thousand* times! Far distant, the pyramidion flashes against the pastel ceiling.

'So...there's absolutely no handrail or any kind of safety barrier!' He urges me to read.

'Go on!' I crouch down, studying the finer patterns.

'Gottit...! It recommends advancing to the edge and lying flat while gazing over!' This of course we start doing.

'It's like looking at a floor... with the whole room turned into a wall.'

'The drop must be fifty metres.'

'It's more! And this is just the top ledge.'

The terraces face a scene that is far away. It includes the beginning of an ochre or buff-coloured road. To either side are walls of angled granite plates receding into the distance. Water cascades over the cut slabs. Up the middle runs the road or avenue to a region which looks perfectly black. And rising from within is the stone-and-copper pyramid. Across the void, the air's stillness is surely total and complete.

'We'll get a better view further along, at the corner.'

After wriggling backwards from the edge we continue, the drop to the left. Well behind the sofa ascends the unsettlingly enormous mirror, a reflected bar dominating its length. The niche is so high its summit is steeply above. Something of the glassy engraving is visible.

'Row, getting back to the defect you mentioned. You're asking me to help you?'

'Yes, just so. Would you object?'

'No, of course not. But can't you be more explicit?'

'Visualise an imminent event and yourself as being the last person, the only person left to take it in.' Suddenly I start laughing.

'But I'd lose my way, get overwhelmed! What's this all about?'

'It is to do with the closing stages of the course taken… by the hexagon of life.'

'The hexagon! Really? When will I see the Lady?'

'Soon…' We pace towards the corner. Moving cautiously nearer the left to enhance our viewpoint he gestures downwards. '…After you get back, we can explore this room if you want. But it'll mean taking the steps all the way down to base level.'

Fresh warnings marked on the floor alert us to the corner. After several minutes we are gingerly crouching, then again lying flat. Near the very meeting of the crescent face with the stairwell, occupying these few square metres, we gaze over the edge.

'Look! This repeats at each ledge, all the way down to the floor.'

'Makes me dizzy… four stages. Can see every flight.'

We are on the immense platform which at the same fixed level encircles the entire room, and which forms the top ledge of each amphitheatre. The ledges below us are simply parallel, incurving steps leading down from this platform to the main floor. The bottom ledge especially can be studied: there are bizarre installations, outsize pieces of art brut.

With a slight sound Row pulls back and gets up.

'Come on.' I snake inwards and to the right, away from the corner.

'Have to be a bit careful!'

'You do!' Two metres in from the edge, our route has thus taken a turn to the right. He points out something, 'This flight is different. See… there's a sunken floor like a stage at the top of it, with small access flights either side.'

'What an insignificant feature. Surprising that it's there!'

'But can you see various items in the area: table, chairs, a divan? Our size!'

'Sure. No-one around. Deserted.'

'Well…we must get over there.'

Bands of text lie at and near the edge. On the other side it is possible to see behind the sofa.

'That must be… over fifty metres long!'

'Hey! Watch that drop…!' He continues, '…You may find this room rather much to take in at one draught.'

'*Ha ha*!'

'But... I don't know what sort of mood the Senator is in. The Lady might just show us something a whole lot worse!'

The centre flight rises into the vast platform area which surrounds everything. As we follow its cutting, the drop to the left lessens. Access steps from the marble stage rise to the platform on either side. And on this sunken floor rest the items of furniture: two or three chairs, quilted divan, narrow quartz table. For some moments, Roland has been gazing in that direction as if distracted.

4. Alter Ipse Amicus

Now, he circles behind and... calls out my name!

'Yes... Row.'

'I'm so sorry. I suppose we're not to be trusted. Just wanted to get you to look this way!' It is conceivable there could be people who've never seen a car or electric light; who are then confronted with these things: only to find the inventions seem to make perfect sense. This is exactly how it feels now, as I turn from him.

'Oh... so many! You caught me out, sir!'

Filling the stage area is a crowd of people. One figure – it appears she has noticed us – stands out, although for no apparent reason. Many men and women in close discussion stand around or nearby. Distances are deceptive.

'Keep in! The drop is still lethal!' We start walking briskly towards the sunken stage, bearing down on the area.

The last few paces seem uncoverable, until the access threshold provides a last viewpoint. We stand over the gathering, staring as perhaps at a news headline or peering as down a microscope.

Before turning to Row there's an impression of tall, smartly but equally-dressed individuals ushering people away from her.

'To avoid abandoning the central location, Aza uses a personal intersurface.' Without turning he whispers, almost hisses, '…This person is older than any of us!'

Even as the Lady deals parting shots to those around her, all are fading into memory, the last recollection is of someone joking. Only the Senator remains. The far-away authority motions us forward, before assuming a throne-like chair. Suddenly, we're rushing down the access steps.

Before us is a person of outstanding authority and dignity. The age is beyond all familiarity, elderly is not the word for it.

'Allow me to introduce Aza, Paramount…' The civilities are dominated by her gaze, it overflows with eminence, power. Her hair, entirely white, is short in fine curly locks. The cushions rest on a stone chair, perhaps obsidian or ignimbrite.

'You look well! Very glad to meet you…!' The words are clear, there's a smile, brief as a sword flashing. '…Roland! Much honoured! Come over, yes here…!' Row takes one of the fine chairs, I sink onto the decorated, mauve divan. The Lady opens with a sharp, declarative speech to the effect that a serious contribution is expected of and from me.

There are no deputies, attendants, bodyguards. But as he watches her from close by it is impossible to avoid seeing Roland anew. Somehow it becomes clear that within a normal frame he hides immense, robotic strength capable of shielding her from an unimaginable strike.

The statesperson fixes me with a deep gaze. Perhaps at last there are going to be some answers.

'Your astronomical universe is fine, indeed many of your theories are not so much wrong as short of the mark…' Roland moves his chair back a little, it is almost as if I am alone with the highest Senator. '…But there's more to it, a great deal more. You should think of the stars as raw land, hardly giving a clue as to the results of cultivation…'

'Such a mood has been building up anyway!'

'…Higher attainment, new advance only bring fresh knowledge of the greatness of darkness! As everything gets larger, the actual proportion we can call ours gets less. Take this tract for example: just the sort of unexpectedness we've had to steer round!' A glance is darted at Row.

'This place is made of paradoxes!'

'So! I understand you've been persuaded to help us.'

'That's correct, ma'am. At your service!'

'We're indebted… You'll be in a region much nearer your own world, full of quasi-familiar things. It lies just through that door.' The Lady points to what I'd taken to be a marble wall.

'There…?'

'Yes! You want to ask something?' The statesperson fixes me with a deep gaze. It is as if further enquiries from me will throw a barrier across the proceedings. But I push ahead.

'This room… Row was saying it's actually somewhere high up in a building.' Her slight, upright body tenses.

'Yes, you've got it. The whole building is itself a curved, screw-pyramid. This is its grandest room, occupying as many as a hundred floors somewhere near the top. All you see is thousands of floors above the main entrance...' A deep breath is needed.

'Thousands!'

'...This chamber is surrounded by lesser rooms. Others above form the apex...'

Again the Lady moves to break off, but, 'Wait! Before, er... what I mean is... the two of us were gazing at swarms of buildings, just an abundance of incredibly vast towers!'

'Yes. It was agreed earlier that Roland should get you to gaze along and into a vanishing-point. To appraise you of realities here.'

'But it looked like... a fresh corpse. I got the impression the Sun does not move!'

'The city itself, everywhere around it is dead...' Before I make the slightest move to speak, she concedes, '...The Sun remains fixed in just one place. You may find this baffling, but the evidence is this metropolis has never known any form of life.'

'From what I saw, death becomes it.'

With a gesture that this conversation must end, Row cuts in, 'Surely he should be allowed a proper viewing. Besides...' he glances at the floor. '...I haven't seen it myself.'

'We've an operation ahead. Time is critical... we can't let ourselves get diverted.' He is brave.

'But to miss the chance would be an outrage, so contrary to...' Anticipation flashes over his face as Senator Aza reaches for a control in her wide arm-rest.

'Some familiarisation now will be time well spent. We can arrange a short demonstration!' Row involuntarily grips his chair, looking at me with a wild expression. The Lady:

'Make sure you're seated securely. Hold on!' A key is touched: the pyramid... *disappears!* Something above the ceiling becomes visible. Indeed the ceiling vanishes: a huge structure above it comes into view, resting on flimsy, withering tails. From one side the full daytime power of the Sun falls on us, as bright sky eats the structure away.

'What's happening?'

'Don't worry! It's all still there. For a very limited period, it's possible to make our surroundings as transparent as vacuum,' the Lady explains, retracting her jewelled hand from the panel. Walls of the square chamber turn to a fuming smoke and dissolve without trace.

Most alarmingly, the substance of our tower itself becomes clearer than glass and vanishes. A material tongue is left in place, the very tip of which supports us. We see below the walls retract to the massive ground-level emplacement.

All around is amazing, Sun-baked vastness. There are forms, exterior designs impossible on a smaller scale. Serrated diagonals compete with swooping occultations. One building is the locus of a classical skyscraper as it moves in a wavy line. The stately apparitions do not even resemble machines. Made possible by super-light exceedingly strong materials, the structural elements are so slender that weight and strain can all but be ignored.

'I've never seen anything like this!' Row exclaims to Aza.

'Dire enormity!' There's a plainness to everything. The structures show a certain level of detail, and that's it. This city is about the buildings, it is only about the buildings.

'The metropolis stands alone in an unexplored, arid zone.' Our group contradicts the lifelessness of the place. Where it is visible, the horizon is perfectly level... this is not a planet! The curvature of the Earth can actually be seen from far lesser heights. And a vaster planet would crush the city under its gravity. Yet there's nothing virtual about this place! She picks up on my ruminations, her expression would befit a specialist passing on tragic news to a patient.

'Yes... miles and *miles* down to street level!'

High in the sky, the Sun's disc is larger than expected. A yellow sky extends beyond the summits rising to more orange, much darker colours above. One or two stars are brilliant enough to shine by day. Somewhere behind lies a pure black region, many needle-sharp stars glitter in unfamiliar constellations. But among them are several known constellations, but on a much reduced scale! There is Orion... this sky has nothing to do with astronomy!

There's no limit to how far the gaze can penetrate, how much detail can be taken in. Shimmering slightly in the heat, line of sight reaches through the towers to the surrounding terrain: it is possible to stare into a fantastic desert, to go on getting deeper into the intimidating natural formations. Scarps, faults, rocky basins extend without repetition. There is no sign of life, nor of any limit to the scarred surface even from this altitude.

'Do not underestimate the scale of the desert...' Aza too is peering into the far distance. '...the city takes up only a lost crevice!'

Some buildings are pinnacles, many others soar to astounding structural climaxes. We can see the breadth of one street, I dare not say how far down. In near panic I look up at something else. There are towers well larger than ours. At a point about level with us, one of these appears to have huge roads entering its heart! Aza speaks, 'You two! I warn you, this process uses up more power than you might think. It cannot be sustained much longer!' A digital pattern flickers and vanishes: we grab at the last few seconds of the scene.

The display falters. From far below, rising rapidly then all around us our tower re-asserts itself. In outline, the building fills the sky above. Sectors of ceiling reconstruct, walls re-possess detail in sudden swathes. The familiar lines cannot return soon enough. Exhaling noisily, I grin at Roland. Aza is the first to recover, taking a sip of fruit juice, she addresses me, 'Young man, take my advice: just regard this room as a place to receive you.'

CHAPTER 3
THE BLAST CONE

1. Remnants of a City

We take turns at a wash room leading off from the Senator's recess, not leaving the Senator alone. Yet during my turn there is an unaccountable, fading memory of having just left half a dozen people with her.

The contrast between my companions could not be greater: Row is inspired, braced by what we've recently been seeing. But Aza has adjusted already, so preoccupied as to have forgotten it. Indeed her advice continues, 'By the way, there is nothing else for you to fulfil...' With an ironic smile, she adds an aside to him, '...as far as I am aware.' Then to me, 'Once you've done what lies ahead, your time here is well... a holiday.' She glances back at Row, who turns to me.

'If you're willing to accept me as your tour guide...'

'Yes!'

'Senator, are you quite adamant that I cannot accompany him?'

'Of course. You shouldn't be asking, you're aware it's impossible. That would involve circumventing the very law which protects our visitor.' Once again the Lady turns to me. Embedded in the back of her hand, a jewel glitters.

'Now… as we've been discussing, we have a place, a task ahead for you…' Momentarily, her speaking is no more than a reassuring noise, invincible memories rush in. Memories of the horrifying realm beyond even this room. Visible between sheaves of towers were depths that defied the ground…

'…You understand? Are you comfortable there?'

'Yes. Fine…' There is a feeling detailed disclosures are imminent. '…Well right. The main questions are when? Where? Why?… What?' Row smiles.

'You'll be given concrete answers in the most direct way. The place will be on a scale more familiar to you, surely. You'll know exactly what to do…' As I try to focus and concentrate, a change occurs at the boundary of our sunken platform. '…It will be no more than a circumstance for you to fit into.' Now the change takes form in the rippling marble wall.

'Is that the entrance, Aza? I'd not noticed it… wasn't there a minute ago!' Row turns to her.

'Once more, for the sake of being clear to our guest: you are going to send him in there alone.'

'Quite so. As long as he consents…'

Lengthy assurances are given, a gesture from me satisfies her. Aza says to him, 'Proctor, this I know is a disappointment for you. I am sorry. You've already had your turn of course.'

'That was a long time ago… er, yes, true.'

'Right. Well now for background on what you will witness…' They break off on seeing me suddenly get up. '…No! Not yet…' Row is instantaneously on his feet and close by. '…I've things to say beforehand!'

'Is it all right to take a look?' The sworled gate is tilted so as to conform to the distant main wall, not the offset.

'All right. Don't enter though!' Pacing toward the frame, I gaze through.

'But this is somewhere outside. Out-of-doors!' Quickly, I turn to face Aza. To my shock both figures, indeed the whole vast room fleetingly appear in *black and white.* Abruptly colour springs back.

'What is the doorway? And that ash-tip... where is that place?'

'You faced a multiple entrance, linking different locations: where you are, where you can be!'

'It's possible to go and... come back?' With a long stare, Aza lets it be known this is the whole point.

'Indeed. The gate is even more versatile: "multiple" means the same interface can occur in several places...' Lady Aza begins a kind of prepared speech. '...Getting back in one piece will be enough. While away you'll undertake a wholly detached scrutiny. As we've stressed, it will be possible for you to see only a vestige of the true evidence.'

'Wait a moment, ma'am. I don't want to get involved in testifying, passing judgement... anything like that.'

'You must understand these events will be unstoppable, you'll have not the slightest control over them: alterations which can happen to the world only once.' Our surroundings, the main flight, the space which hangs before it gradually take second place to the discourse.

'Discovery, invention? Records, the wheel, weaving? Those sorts of events?'

'Well, the reflex of these...' she says rather testily, continuing, '...If all goes well you will contemplate a destructive climax.' There is a recollection of the grey place.

Roland suddenly contributes, 'Just an example, a hint of a development reaching beyond any scale.'

'Mmm. All right. So, when will it be time for me to leave... now?'

'Shortly! Not just yet...' Row offers her a glass. Her hand hardly moves in refusal, when to my surprise he presses it on me, as if we're going to be here a while, as if I will need it to keep up with her.

'...It would be imbecilic to claim that the world could guarantee an indestructible foundation for modern advance, without first getting rid of its greater part.'

'Er, yes,' I say faintly. As we speak, Row is somehow smiling and pursing his lips at once, while beaming down indulgently on the proceedings.

'But in categoric terms, this means oxidising all of history as in a reverberatory crucible. You will see the catalytic disposal of the tortuous wasps' nest at inhuman pressures, blinding temperatures. You will actually, personally watch history discolouring, smoking, deforming... vaporising!'

Re-seating myself up straight on the divan, I strive to assimilate all she says; helping this process by taking a noisy draught of the exquisite juice.

'...You'll actually see the substance of history choking on its own poetry, going sing-song while it is being *magmatised!*' From my eye she receives a steely glint.

However, the solidity of her words, the steady, vehement pounding are taking their toll: even Row is beginning to look glassy-eyed.

'Well, is that it my Lady... you've covered the briefing, orientation?' Wind from the entrance blows at her robe, at everyone's hair.

'Almost... Practicalities prevent you seeing history jerked up and down thousands of time very minute for hours, months, centuries even, all this repeated many, many millions of time over...' With an effort I stifle a laugh, but her gaze tells me that soon I won't be laughing.

'So too the application of the very fragile wand. Sheathed in glass, protected by electro-magnetic and strong nuclear fields, it is upon this filament that the whole of history is lugubriously impaled. Fully penetrated, in at the front all the way through and out the back, there is no hope of escape or survival. But on this journey you will not see it.'

'This I will *miss?*'

'I am again making the point that this is an occasion for the incident, the fragment of the larger picture. There are many auxiliary processes, such as the printing of history as a charred shadow on the wall by the very powerful light, which cannot be revealed.'

As we discuss these arcane matters, I ask, 'So with a hundred thousand others, I will watch this performance from some kind of hazard-resistant grandstand?'

'No! On the contrary. That's why my colleague, your friend Row has to remain here. You'll be entirely alone...' There is a sensation of adjusting, of coming to rest after a series of shocks. '...Besides those fleeing don't look for anyone else, it will be a waste of time!'

'Will I need to take supplies, kit of any kind?'

'For this short excursion, none at all. You'll find your way as you go along. It is a place you're sure to find interesting. You'll be able to handle it, able to get back.'

There is a brief silence as we face the pyramid in its appallingly vast setting. Then she tells me, 'It happens relentless demands are pressing. But be assured...' Her stare says these are not idle words. '...I'll return to this place shortly before the earliest time at which you'll be able to return. You'll find me waiting!'

'All right... Er, how will you know when that time will be?'

'To within a matter of a few seconds, I already know!'

'Really?... Anyway, of course I undertake to come back. Would it be all right to try a preliminary pass...?'

Row backs me up, 'That is possible?'

'Yes.' She turns to me. 'Go ahead. It's better that you do.' I spring up.

'Will come straight back!' Glancing at Row, sending her a half smile I dash through the wide, almost square entrance.

The ground slopes downwards. Hardly glimpsing back at the structure holding the interface and pausing only occasionally, I take in the scene. This is a wasteland on the fringes of a deserted factory: it quickly becomes clear how large it is. The gentle slope falls to an immense square area containing the sunken complex. Within this, awesome industrial installations rise into the sky.

I run to reach some vantage point in the desolate place. A large, broken rock rests on ash and debris. By climbing the sharp faces to its top, I gaze straight along what is an artificial escarpment. Soon it is possible to make out in the far distance that the perimeter forms a corner.

The entrance! Where is it? There... this side, it looks like part of this scene! Keeping the bargain, I sprint back towards it. It suggests nothing of what lies on the far side: near the threshold, a slate-coloured plane divides in two, not into areas but: life and room! The life subdivides into clothes, hands, else; the room into 'right angles, vast. Details play games with one another, as they rush in. Suddenly attaining completeness, everything is there. Wwoooooh! Back again. Back on the mauve divan before her chair. There is the impression the Lady was talking to a third figure, someone who departs as I return.

'Who... was that?' But she ignores my question.

'And you're all right? Of course you are!' I focus on the windswept site.

'That place *looks* cold, but doesn't feel too bad. How long will the trip take?'

'You will be entering an hour before noon. If all goes well, you should get back today. Be aware there will be... an element of danger!' Stiffening slightly and with a new seriousness, I reach close to her hand. The Lady acknowledges with a brief, slight contact. Roland steps forward, we exchange grimaces. Without speaking, I rise to leave.

From within the absolute stillness of the vast room, framed in marble, clouds can be seen moving. Wind snatches at my clothes and face as I pass through but it is hardly chill. Devoid of all decoration, the door emplacement is instantly forgotten. But recollections of Aza's recent, obscure words play like a record.

...Contemplate history torn to pieces and fed into cavernous, insatiable induction-manifolds. Hear the roar of the degradation chambers. Observe waste bursting from the awesome discharge horn...

The special exit is located somewhere near the top of the artificial escarpment. Buffeted by fresh wind, I spend many minutes taking in the scene. It becomes clear that one structure, a smoking chimney, dominates the vast site. A brisk and long walk lies ahead, the way is apparent. I take the slight down slope.

2. The Retort

A groove winds over the steepening earth-ash surface. I wrestle with the formations, trying to gain some kind of track or water-course cut by recent rains. All the while the distant basin and its purposeful installations call for scrutiny. Flues serving the complex are on such a scale that even from here vertical, ochre rust stains can be seen running down the concrete from the steel collars of the inlets.

A low cloud approaches the dominating chimney. Surely! The belly of the cloud is going to be torn by the chimney mouth. Not only anomalously low, the cloud seems to be made of tight stuff, that tries to hold together as it is ripped by the concrete, brick and steel shaft. The plume stains its innards, mixing only partially with the vapour. There is a period when it is not clear if the cloud will continue, but it passes to the far side. Amazingly, ribbons of it gently float down into the factory, some large enough to come to rest on the roofing while disappearing.

The scene is so compelling, detailed recollections of what Aza said are fading. What was that about a grand picture? Oh yes! Loaded words float back, aimed with accuracy and timing.

'Get ready to watch the very embodiment of waste-matter being boiled in acid!'

Near the rim of the escarpment and fused unintelligibly with one another, faint noises reach up from the complex, only to be carried away by the wind.

During descent the weather feels ominous, perhaps because the chimney discharges its plume so far up to the sky. There's a strong steady wind, often with a forceful gust or an occasional stillness. Clouds rush over me.

Noises increase markedly during the walk, generally sudden and alarming, even apparently out of control. Although no one is to be seen, either at work or simply about, the functionings do not seem to imply any particular automation, as with robots. More as if brute processes remain unstopped, without human supervision. Down now amid the desertion, everywhere there is sound without direction: grinding, mechanical impacts, vibration. Through this, a dignified warning seems to reach me one last time.

'Remember, there will be… an element of danger!'… Wind mindlessly howls in the factory roofs. Often there is movement, but only of loose packaging or corrugation torn from temporary sheds by the gale. Grey vestiges resemble people, vehicles even.

They *are* people! Many are getting into cars, the traffic is coming towards me. Swarms of people, men and women. Soon I am waving, within shouting distance.

'Are you all right? Why are you leaving?' two burly women shout back.

A man in overalls says, 'We're all leaving. Look!' He points to a distant part of the slope. It is carpeted with crowds of people moving up it, away from the complex.

'Danger? Is that it?'

'You must be cracked! You want to get nearer?' I know the answer to this. Explaining is not so easy, the main thing is to stick to the plan.

'So it is safe?' But how could this possibly be? I ask to myself.

Several speak at once, 'We can't say. All we know is we're not needed here any more. There's nothing any of us can do about what is going to happen.' Amazingly, I am stiffened by an unaccountable authority.

'Do you know what is going to happen? Do you care?' Sullen faces turn away, aside from one or two.

A younger man says, 'You can come with us... but you're not going to, are you?'

Indeed not, I think to myself.

He continues, '...I would never wish to be in your shoes. That goes for all of us.' He sweeps an arm to indicate the now thinning stampede.

'You might meet one or two more on their way out. Otherwise you've got the place yourself!' Soon only backs pacing way, retreating vehicles churning up dust are to be seen.

The way to the chimney base is wide open. Feeder pipes clustering around the area widen into manifolds of rusting steel, the surfaces have a roughened texture apparent even from here. After a further considerable walk, I approach and actually stand at the very wide foundation of the chimney.

There are steps to the top of a ground-level collar; after taking these I get a feeling of slight radiance, heat on the face. The base of the tower is so wide the curvature seems to disappear on getting in close. I glance up along the cat-walks fixed to the chimney. Before my gaze can reach the top, it is necessary to contort the neck, arch my body, roll back on the heels.

From the distant chimney-mouth, a rich, opaque smoke is unloaded; it folds with black force into the horizontal. Now and then an orange flame shows in a cusp… from the orifice, crackling outbursts strike down. This would surely account for much of the background noise heard from afar.

The edge of the smoke cuts sharply against the cloud cover: in a moment, the sense of their relative motion is exchanged; the smoke appears as stationary black ink, pasted onto a clean sky by flowing, inertial strokes of the chimney.

Steadying myself on the warm outer surface of the tower, I retreat a few paces and turn round. It's not particularly easy to make out detail in this light, but there appears no sign of the workers, nearby or farther up the slope. There were hundreds of them, with many more behind passing in the same direction. After so purposeful an approach, now it's up to me to get away from here! How much time is left is not clear. But I must plan a route, then make tracks.

Besides the several large flues running directly into the flanks of the chimney, nearby is a rambling, filthy retort-house, almost a small city unto itself. Rising out of this, an enormous S-shaped pipe swings round and plunges below ground level, while bending towards the chimney. From this the outstandingly tall vent is evidently fed, via a wide-bore flue passing under the concrete surface on which I stand.

Surely a knowledge of this place is likely to help me get away from it! With a cautionary glance upwards at the chimney mouth, I decide to walk round taking a look from the far side. Rusty, patterned covers clank underfoot. Up there…! Folding of the heavy clouds produces a short-lived breach. Amid the brightness comes a give-away… for a second and a half the Sun's disc rides in the vapours. Given the time, this is quite enough to work out basic directions.

All the way round colossal manifolds converge prior to entering the base. Continuing, I pass so as to allow a look inside the retort-house before leaving. From the entrance it occurs to me that, large as is the flue-pipe coming out of the building it is small in comparison to the girth of the chimney, even to the conduits approaching the manifolds. There could be still larger flues feeding the giant exhaust, there's no knowing what lies under the expanse of concrete.

It happens a road leads straight into the house, in fact past the retort itself. To the left is a considerable drop, on the floor below lie mounds of a grey, metallic powder. Chains hang in the darkness over this from a roof obscured by the immediate ceiling. Every few paces, flanked by steel railings are steps running down to a dust-heaped floor. It is to be emphasised the equipment is not an ordinary crematorium retort. This is an industrial retort, very many times larger. The pavement now passes close to the alembic or stomach of the apparatus.

Pausing to grasp a handrail, I look down one of the flights to see a dim, oval patch of light. The makers have inserted an oval glass window, heavy bolts around it make it resemble a port-hole on an early submarine. By gazing directly in, it is possible to see everything. After standing there for some time, while the level of background noise rises I learn the secret of the distillation-house. New, louder noises from below prompt a move. Further along the road becomes darker, but fortunately some distance beyond the apparatus is a door. I step outside, the retort-house now behind me.

At low altitude in the sky is a small blue patch. But as I watch it is shut away by clouds. Northwards between buildings appears a sliver of one of the straight dykes, these form the square ramparts. It is so distant that even in clear air it appears slightly hazy.

Using this, it is possible to roughly chart out a route through the factory complex away from this area, but one which will still allow an occasional look back. So after turning for a fleeting glance at the disproportionately tall chimney, I begin to stride along concrete roads, clanking weighbridges and metal grids. Bordered by grey corrugated walls, the route is cut through with railways. These run along the road or pass into the factories, pairs of rails flash in the daylight. The avenue takes me near, if not through numerous unusual buildings.

During this journey on foot, there's a rising feeling. One of being the last to leave the site of an imminent, devastating event. This could be the testing of a nuclear device. But the keenness to get away does not altogether overshadow another interest. This is the urge to observe things laden with all their details, as surely they have long been: acronyms stencilled on concrete pillars, yard-lamps, sirens, entrances, signboards. An urge to take them in now while there's a chance. Before the event for which they mutely, unknowingly wait.

What had Aza been saying? There were words I'd scarcely assimilated.

'...diametric   misinterpretation...   empathy   of penetration and elimination...' But the Senator spared no pains in laying out temptingly her many inducements. '...You can watch unscathed as history is screwed with unprecedented torque, round and round at appallingly high temperatures, made to rotate so fast that echoes of the whine seem to take twenty minutes to pass...'

'If I survive, that is!'

'...You'll survive. You can stand secure as you watch history flung from its terrace on a certain mighty platform, hurled into the abyss. And which platform might that be? The one so high that to it the most tremendous achievement adds only a modest increment...'

Your mind's wandering! Think! The route must get me away, but it must give me a view. So it should take a line as straight as possible to the perimeter dyke ahead. This would make a huge corner with the dyke just seen to the north. The square does not quite correspond with the compass: but the path will head for what can be called the eastern dyke.

There is the roar of exhaust. A car draws close, window wound down.

'What are you doing here?'

'What? You startled me!'

'You're not supposed to be here. No one is, not today. Too bad, anyway. It's too late to enforce the regulations now.'

'Is this yours?' I pat the scratched, dented roof of what is an expensive five litre vintage sports car. The body and inside are in battered condition, it has suffered deep grazes and impacts. Boxes of tools appear to have been thrown in and out many, many times.

'Of course! Like it? Was in worse condition when one of the furnace lads sold it me. Needed attention, a few parts. Look, I'm sorry I can't offer you a lift. You'll have to find your own way out. Sam and a couple of the ladies are expecting me at the retort house. Been getting together supplies. There won't be an inch of room. Have to go.' I stare at him, at the car, back at him. All I can come out with is a laugh.

'*Ha ha*! OK.' He is gone, and after a distant growl or two there is silence. It takes awhile to re-focus on the dyke ahead.

There are many types of water-tower: concrete, bulky, aluminised, utilitarian. The route passes fenced industrial estates From within these, here and there the sky is threatened by blackened chimneys. Some factories appear years, decades out of date... centuries even. Not only this: the styling of buildings and machines in a nearby estate appears unfamiliar, more than new, as if borrowed from the future. There is a mood of no particular industrial attainment, every epoch is represented!

3. Power

It is not possible to remain outside all the time: keeping to direction occasionally means passing through a building. And before entering, of course it feels safer to plan a way out. But this is not always possible, some mills are themselves contained in larger buildings: inside and outside become relative. Now there is no choice but to enter one such factory-labyrinth and hope for the best, for an exit on the far side.

The route thus leads through a dark, nearly empty shed. Like the retort-house it holds equipment on chains, every exposed surface is coated in grey dust. But as well the air holds a whiff of lacquer, some kind of proofing. One place inside has been used for loading, there's interesting equipment for manipulating and treating large rolls of paper. All is switched off, disconnected. Finished products have been thoroughly cleared, some litter remains: I pass a vat with varnish residue stuck to the bottom. Discarded curls of treated paper have been torn from completed rolls. Here in the middle of the abandoned, prefab shed the background noise is less.

Leading past floors at various levels, an interior walkway takes me through a series of unpredictable room-shaped spaces. These open into each other to make a single cavity; the roof is less than a metre above. The windows let in only a dim light, merely looking out into other rooms; yet it is not completely dark. The turns and corners end at an extensive closet. In this place, the background is scarcely a murmur.

This is the cabinet-work of a certain installation. That which is to cremate history! Briefly the threat from what is going on inside the retort is forgotten. Now the phrase: 'altered the course of history' sounds rather ridiculous. This is not to be the discovery of glass, the navigation of Atlantis, the invention of the power-loom.

Luck seems to have run out. Built against two walls, the closet occupies a corner. Reaching short of the ceiling, still it's high up enough for me to stand in. Opening the door, I enter near the middle. The fixture plops audibly, as thick felt lining inside brushes against the frame. Amid slightly more noticeable fumes of varnish several boxes are stacked, each perforated with patterns of air-holes. In this light, nothing can be seen through the holes: there might be danger of explosion. But the vapour passing through smells stale, faint. Perhaps articles in the treated paper were stacked inside, then left to dry long ago. A lanyard is fastened to the felt, so that from inside it is possible to pull the door shut.

Everything goes black, the background noise all but disappears, aside from a deep pulsing or heaving. But these effects coincide with... vibrations coming through the floor! This man's an ostrich!

In the stuffiness and gloom three faint lines show, outlining the rectangle of an external door. Stepping over various loose objects, I lean against it. There is definite give. More force: it bangs open. Out-of-doors! At one step I have exited from the closet, the cavity which contains it, and the prefab shed with its chains and mineral dust.

Duck-boards... the sill leads over railway tracks! Granite chippings crunch underfoot. There is the smell of dirty mineral oil, of coke, of solvents: not a weed grows on the poisoned ground. But to me the air smells marvellously fresh. What stands outside the shed door is of great interest, but for many seconds I totally ignore it, bracing myself and breathing deeply. The next few seconds I spend looking for the chimney: no sign of it, aside from a plume of smoke hanging in the sky and not-so-distant, bass noises.

On the rails by the shed, is a diesel locomotive. Silent, magnificent... it is so close the door almost struck one of the elliptical steel buffer plates. I push it closed.

Looking forward to checking over the huge loco, I glance up. Imbalanced cloud cover casts a peculiar light. Most of the sky is dark, filled with heavy grey anvils; but in one or two places whitish clouds are moving, and again there is a patch of blue. I knew it! How often this seems to happen: a full Moon appears, the colourless silver-white always it presents by day.

This locomotive is the only chance of putting real distance between myself and the chimney. It is up to me to get in and start it!

The engine rests on the rails, massive and inert. Scored metal steps lead to the driving cabin. I enter. This benign monster is larger than any I have seen before: calibrations on the dials herald a truly awesome machine. Still it feels familiar... once watching diesel locos from a window, I recall trying to decide whether the rectangular slabs of power were males or females.

To get more of a feel for the system, I get out and walk round the back; on the return regaining the driver's cab, sitting on the smooth seat. Much use has allowed an air pocket to develop, the weight squeezes out a stifled fart. Feeling the worn controls, it seems possible to actually work out by trial and error how to start the engine, without committing myself. Don't want to start something which cannot be stopped. But the push-buttons, handles, actuators are jammed, they do not respond to the manipulations.

An insect scuttles across an area of the console holding a red control button. It approaches the grimy disc with caution. Right and left antennae move independently. A dark residue stains the button. The antennae ignore this, to make contact with the red surface. Both antennae. Barn! Barn! There are two deep throbbing vibrations some metres behind, the noise of motors and gears, and suddenly the great diesel engine thunders into life.

Instruments indicate that the loco is equipped with batteries which slowly build up their charge from some source. Once the charge is sufficient, current will then be taken to operate starter motors, and this is what's just happened. Furthermore, the throttle is locked so that the idling rate of the engine will automatically engage drive.

The exhaust note becomes a howl as the engine takes on load, and the loco gently shifts forward. The speed, however, barely exceeds walking-pace. Without looking, I know the chimney is behind me. Still the controls do not respond at all, the speed holds for some time. The machine passes through a marshalling yard containing coupled mineral wagons, some filled with the grey ore seen earlier.

The system is accelerating, the engine note drops as a higher gear is automatically engaged. The throttle opens to reports from the exhaust. Now it would be impossible to jump out of the cab without injury. Continuous rail under the enormous weight sounds marvellous, if slightly unfamiliar. The climb in speed passes, the machine holds.

Most of the way the track is straight, but in some places the locomotive takes a turn at catch points, and in others the rails lead into and through buildings. There are walls largely submerged, their foundations underground. Turbines, bolted domes, anchored storage vessels, ribbons of parallel pipes can be seen on floors going down level after level, supported on immense rolled steel stanchions and joists. Indeed, other railways can be seen further below.

Something is going on behind the clouds, the Sun is trying to shine. A furtive sunbeam reaches the ground. But heavy clouds twist it away like paper. There are glimpses of distant ramparts of the sunken industrial city. One of these, that lying to the east, is evidently getting closer. It feels decisive... this is it! I'm covering the distance reason demands. Now it's all right to switch priorities, to let the threat take second place and instead to make the most of the opportunity. It's time to find a place to watch the spectacle! Well, Aza gave me a fairly clear idea of what not to expect. Just what *is* going to happen?

The track leads under a building, a brick warehouse or mill rising floor upon floor. The heavy, slightly decorative facade seems out of place amongst modern factories: from upper window-sills foxgloves sprout. The loco approaches an ornate, dirty arch leading through. Thus the bank rising ahead disappears; in the blackness of the tunnel, light shows on either side through brick cloisters.

Luck is with me, several things converge. At the far end, after leaving the arch noise from the giant motor becomes much more relaxed: by itself it throttles back. Ahead the rails gently curve away from the embankment, mounds of gravel pass on one side; immediately I think of jumping off.

But all attempts to further restrain the locomotive fail. The lower flanks of the east dyke rise from behind deserted factory and office buildings. The slope is now so close as to appear to wheel beside me, but there's no opportunity to give it even half a glance. Can't find any way to reduce the revs, or bring the engine out of gear! As the system leaves the bend, my efforts become more strenuous. A lever to one side might apply the brakes. With almost a frenzy I wrench at it: but then stagger backwards, rejecting the handle. A heavy steel pin locks the lever in place. With the locomotive now entering the straight, its speed begins to increase.

Departing the cabin, I climb down the steel stairway and jump, by kicking towards the loco and forward against the edge of the bottom step. And so fling myself off while trying to lose speed. Crump! A sudden dip by the tracks means there is a drop as well, making landfall rougher.

'Thank you!' Ridiculously I speak aloud, after rolling on the gravel and getting up. But it does not hear me. It is a machine, still accelerating. As the loco leaves, I stand and watch. A crackling boom accompanies a widening of the exhaust plume. Shortly after the track straightens, it enters another building. Thus I remain, staring at the space where the engine has disappeared, until its sound is gone. With one ear to the track, the scratchy ring of its progress can be heard for a fair while longer; the speed apparently still increasing.

4. Distant Escarpment

'Oi...! You all right...? Saw you take a bit of a fall back there.' My look of alarm changes to a smile.

'Is there no privacy in this place?'

'Fraid not. Not with a dedicated night watchman like me. Jeff, by the way. Not that there's "night" about it particularly. I am supposed to be here at all times.' Together we pace the gravel.

A short while after, we leave the track, it occurs to me the chimney should now be visible, back towards the west. The stranger notices me craning to get a look. But here at base level even its unusual size is not enough; buildings cluster around the large warehouse through which the rails pass. The chimney lies somewhere behind either these or the brick edifice itself.

'Magnificent is not the word for his plant. What it for?

'Full of questions, are you?'

'And observations. The central compound of the works is the retort area. Why is the output of smoke there increasing?'

'You'll just have to wait and see!' He swings round a stiff canvas haversack, pulls out a sandwich and offers it to me.

'OK. We'll do that.' Obviously, the best vantage point would be somewhere near the top of the escarpment. Turning, we continue briskly towards the foot of incline. Above the rooftops the black pall is visible, there is no question it has grown in bulk. Ground texture is damp, morbid: on the cinders are sparse, discoloured weeds. Jeff seems to be agitated about something.

'Look, I tell you what. You're planning to stay and watch. True or false?'

'Yes... True.'

'Then you can take over my responsibility. Aside from being here, there are no further duties. And I'll be able to leave.'

'If you say so.'

The nearby rampart meets the north dyke, forming a corner of the site: a road cutting through factory buildings gives a glimpse of the actual corner. Adjacent to the floor of the complex, this area of the bank is covered with buildings. Pipes, roads even pass into it; rows of street lights converge, their concrete pillars showing pale against the dark sky. As we approach the foot of a drainage channel, he issues a further proposal:

'You see that culvert. It leads straight up. I can reach the rim from there, while you continue toward the corner before making for the rim.' After swapping goodbyes and watching the figure climb the storm drain, I head northward.

Where the factories covering the bank do not give way to open ground, they have flights of steps leading up stairwells or against concrete walls. There are roof stairs giving access to the next tier of buildings higher up. Thus it is easy to ascend on foot, towards the summit of the artificial escarpment. Now standing on one of the roofs, still not halfway up the slope, I wheel round.

In dull light there is no glare; the air is clear, every detail can be seen for many miles around. No sign of Jeff... a stark brick tower rises to the right, the foundations are very wide. Does this rival, surely not exceed the chimney in height...? No chance! The whole view is dominated by one feature:

the large funnel of smoke straight away pinpoints the retort-fed structure. Orange flame surges at the vent, now obviously climbing further up. Attenuated by distance, and several seconds after each growth, a whispery crackling is audible.

Carrying on through the buildings, covering the distance up steadily rising ground, I reach a fine vantage point. The sky is shifting, voids appear between deep masses of cloud but these race past, seldom recurring: it is getting darker.

Now for a diversion: I must find a place to watch what happens. Further up something glints, from just by a reinforced asbestos shed. An ingot of clear greenish-white glass has been left to congeal to a solid. The hastily-made mould must have collapsed, refractory blocks lie nearby. Fractures pass through the ingot.

It will easily take my weight, turning around settling myself on top of the massive throne, slowly I elevate my gaze in the direction of the chimney. Well beforehand it's clear the flame at the tip has further enlarged: the surges and fluctuations are hypnotic.

Now near the top of the escarpment I've a clear view of the north-east corner, in the near middle distance. There is a wildness, the land has been raped by the complex. Evidently dangerous plant is sited in hardened concrete bunkers. Areas appear to have been reserved for testing explosives. Yet in several directions, between colossal industrial installations, streets of small buildings wind and extend. Steps, doors, windows, upper floors, shops are clearly visible. So. Roland has already seen something like this... we'll be comparing notes!

Continuously playing, flame surges up into the smoke plume. The black trunk is carried behind the chimney by wind, although it maintains height: never dipping below the level of the mouth, not losing a sharp edge. Around the lowest stretch, it passes over a mill. At first the building appears empty, it is possible to see through the windows. The heaving swathe then rises until merging with heavy, dark, clouds.

Amongst many sounds, the shattering of strong glass vessels is often heard; metal lengths grind together. Erratic, bright bursts accompany gradual growth of the flame, the torso of smoke bulges irregularly. Through the roar of fire comes a distant, expletive crackling.

The mill is not after all empty… at its brightest the light reveals a silhouette: a turning wheel.

Life! An animal like a grey dog, it's large, is running towards me. A lone scavenger disturbed by the sudden growth. It races past totally ignoring me. The beast is exhausted, it has run all the way up. Still, it shoots over the top of the dyke.

5. Titan's Goblet

The flame often exceeds the height of the chimney! Its smoke coils into clouds of its own, darkening and filling the sky. Frothing, agitated matter floods down the chimney. One stream of burning liquid reaches almost to the ground. To think I steadied myself there, on the warm outer surface! Whip crack noises ride on a dull, variable thunder. Pieces of flame become detached, flung forcefully, some actually falling to the ground.

This is the exhaust of many installations, the plume cannot be accounted for by the retort-house alone. Now the bottoms of the heaviest clouds in the sky are within striking distance of the fire and carbonaceous matters. Chimneys close to the furious tower begin to smoulder and spurt fire of their own.

The feeder pipes clustering around the chimney base come together as manifolds of roughened steel. Of course! The rough texture of the surfaces stood out earlier. Now the pipes glow visibly as they blast their discharge into the chimney. One of the pipes develops a more brilliant, orange-yellow patch. This lengthens, suddenly the vast pipe splits: incandescent slag rushes out, producing a frenzied reaction with the stuff of the ground. Bubbling slag appears to set hard, domes of it obscuring much of the chimney base; the solid has the effect of re-sealing the split manifold. Are the precautions I've taken enough? Even at this distance, warmth can be felt on the face!

It has not climaxed. The flame grows with sudden and tremendous power. The noise gets very much louder. There's brightening, heightening of the explosive column; clouds far above thrash into a dancing annulus. Balled smoke flattens, the black mushroom spreading out, very far out, eventually reaching the horizon, devouring it. Ground beneath the concrete and brickwork vibrates, buildings shake and collapse!

The insuperable energy of the fire is overwhelming! Even in the magnificence of the radiance and darkness, I am seized with another spasm of shock. Across the complex to the south-west a small range of mountains appears, the highest peaks reflect a ruddy colour, this is the first time

I've noticed them! In the desolation, I turn as if to Row. He is not here... this is for me.

Inexorably the rate of growth fits a curve, pointing to an explosion: the refractory chimney will split open from the top, ripping to shreds in hardly a second. The fire will grow and convulse, the core throwing out searing bars of light. Details will become discernible on the mountains. A few brilliant-faced objects capable of withstanding the onslaught will cast impenetrable shadows into the distance. Suddenly the bars will become a block of pure white: all that confronts it will be incinerated, vaporised.

But myself? No. Simply being here bestows a guarantee beyond all ideas of invulnerability. And indeed events override reason! For some time the metallic smell of the smoke has been reaching me. Exceedingly thick smoke now shades the central flame to a diminishing reddish-orange. Instead of fire being the threat it is darkness. The struggle has turned: there is the vile, obscene sound of the appalling fire *choking to death*. First the vertical thrusting is gone, now the body of flame passes out of sight altogether.

There seems to be no movement in the enormous, dark mass: as if the smoke above has solidified. Peering into the murk, it is clear the central fire plume has become vitrified ash. A putty-coloured solid, the material merely reflects light.

Flames at other chimneys fail, turning into fragile ash. There is light somewhere, but fast fading and disappearing. Every plume is dark. It is possible to make out little but the feathery silhouette that reaches up forming a roof in the sky, dimly caught by distant light.

As the air clears, the eyes adjust, I study the central column. Once a pillar of fire, now it supports a lacework of funnels and sinuous ridges curling into the distance. How long will this flimsy roof hold up?

Low and distant illumination leaves the ground practically invisible. Slowly levelling my gaze, gradually I notice… an inexplicable needle of colour. Passing to the right, losing foothold once or twice on the cinders, I'm in no doubt the needle is widening into a parallelogram of pearly light. Things beyond can be seen clearly. The vast room, Aza's cushioned chair… the Lady approaches, taking her place on it! Walking, staggering to the multiple entrance, I sway through and rejoin the company. There's nothing else for it, in sheer exhaustion I collapse onto the divan and fall into deep sleep.

'You must wake up now!' Where is this? In a garden somewhere? The stricken landscape is washed away, the dry reek gone; sharp, linear forms abound: back in the vast room! Astonishingly, there's an impression Aza is a young woman standing over, grasping and shaking one shoulder to awaken me. Row is close by, contemplating us.

The Lady's weightless shawl ripples with her movement. He remains standing, she resumes the chair, smiling perhaps at my condition. We talk, pass time taking refreshments… now there are baffling, recent recollections of having seen a number of figures, a crowd seated or standing around her, they were on the point of leaving as I appeared:

'Who were those people?'

Her eyes seem to recommend acceptance that there were no others; instead she says, 'You have observed the digestion and passage of history!'

'Umm. Did you see the build-up... the climax?'

'I knew the sort of thing it would be. Otherwise, no: it was for you! The memories can be left for later. You should relax now!' I take quantities of chilled juice.

Dreams of the industrial ruin are still falling away. Was it worth it? All but gutted with terror! To her I confess to now being in the strange position of having more answers than questions; then ask, 'Can we stay here?'

Row adds, 'That's the plan. It'll be OK?'

There's an edge to her voice. 'This room is habitable. It's been checked. So you both just want to remain and find your own way out... All right. That'll be fine.'

'Your glass.' Roland takes it from Aza and sets it on the table; now in turn she fixes each of us with her stare.

'Time has run out! From here then, you must continue as best you can. Take care...!' A roughness rises in the throat. '...Stand over there. Yes! Farewell!'

CHAPTER 4
THE HORN

1. Obsidian

The Senator lifts her right hand. Under it, set in the wide feldspar arm-rests of the chair spreads a chequered design, like a chess-board but cut along the diagonal. With the index finger, she touches a sequence of impassive squares. Then as Aza looks up: the lady, the chair, its plinth, all turn transparent. Seemingly from a point deep inside her shines a radiant light, growing brighter until it bathes the farthest reaches of the vast room.

For a few moments, the largest features, the pyramid included, stand facing the scene in silence: how can one survive near so powerful a light? A huge shadow forms behind my companion. Yet the emanation is subtle in colour, not altogether white, a satiny copper. For a while there is no variation. Now, as the illumination lessens, there is an urge to move forward. After a brief, final display, the light fades and vanishes. Aza is gone.

Turn! Yes… at least Roland is still here. For a time, we stand gazing at the spot on the floor, where rested the plinth of her chair.

'*Ha, ha*!'

'What are you laughing at?'

'The things she was saying!' The mood pivots to shock at our isolation.

'Maybe staying here wasn't such a great idea!'

Sobered by our loss, we wander the top platform. It is vast, of synthetic marble and otherwise quite featureless. A clear glass table stands beyond the summit of the centre stairs. Walking up to it takes time: tall in proportion anyway, on everyday scale the stainless steel legs are huge. Passing under the centre Row wheels round to survey the abyss; I glance up through the scarcely-tinted top at occasional items laid across it. We are standing in the central plane of the amphitheatre. Behind ascends the overbearing, steely vitreous envelope; owing to the room design it is offset to the left. But so with the other walls: in terms of the pyramid and its apex, there is symmetry in the whole.

'How did we withstand that light?'

'It passed through us... an hallucination.'

Suddenly, we gaze at one another, Row exclaims, 'Not the only one... was it? There was an audio signal. A tremendous sound!'

It is true. When Aza looked up and as her world turned transparent, a powerful, chord-like sound arose. It gave the impression of a circular saw sinking into a plank of timber. The signal fell away as the light faltered.

'The shadow must have been something!'

'Which?'

'Cast by the pyramid... onto the far wall of the chamber!'

For minutes on end there is quiet. The ceiling streamers somehow work with the offsets: the entire room seems to be turning, orbiting round the pyramid. But even from so appalling a vantage point restlessness, keenness to continue stir.

We walk forward, regaining Aza's sunken platform, standing at its rim. Below, the first of the series of immense and very wide flights of steps unfolds. They run over all the lower ledges, down to the elliptical floor and beyond.

'You've returned to what is only a reception-facility. We can leave now.'

'No, no! Surely, we should explore it. Some of it?'

'Of course! But you must still be reeling...' Memories of the ruined industrial complex flood back. '...Don't you want to rest awhile?'

'It's OK. Feel fine... I've done my collapsing.'

'You were in deep sleep. During that time Aza left... and returned to awaken you!'

'Anyway, the refreshments seem to have worked...' I gesture down the flights. '...Are we going to take the steps, head for the middle?' Scale allows the wide treads to be flanked by tablet-like steps of much increased size.

'Sure...! Let's go.' Exchanging a glance we take the daunting flight.

The descent takes a long time; with now and then a pause to look up at the vitreous reflector. It's a vertical sky, rising behind everything. Near the foot of each flight, a quarter or so of the steps spill out of the huge cutting, making an 'entrance pattern' before reaching the level of the next marble ledge. This extra height makes it possible to see more. It is awesome to have such depths, such areas spread out before us; while walking down... down... but without seeming to make a great deal of progress.

Of the recent journeys by rail and on foot there are forceful recollections. Images of the escarpment have not faded. For a while no word is spoken, footfalls on the marble are audible.

'I didn't understand what Aza was getting at, you know before I left until the last minute, the last second actually.'

'Now you know, eh?'

'The ramparts there enclosed only the surface workings. In places you could see underground installations, going down level after level...!' He is preoccupied, surveying the room. '...Row!'

'I'm listening! Tell me, did you wonder if a better vantage point could have been set up for you?'

'On the contrary!' There is something contrived about his smile.

'Or that perhaps a grander display could have been arranged.'

'Absurdly absurd!'

'Well, these might have been. But instead Aza insisted on going over the calculations again, to ensure your safe return.'

I draw a deep breath, and admit, 'There was danger. Had to move pretty fast a couple of times.'

'Of course. However... if you'd picked a slightly different time or place of entry to the site, the outcome could have been very different!'

'For me?'

'Not only for you. With a different set-up the event itself becomes different. Suppose you'd entered the complex using the coordinates we were given. Owing to a slight miscalculation which the Lady uncovered, to get you back we found that the multiple entrance would have had to have opened right next to you. I then would have had to push you violently to one side, while the baffles inside the entrance were closing!' Most of the way down lies ahead.

'Why? Because the power of the fire would have gone on increasing until there was an explosion?'

'Highly likely. Your clothes might have been scorched by radiation from the source!'

'It became so bright I could see mountains in the distance!'

He continues, 'You may find this interesting. The refractory baffles would still have been closing at the climax: a tiny rectangular channel into the vast room would have remained. Senator Aza's computation showed that a concentrated beam of light would have shone through, a beam so focussed it would have impacted and destroyed several square metres of the far wall.' This sinks in.

'Roland. Why did you not come with me?'

'It's true that because I've used an entrance myself to get here, there could have been complications. But in theory these could have been overcome. We did not give you the real reason.'

'Whatever the reason, my true anxiety was that something would spoil what was going to happen!'

'The defect of which I spoke is no more. It is gone! My presence could only have been a distraction to you. You have ventured through the outer or senary door, which opens only very seldom. The opportunity was too rare, the operation too important, for us to risk compromising it.'

It is so still. Profound stillness. Nothing moves, nor has moved for a very long time. Possibly nothing here has ever moved. This produces an alarming feeling, one of precariously leaning over time's edge.

'Hold on... Perhaps it's me... no... the whole room is slightly darker on one side than the other.'

There's a pause, then Roland agrees, 'It is... I hadn't noticed!

'Why would something like that take so long to notice?'

He has a ready theory. 'Because of the offset, the far right corner looks further away... perhaps that was it: we put the difference down to the distance. Look... it hangs in strata. Not smoke or anything. Just part of the decor!'

2. Hierarchy

'Have you been here before Row?'

'To this world-room? No, it's the first time. But... I was in the one depicted on the mirror's surface!'

'Were you? I studied the etching through the scope. Interesting room but it looked quite different.'

We are free to explore lower terraces of the immense recess: with one or two exceptions, the ballooned articles resting on them are familiar. In so wide a space, footsteps are not loud enough to ricochet. We fool around, make sharper noises, these have unique curling echoes. Suddenly, the backlog of questions can no longer be restrained.

'Why did those people with you disappear like that...? Are there millions of them? Trillions...? So we have this place to ourselves now...? Do you meet Aza regularly...? You're a colleague...? Tell me: will I see the Senator again?'

'...No kind of. Getting warmer. Yes. Sometimes. Yes. No. Exacting conditions have to be met, subtle protocols observed...' He smiles. '...before gaining admission to the world line of the Lady.' Now he peers at me as if sizing up a recent acquisition in a gallery. 'You would have to leave and then come back, and even then... Actually, it's very unlikely even I will see her again while you are here. Her seniority, her position in the hierarchy is so far above mine...' We pass down the middle of the flight.

'The hierarchy?' His manner with Aza was unlike anything I had seen before: at one moment the utmost deference, more even than I as a stranger and interloper could muster. Yet the next instant, he was joking with her, almost sarcastic. Now it occurs to me: not only in a different consciousness, I am in an alien society.

'Few but the guarantors of permanency...'

'Come on, Row, who are they?'

'...Members of the senate! It's a synonym, quite helpful, as it describes their only duty or obligation. I was going to say few others actually accept there is such a thing as the government. It's regarded as an irrelevance, a total myth. I take an assumed name, live in a common place, occupy myself with ordinary work!'

'And the vote? The veto?'

'Long ago we left democracy, indeed all other systems, corrupted or uncorrupted, far behind; we've perfected spontaneous government. If it exercises any control at all, it is by secret gestalt.'

'But you're keeping everyone in the dark!'

'The secret is anarchy! They're not in the dark. Everyone knows the score.'

'Perhaps I won't measure up to this society. It may take a dislike.'

'Why don't you take Aza's advice, enjoy the trip. I can't think you'd want to become mired in the sordid complexities of our lives.'

'Really? Sounds so interesting though!'

'You've made it possible to fix an unlimited problem. But. Just because it was a success: beware! Knowing how things are, they'll try to get you to help out with a couple more.'

'Do you mean that? Well, maybe… after I've recovered a bit.'

'Anyway, you've been warned. If you consent… at any time someone may try to bribe you to change your course…' I gaze almost straight down. '…you might be arrested for a crime you've not committed. Brace yourself to say "no" to older, more influential people than me.'

By now our descent has changed angles: larger features appear to have shifted position. He seems to be hurrying down, almost ignoring everything, keen to reach something.

'Sounds crazy, but this room has a quite low ceiling!'

'It's true. Reasonably aesthetic proportions, wouldn't you say?'

'Surely, I would. So this is the usual shape?'

'Not necessarily. The state room of a great building may well be deep, tall. Or wedge-shaped, or a…' Row inhales mightily, snatching out a handkerchief. 'Aargh… *ATISH*!' He sneezes thunderously, powerful echoes batter the vicinity. The man tries to make as if nothing has happened, but:

'*ATISH! Aatish*!'

'Are you all right?'

'Oooh… Yes, of course! Vehemently all right, thanks.'

'Did you know sneeze-particles have been detected travelling at supersonic velocity?'

'That's nonsense…!' He forcefully stuffs the piece away. '…*Ha, ha*!'

'It is! *Ha, ha.*'

In height the tremendous amphitheatre is well less than a quarter of that of the steel mirror. Our descent of it has made a big difference: overall designs on the piazza-floor are too flattened to make out, furnishings look more like buildings seen from street level.

'Well, go on. You were saying!'

'About other vast rooms? Er, I was just… Imagine the shape of a chamber inside a termites' nest. Or the shape of ashes after a fire has gone out. The concept of shape does not have to be geometric.'

'Look! You can almost count how many steps are left.' At this level, the patterns below mean nothing: cutting-sharp, polished divisions between artificial slabs draw near. The final steps are black, at last we reach the foot of the amphitheatre.

'Floor level! This could be as far down as we'll get.' It is made from synthetic stone! For a moment we relax. The pyramid glowers down, looking slightly bigger, nearer.

'You like lying on this stuff. I'm going to sit on the step!' Perfect flatness opens ahead and to either side, especially to the right. There is no particular incentive to remain at the base long, and after gazing all around and back at the overwhelming mirror, we head out for the walled road.

Very extensive, the open area is transversed by a perimeter road wider than the way to the centre. Thus to approach the pyramid, it is necessary to travel this width; with motifs of huge designs just below us. Near the middle Roland pauses to glance at something ahead, then turns right to gaze along the main road.

Taking in each side from the far-reaching plane is as giddying as repeatedly whirling around; after getting over it we carry on into the buff-coloured road. Flanked by stately, autocratic plates of granite, it leads straight ahead. The facings look even larger than at the first, disturbing encounter.

3. Foundations

The road has a slight downward gradient, so that the series of granite plates, which remains horizontal, appears gradually to rise. On the slope between the lower margins of the plates and the edges of the road are terraced gardens. These have shrubs, exotic trees, water-courses, fountains. There is a peacefulness in the deserted, silent room, in the immense pyramid. But I catch my breath as he almost whispers, 'Over there… to the right! One of the layered, dark areas!'

'It is…' Hair stands on end as I realise how near it is. '…almost next to us!'

'Look! It's all around that black marble block.' We walk over, causing us to lose sight of the layering.

'Mmm. Nothing here. Just polished walls. No windows.'

'OK, let's head on…' He passes round towards the back. '…Hold it over here! It's like an entrance to some kind of station, an underground maybe!' On the far side, hidden from the road is a wide downward flight, glare makes it difficult to see where the steps lead.

'Where are the passengers?'

Now he announces, 'This is an entrance to the foundations!'

'But we're a thousand floors up.' Row seems to be taking the find very seriously.

'You can think of the central pyramid as just the capstone of a much larger obelisk, which runs down through the building and into the foundations. The obelisk is hollow, it allows you to gaze directly into a black void confined under the foundations of the city. The whole thing is known as the reservoir.'

'OK. Let's do it!'

'We can't. The pyramid is too far away. But we may be able to reach the top of a very long staircase which leads down to the reservoir.'

'Then let's do that!'

'*Ha, ha*! You realise this has nothing to do with your meeting with Aza?'

'Who cares!'

'Look. This basement won't have been done up specially for you. And we're not properly prepared to go down! You're still interested?'

'Sure, of course… Let's at least see how far we can get.'

Only a metre or so below road level glare lessens, it gets much easier to see. After a fair sweep, the flight reaches a wide landing. This opens in all directions to an entirely different prospect. The self-luminous property has ended, the further down the darker it gets.

In fact, the entrance flight is black as coal. Grey and variegated marbles now make it easier to see. Surprising illumination filters downwards, perhaps as a result of alignment and reflection. The vast ceiling seldom completely passes out of sight; but as we continue it appears only in strips.

'Navigation has to be by light from above. Very little reaches to the lower chambers and labyrinths. Still it will be enough.'

'Surely not. We won't be able to see.'

'You remember staring earlier, over the cushions along into a vanishing point?'

'That was vision to any distance!'

'Well, this time it's... to any faintness. Unrestricted night vision, you could call it. Allows you to see stuff you'd never see in ordinary light.'

Our change of plan is like surreptitiously going from a shop into a stockroom, a place barred to customers. Although nothing is untidy, it is as if what is down here is not yet finished, or even waiting for disposal. And of course all is in night.

Row pauses, turning, hunting around.

'What are you doing?'

'Just trying to find the best route to the source of darkness...' He motions toward a handrail. '...We need to reach the beginning of the vast flight of stairs descending in the direction of the pyramid. The flight keeps going until it passes into the side of the shaft underneath.'

'What then?' Dark shadows fill our path.

'It's a sheer drop, straight down.'

'So from the top of the flight we'd be looking into the shaft from the side?'

'Exactly. We'll be lucky to get as far as that. And from there it will be only a modest viewing. Of course, we won't be able to get to the lower end. From there you could look vertically down the shaft!'

We make our way forward.

'This stretch here... there's almost no light!'

'It gets better further along...' Row appears to be concerned about avoiding a disappointment. '...Remember, I'm not supposed to be taking you down here. We might not even reach a true vantage point.'

'What actually is the reservoir?'

'A space, no more. But it contains voids which can only be viewed via night vision, in contrast say to the pyramid, which is best seen by daylight or brilliant artificial light.' The light improves slightly.

Razor silhouettes loom everywhere: a silent bust, a classical architectural motif, the outline of a machine. There are tumbling, sinuous forms.

'Take care! Slow down a bit!' Among the supports of a steep-sided pyramid are vertical shafts and slots.

In single file we take inclined galleries and wall-hugging staircases; with grasping or just touching handrails the going gets easier. A gallery widens into a cavity with a downwards-sloping floor. Vague, shuffling patterns fill the ceilings to the edges. He returns to the matter of the voids.

'The pyramid and the contents of the reservoir are opposed. In mass, material substance the pyramid is vastly greater. But in terms of emptiness the reservoir is infinitely larger than the pyramid!'

Visual adaptation to the dark has improved surprisingly with the passing of time. Above pitted bronze walls, there are still occasional flashes of the ceiling. But the great depth makes it appear hopelessly beyond reach.

It is easy to detour into cobweb-like galleries flanking the route. There are irregular cloisters or palisades. Are these here for furnishing, decoration? Do they represent some process long out of hand, which started quite aimlessly?

'We have to ignore the artefacts. Otherwise we'll never get deep enough.'

Eyes further adapt to lessening illumination. Sworls of greys, colourless reliefs, umbral streamers become visible. Shadows wait patiently to spring.

'Imagine how it would be to be alone down here!' It gets still tougher, ledges have to be felt where nothing can be seen. Yet he seems almost in a hurry.

Ahead, our sloping corridor is barred by a balustrade, the path branching on either side into short passages.

'This is the upper circle! From here we can gaze in.' As he speaks, there's a curious feeling that no one has come this way before.

The barrier is seemingly there for safety; its glassy material almost imperceptible. Gazing, raking to left and right the space beyond, it appears as pure black, a sheer drop. But... No! After long staring, we take in an awesome void beyond the balustrade, into which descends a bottomless flight. Undoubtedly forms hang somewhere above the stairs, although very diffuse, difficult to make out.

A recess of some kind perhaps. Is there slight movement? No, an illusion which passes as we become still. Yet dimmer images resolve, much further away! With passing minutes, every demand of the eye is met and more than met. Silently we gaze. At the distant perspectives, my jaw hangs open!

'Tell me what you see,' he asks.

'Everything is still. Neither natural nor artificial. Never seen so much information... Blanks suddenly fill with detail. There are no colours.'

'The key is faintness. Things go on getting fainter and fainter, there's no limit.'

'Yes... how it takes time.'

'Vision is capable of surpassing any camera. Remoteness and faintness go hand in hand: the fainter the light you're able to receive, the further you can see.'

Like two consuls, we hold the glassy handrail, gazing forwards. He explains that a very small eye movement can produce a whole different perception. For a while we are silent.

'Have you seen enough?'

'Er... What did you say? Hang on Rolls... Can we stay longer? The distance... this detail is far beyond anything I've seen before!'

'Yes, of course! The longer you stay, the better will your gazing adapt.'

A renegade idea takes shape: the flight is waiting for us. To either side of the balustrade are openings leading onto it. Fascination overpowers fear... the real challenge is to take the stairs... to gaze vertically downwards... After a short while, I make a move for the shrouded flight!

'No!' he restrains me. 'We are not equipped!'

'Ah! Don't know what I was thinking of Madness. Sorry.'

We take one of the short passages. Facing us in a vast cellar… slowly floating into view, are ascending steps. We pace toward them; above a slot passes straight upwards, shedding feeble illumination. The eye scarcely catches the surfaces of the steps: they are glass. Rising in a wide curve, the treads look perfectly black. The feeling of uniqueness returns, an intimation no one will again take these stairs.

After contemplating the foundations, we pass through sunken galleries with hardly a word or glance.

'Foundations provide support. Why doesn't the whole city collapse into the void below it?'

'Yes, you've got a point. The foundations, if there are any, will be purely ornamental. As I mentioned, gravity here is artificial.'

Somewhere a grey rectangle appears, lighter than anything seen for hours. Everything gets brighter. Soon it is a struggle to look at the dazzling room.

4. Urn

Overhead the ceiling is in full view. But still we're lost, not quite at floor level. Now with a sudden, happy appearance there are nettles or salvia plants, they hang over the two sides of a stone-like passage.

'This is it…' We are back on the pyramid road! '…Look where we've come out. Couldn't be better!'

Ahead in the middle of the road stands an unusually wide urn, home to a sub-tropical cactus. Judging by the size the plant is very old. Most of the spiny blades, lobes and branches can be seen over the urn rim.

'I'm whacked! Let's stretch out here for a bit...' Not waiting for a reply, I tumble onto a sloping lawn at the roadside. '...Look! I've some of Aza's fruits in this pouch.'

'Uhhh...! Thanks.'

'It's incredible what you can see directly above...' Craning my neck back slightly, the acuity returns... again I can see into unlimited detail! '...This is amazing...'

'...Uhhh... Row, sorry I fell fully asleep just then!'

'You did! C'mon. Let's make a move.'

The urn! How could we have failed to notice it earlier, there directly in front? The cactus is unmoving yet living and aggressive, certainly it has fearsome spines. Vital, exceptional, the outsize succulent looms down at us. It stands in an open vicinity, where we have resurfaced. This stretch of the buff road is just after the place where the series of reflective plates ends. Row gazes absently at the ornament.

'You got on crackingly with Aza!'

'How could a person in her position afford to have given me even a moment?'

'From where you came, it's possible no visitor might ever come again.'

Even though we've spent hours swapping personal details, questions and answers have flown back and forth, still the greatest questions remain unanswered. I strive to really get to the point.

'Her age seemed unfamiliar... trees can be centuries old. Frankly, she seemed older.'

'Actually, I'm a bit older than I may look. But I can introduce you to a shocking ruler of the underworld...'

'The underworld!'

'...Zircon! The sculptor! He's much older: someone of rank comparable to Aza's but less, really much less preoccupied, he is not jammed with schedules.'

'Now wait a minute!'

'You should take the chance of coming under his influence, he's a man of profound age. There are things he can demonstrate which I cannot.'

'There's nothing more I'd want. It'll be a matter of doing justice to the encounter.'

'You'll take him in your stride. It's true he's difficult, stiff. There are people who try to avoid him, the lectures, his strong opinions! However, I'm sure all this won't put you off.' The urn casts a vague shadow.

'When would you say this would this be?'

'Fairly soon... Then if we escape him, we can find a bit of anarchy, maybe by joining in what is going on.'

'Look forward to it.'

'You can get a glimpse of the natural world. See one of our megalopolises, live there for a while. I will take you to the last door, your journey home will be alone.'

There's almost a sense of foreboding centring on the plant, actually of coming mischief which must not be unsuccessful.

As to scale, the urn is rather larger than the sofa. More comparable would be the piece standing over the marble flights, a certain glass table.

Steps beginning at the urn's base wind round the outside of the narrower support. He makes a move, indeed going up here seems a great idea. Soon we pass into the bulky interior through a porch built from slabs of malachite.

'Look! Favourite stuff, this.' Brilliant greens swarm in weird shapes over the finely polished slabs.

'Yes, but it's not strong... lovely stone... easily dissolves away.' The staircase exits near the rim, facing in towards the cactus. The organism has several features. But foremost are the oval dinner-plates, lobes of powder-green flesh seemingly rammed together and arrayed with clusters of needles. Its patterns of defences twist and converge towards the tips.

'The size of it!' Underfoot tilled soil is firm, slightly moist. One feature Roland seems to find of particular interest: dry pods on some of the lobes.

Below the rim a paved pathway encircles the plant. This makes it possible to walk round, to study the clawing lobes against distant objects in the room, the pyramid and its boundary included. Soon Row and I are on opposite sides, he doesn't seem much interested in looking around. In fact I notice him looking at me, it's difficult to place his expression. Perhaps as a tailor, wondering whether a garment being tried will bring his customer satisfaction. Above Row's head, over a mile away two main spars meet spectacularly at a corner. He turns to the pods, looking them over,

'Why don't you take one of these...?' Dry husks, they are almost smooth-surfaced, perhaps porous. '...Here's a fine specimen. You know, there's no better way to leave this vast room than to get it to spit us out!' The pod is just within reach, I move my hands near to its sides.

'Spit us out?'

'Don't touch!' My hands stop short, avoiding the dry, fawn surface. With an inch or two before contact, there's no opportunity at all to pull: yet the withered stem gives a faint, brittle snap. Into my hands the pod drops from its stem.

'What is this? It's completely dry.'

'Full of seeds, wrapped in fur. Not poisonous.'

Examining the pod, I turn it several times. A small passage or hole which leads inwards marks the place where the gourd connected to the plant. Opposite this formation sprout bundles of dry stems, each with fine hair at the tip like dandelion seed. As I look Row raises his voice.

'Careful! Hold the furry end away from your face!'

'The seeds are protected with needles that shoot out?'

'Something like that. Try blowing into it, into the dark hole!'

'A wind instrument... all right.' Inhaling deeply, I lift the gourd.

'Remember, this is it!'

'What do you mean?' I ask, releasing the breath.

'Well, you might get another go... but this could be your only chance! You've got to really *blow!*'

Taking another deep breath, placing the pod firmly against the lips, I blow hard into it. Force is required at first, almost no air goes in. Then the seed needles burst from the pod, immediately it gets easier to blow. But by the end of the breath, no sound has been produced.

'So. You have obliged Ferocactus... look at the horn it has given you in return.' In places the pod has become iridescent!

'Go on! Try again! Do it!'

'You think it'll produce a note?'

'Move round, away from the plant... aim towards the centre of the room! That's it...! Up, higher...' Still he pushes. '...You've got to absolutely blow! This is your only shot!' Inhaling fully, really scraping the barrel, again I position the hole. Violently, I blow into the now steel-blue spheroid. With the first passage of air, a deep note emanates. Suddenly, there is a rush of air, indeed the wind seems to be actually sucked from my lungs. The loudness and pitch both rise. There is the feeling of having started something beyond control. The sound goes on getting louder with the draught! Possessed, I blow as hard as I am able. Just past the gourd in the direction Row suggested I can see a kind of wiggling haze, connoting heated air.

Echoes returning from the nearest artefacts already clash with the primary sound. It is possible to see like a bat, with reflections from individual structures.

In the midst of the effort, my glare hits another pyramid. Of glass! Wild. sounds return, they do not correspond to anything familiar. Shock-waves reach distant features: bronze curtains, fans of synthetic rock. The blast slams the far wall: scarcely diminished in power the echo charges back. As if acting by itself the pod falls to the earth.

Sounds arise like the opening crack of thunder, like an impending catastrophe in the foundations. Could this threaten the exquisite marble?

The volume remains very loud, it does not diminish. But... the energies distributed over the whole room threaten nothing, of course. There's no danger of seeing the beams come crashing down, fragments trailing powder falling unhurriedly. Of being crushed by masonry dropped from a mile above!

As the huge sound tumbles it is like hearing an extensive collapse, although the room and all it encompasses is perfectly still. More than once we are taken by surprise from the front, from below by colossal resurgences. But the great loudness has passed. The main echoes gradually recede and fall away.

Still we are bathed in sound of course: I turn to him, perhaps expecting congratulations. But he is looking straight at me, as if nothing has been happening.

5. Capricorn, Taurus

'Look, you must get ready for a spell of travel. We both have. You may find the trip alarming…' He lets slip a sly smile. '…Brace yourself!'

'Why? When?'

'You'll see! Soon. In an hour or so.'

Seed-needles slowly settle, some beyond and far below the urn rim. The majestic echoes plunge to their deepest levels. Silky, almost percussive sounds accompany them. For a long time, the motifs chase and play, as impetuous waves, stirring ripples.

'That's it. Over…! Hold on…' I glance round, half looking at him, half commenting. '… No… Can still just hear something!' Dregs of sound repeatedly postpone the inexorable advance, and eventual triumph of silence. Unblemished, unending silence.

To have stood on the urn rim long enough to be certain of the extinction, surely has taken an hour. From this fixed vantage point we remain a spell longer, surveying our place of entry to the room, the pyramid, the lacework evolutes of the ceiling.

Tulch! From the spiny nucleus of the cactus comes a sound as of a water-filled glass dropped to the floor. Rich, buoyant smoke is released. The fumes are dense, they drift lazily without breaking up. Raising my hand, fumes roll against it. There's a slight fragrance, as a neck of white vapour passes before my face: a length is inhaled. I cough and gasp for breath, taking in more fumes. It is just possible to stagger towards the plant, then sideways to get out of range; by now the whole body is helpless with drowsiness. Patterned sounds scythe through my head, as the drug's effects get worse. Twisting, fanning out to the farthest reaches of space, the sounds push away a straggling thought: the same is happening to Row.

Aiming to sit on the urn rim I slump forward onto soft earth, falling into a conscious sleep, the eyes not fully closed.

In seconds, an extraordinary thing becomes clear: it is not only myself but gravity as well that is affected by the fumes. Helpless with intoxication, in two stages up and along, I am levitated without contact over the rim of the urn, then dropped towards the hard floor. Falling to scarcely a metre from it, my sense of up-and-down abruptly changes. Now it is as if the buff-ochre road becomes a wall, a precipice with the vitreous hollow lying below my feet. Without any sense of air rushing past, I tumble ever faster back towards the glass-like canopy. Row can be seen clearly, falling along the same path but hundreds of metres behind My flight so near the road surface is not quite a straight line, it alters occasionally to compensate for the gradient.

Soon I am less than a thousand metres from the glinting vitreous reflector, approaching very rapidly. The amphitheatre and huge flights spilling through it seem very near. You might say the gravitational field again suddenly alters direction, but there is clearly more to it than that; for now I suddenly make a sharp turn, in the wide space above the floor, falling this time along the smooth-surfaced perimeter road. There is no curvature to the turn; nor do I feel it at all. Clearly my speed is still increasing, just as if falling in a straight line.

Elegant, off-set barriers and wall-sculptures whistle past nearby, structures further away move more slowly; the pyramid appears almost stationary. With my companion lagging furlongs behind, I drop at great speed towards another bend, no less than one of the four corners of the vast chamber. The wall side is decorated with a contemporary frieze: figures and symbols clash with panels containing natural cliff faces; Row appears as a faint dot. The perimeter opens in the new direction, passing outside one of the massive obelisks. Flashing just above the floor, instantaneously I take the corner. On the side of the interior, often there lie sunken tracts.

Guarding me like a steward moon of Saturn, my companion takes the corner far behind. But hardly can I make him out, acceleration is rapidly widening the gap, soon he will be invisible.

The wall to my right has abruptly fallen away at a different amphitheatre, it also is surmounted by a tinted steel. The pale marble ledges are ruled with flights of steps, but there are no sofas. Instead sculptural pieces in weathered steel, glass and stone litter the terraces. So fast am I now falling that even this powerful asset of the room is gone.

Once or twice vibrating designs appear, pure products of after-imaging and strobing. An attempt to interpret them is cut short by a dramatic glimpse of the pyramid and its foundations from an entirely different angle. This occurs just before reaching one of the far corners of the room, and there another turn. Very soon I will be at the immense mirror opposite to that of our entrance.

We are in the grip of forces beyond us; indeed Roland is gone. With a last, unsuccessful effort to spot him, comes a deep realisation of my position and relationship to the room. These are the last seconds.

There is time for a fleeting glance at the distant copper apex, before the amphitheatre gulf opens before me. I peer into the space: it is not quite the same as the one we walked down. The vast steps are punched through by an ornate, square entrance. At the point of reaching the plane of symmetry, there is a sudden turn away from the pyramid. I am leaving the vast room, shooting out of it through the ornate entrance. There are a few torn fractions of a second to arch round for a final glimpse. Then a last, abysmal effect of scale as the patterned walls snap past: the contents of the room hardly seem to recede, just to become enclosed by the shrinking square of the entrance.

Very briefly, there is the impression of approaching at great speed a much smaller square aperture, in the wall at the end of the huge entrance. Although surrounded by snaking, dancing patterns, it is familiar. In fact it is identical to the depression which came after the room of cushions. Now I fall straight into, and whistle through the ornately-tooled stone shaft, still accelerating. Again, the internal reflection means it remains illuminated: all the patterns can be seen in complete detail, vanishing to the perspective point before me. This point lies at the convergence of perfectly straight lines, produced by the meetings of the walls.

The inlaid metal designs on the four equal walls are so precise, so cleverly inlaid that it is possible to tell my own speed. There is no effort at all in seeing that it is what it would be, if I were falling down the carved stone shaft in a pure vacuum.

There are periods of unconsciousness or sleep. Each awakening is in the dead centre of the shaft, still accelerating. I am travelling at thousands of metres per *second*. There is no sign of Row. Time passes. Almost imperceptibly, but nonetheless quite clearly, I bullet past a point at which the field reverses. Now it feels like being shot up a square chimney. Soon the patterns as well clearly indicate a loss of speed, just as with a stone thrown straight up. I black out once or twice more, now travelling about the speed of a jet airliner, but steadily decelerating.

Otherwise perfectly straight, the shaft made two turns soon after the room, the first a right angle; the second, definitely not perpendicular. Now these recur, in backwards order. I spring round like some flexible object, never touching the walls but able fleetingly to look back. A dot…! With trainers, clothes, arms… he will close in a minute, in a matter of seconds.

What is that ahead? Where the vanishing point would be there appears an entrance! Of course: by the time I reach it, the flight has slowed down to no pace at all. Beyond is an ordinary room; half-filled with foam-core cushions. I charge through this aperture, and at that instant normal gravity takes hold. The room is simple, on the everyday scale. Entering it I fall slightly, describing a curve over the floor and landing on the soft, blocky designs. 'Stay away from the tunnel,' I advise myself, rolling aside and passing into long, undreaming sleep.

CHAPTER 5
ZIRCON

1. Zircon's Statue

Dreams! So strong… They swerve from scene to scene. No sense of having just escaped gut-wrenching vastness. There he is… Roland appears, but only as a chimera of sleep. Try as I may, he will not allow me to wake up.

I have another crack at speaking… now the effort awakens me. Yes, awake! Gone are dreams.

Cushions support me, quite a pile. Eyes wide and turning on one elbow I roll down, stand up. The springy, soft forms fill one end of an oblong room. The walls are of glassy, reflective stone. The ceiling, the gleaming marble walls share no cornice. An ordinary room. Where is the statesman, my companion?

'Over here!'

'Ehhh! Howdy Rolo!'

'Enjoy the flight? Evidently he's been awake for a while.

'Yes I did, very much! All happened too fast to feel scared. Still feel drowsy though from those fumes, you know, the fumes produced by the cactus.'

'Same here. It'll pass.' The air is fresh, not cold.

'That was flying in perpendicular gravity, Row.' For a while, we chat about the powerful horn, it is pleasant going over the details comfortably supported by cushions. Many scenes are reviewed: the place of the shadows, views from the vast flights of steps, Lady Aza. But he becomes restive, after a while interrupting me to explain a few facts; we discuss the schedule.

'Zircon tends to hang around here, this is his place. About as near the surface as he ever gets. Spends most of his time far below. The plan is to get you two to meet up, the three of us can then travel downwards together. There'll be every uncertainty. It's possible we may get separated! But if we do you'll be in safe hands. Don't worry about me, I can find my way out.'

'Mmm. Very well. All right... after all, I wandered the blasted ruins alone.'

'I'll mean missing out on the journey of course, which for me will be disappointing. But instead I can get the car and come round to the back.'

'Car? Your car? Sounds great.'

'OK. Then after this is all over, after we have taken our leave from the master of the underworld and his place, it'll be time to prepare for a long drive in the desert. You can get practice driving on the right!'

'Practice? *Ha ha*!'

'So. It's some time since my last call here. What I've got to do is survey the entrance area...' With a sweep of the arm, he indicates a lighter region ahead. With a small disturbance in the air, dust rises upwards.

'That's outside is it? Out of doors?'

'Er, yes, you could say that... kind of.' Roland stands up.

'You'll be back will you?' He is clambering down the cushions.

'Do you really think I'd leave you here?'

'Well, glad you didn't leave me under the pyramid!' With a short, benevolent grimace he is gone.

By myself then. Perhaps it may be wrong to say the room has no cornice. Up there is a progression of vertical red and black teeth of machined stone. Just below is a border, in the classical key pattern.

Each of us was flung from the mouth of a patterned tunnel. Where is it? Sensing a square in the wall to one side, I slowly turn while lifting my gaze. It is there. The ruled design vanishes to a dot at the very centre. Detecting no tendency to fall into it, I cautiously move towards one side. It hits: the square has no depth! Far from being a tunnel this is just a picture: exquisite, drilled into the stone. Moving up close, my fingers course over it.

Throwing cushions in the air, some up to the ceiling, another at the design, I make a series of shouts and vulgar noises. How loud they can be, with one hand clapped to the mouth. Perhaps he'll come running.

Descending to the polished marble floor, my eye catches a decorative frieze standing forward from one wall. The work is in the form of a series of figures, the first few no more than mosaics of coloured stone. Next come one or two figures drawn in the variegated wall. These are followed by reliefs depicting men and women. The series ends with a couple of freestanding statues.

Opposite spans a wide arch, on either side are more reliefs; through this is a floor of planed marble. Underfoot lies rubble, some swept up into stout paper sacks; perhaps chippings from work on the frieze. Further away the floor is free of fragments and dust. The polished surface gleams, in light already reflected from somewhere else. There's a mild chill, carried by a breeze. Flanked on either side by caryatids, I stare into the marble chambers.

Returning to study the fine sculpting, this entails examining more carefully the true statues, there are three. Following on from the deeper reliefs, all are surprisingly life-like. Very finely carved from alabaster and marble, the middle one has piercing eyes. The irises glint with grains of mica.

There's a feeling of obligation, not so much as to wonder when Roland will show up, as to try use his absence to organise my recent memories. How long have I been in this realm? Hours? Days? Weeks? As I try to grapple with time and distance, though, a new compulsion takes hold. Nothing preoccupies me more than the last figure in the sequence.

Breathtakingly life-like, it depicts the wiry but upright figure of an old man. Old certainly, a very old man; but virility, strength are extraordinarily apparent. In one hand he holds a steel instrument, a sharp-tipped incisor or piton. Scrutinising the mass of lines scoring the face and neck, I gaze into the eyes. After peering into their sparkling, black depth for an unexpectedly long time, I convulse with fright: this is no statue! I am looking into the eyes of another man! Movement. He bows his head slightly, without breaking his compelling, penetrating gaze.

'How are you? You two have awakened from a long sleep. Welcome! I am *Zircon!*'

'All right thanks! How do you do, Zircon? Wow! I mistook you for one of your statues. I am, er... my name is...' We shake hands. '...But where's Row? What happened to Roland?'

'He awakened first. I tried to dismiss him...'

'What?'

'Without success... as usual with him.' There's humour in his eye. '...Be patient.' The sculptor appears to grow as he springs down from his frieze.

'Row spoke of you before we came here. We discussed you.'

'So, pleased to meet you! With the pair of you asleep on the cushions, of course I had to work quietly. You slept deeply, as did your companion!' Older than me by many... generations... it's impossible... by centuries... his voice is sharp, baritone. The eyes are commanding, they imply skill, power, accomplishment; but somewhere as well amusement, warmth.

'Certainly I was out cold! So tired, from... memories of snaking patterns flashing past... a very fast journey, from somewhere you must let me describe!'

Quietly tapping his forehead, and without explanation, he says, 'Roland's on his way back here!'

'How do you know, sir?' Zircon ignores me, grabbing one arm.

'Come! This way, have a look at the entrance to the marble halls. It is through this that an occasional wind blows. Perhaps you have already noticed it?'

'Just a zephyr. Tell me, did you work on that frieze alone? And the statues? I've never seen such work!'

'They're worth a glance? Thank you. I use machines of course, as well as. classical implements.'

Now Zircon gazes through the arch while speaking.

'These halls are entrances to a labyrinth. The innermost culmination of it forms a maze, a celebrated maze!'

'Can we go there? Is that, er... somewhere we're all scheduled to visit?'

'Of course! Indeed it is, although it lies very deep. We will have to take care... pick up Roland... otherwise there is nothing to prevent us leaving now.'

'Sounds really fine! Very interesting.' He turns to face me then slings his metal instrument onto the small pile of rubble, the steel ringing loudly as it strikes the stones.

Glancing at the paper sacks, he adds, 'The idea is to avoid wastage. That marble can be powdered and ground up with lime, to make stucco. You'll probably see some of the mouldings. Hold it! Hear that?' There are footfalls.

'Yes. Someone!' A figure appears, there are whitish, powdery streaks on the clothes.

'Guess who it is?' Row!

'So where have you been?'

'Just having a casual look around. Checking that Zircon's work is up to scratch! You well? No jet-lag?'

'Better than ever! We're going to this maze... Are you ready to leave more or less straight away?'

The sculptor cuts in, 'How is dear Aza?'

'Can't keep up with her. But then, nor can you!'

'And our guest? When you're not passing the time throwing him down a depression, did you manage to get any work done?'

'That reminds me…' Abruptly, with one or two polite disclaimers to me, the pair engage over statecraft, none of it sensible to me. Suddenly an argument breaks out. They go at it hammer and tongs, as if I am not here. Breaking a brief silence, Roland turns to me.

'The maze did you say…?' But before I can reply he rushes in with. '…Raring to go. Actually I've already done the trip, a long time ago.'

Zircon turns on his heel, rather brusquely addressing me, 'Little more than resolve to penetrate the core of the maze will be required!' With similar instructions to Roland, to whom he proffers hardly a glance, the mason walks away, motioning me to follow. But instead of course I ask my pal what's going to happen next.

'He's someone who will guide us further into your world?'

'He's our best bet, anyway.'

'That sounds a bit shaky… really? If you say so, Row.'

'Remember, finding the old fellow was only our first problem. Worse will follow!'

'*Ha, ha.* What do you mean?'

'It's liable to be rather tricky handing you over to his charge, and making the whole process stick.'

'No, no, come on, I'm truly looking forward to this. But… "handing me over"? You're coming as well?'

'It's hard to see ahead. Something is going to go wrong, I know it. We've had it far too easy.' But the sculptor strides far ahead; he takes a corner and disappears from view.

'Hold on… Where is he?'

'He went down there.'

2. Sun Portal

'I know. But then which way?' There is nothing for it but to take a chance: he motions down one branch of an ornate passage. Even as we are getting lost, I cannot help observing.

'We are still indoors! Row... Since our meeting there's been not a glimpse of direct daylight.' But my guide does not comment.

'Just bear in mind that we need the guidance of the Designated Crystallographer.'

Our branch of the passage leads into a square room, empty as it is ornate. The decoration of the passage ceiling simply continues, flattens out. But immediately noticeable is something above one of the far corners: the gilt and pastel octagons of the ceiling are suffused by a brilliant rectangle. This is produced by a powerful light, shining upwards from below, through a doorway or portal. Given a head-stand, it can only be Sunlight.

There appears to be nothing beyond the empty, ornamental, ridged doorway. Walking across to it, there's a pleasant buffeting breeze. I cannot resist studying the reflections of the patterns surrounding the portal, in the polished floor. Only on breaking this gaze does it become clear: the portal leads to no more than a wide ledge. Beyond this is pure blue sky, up, up as far as can be seen; in front unbroken, cloudless sky without limit. And... this is the real surprise... below as well: bathing his face and mine and surely casting the hard shadows of our heads and bodies onto the ceiling and into the empty room behind, is the radiant, unbearable Sun, alone in space far, far away below.

After several metres to the right of the portal, the wall makes a right-angle turn. It extends some distance outwards, before turning back again. The wide ledge is perfectly flat and without any kind of balustrade, it follows the wall to and around the near corner. The ledge evidently passes as well around the outer corner. The sliver of facing wall to the right extends far upwards. And at the level of the ledge, the sliver contains another portal, doorless and identical in size to the one in which we now stand. Reaching it requires walking to the near corner. This we do, Row first; while both above and below unfolds the blue abyss. So! At the corner, each of us turns outwards, left. Then after a few paces, do we pause and rotate fully, backs to the wall. The travellers face the marvellous and terrifying abyss, dominated by the dazzling brilliance from below and rather to the right.

It is possible to explore the sky, its gradual change in hue. The tonnage of white at the Sun passes through pale then pure colour to deeper blue, tinged far above with mauve or purple.

The breeze has been tugging since before going out onto the ledge. Suddenly, it rises. Then again, now twisting. Involuntarily I draw breath, noticing him deliberating moving. Rotating to the right, we walk the remaining two metres or so of ledge to the far portal. Roland enters, momentarily leaving me alone on the ledge. There is a temptation to back-step from the ledge for a last look. But indeed I turn and walk in, without again glimpsing the blazing Sun.

This far portal leads to an identical square room, it is littered with the sort of sculptors' junk we saw earlier. Ahead lies an exit to another ornate-ceilinged passage.

'Very sorry... I'm afraid it looks like we have lost him.'

'We did pretty well just there. Can we maybe... do the trip without him?' He gives me a withering, almost derisory smile.

'Not a chance!'

Passages, steps, rooms lead into darkness not dispelled even by the powerful light now far behind us. Yet there is a pale, slightly primrose light reaching everything from somewhere. Exquisite stone work has become replaced by places so untidy and rough as to be hardly distinguishable from cavities in the surrounding rock. Columns, a ceiling can just be made out.

A lightish area shows in the shadows of one corner. A dirty white sheet covering a sculpture? Look again! Quietly tapping his forehead, absently yet attentively, it is Zircon. For a moment, Row folds like a sheet himself.

3. The Old Rocks

'How dare you play a trick like that!'

'You have both to be exposed to the nature of the descent.'

'All right. Never mind anyway. We've got to discuss practicalities. I have responsibility for our visitor. Are you sure you're going to get him down and back in one piece?'

'Remember, Roland so long as we are together, I am responsible for him no less than you! All right if you insist, we will make it a party of three. But you're aware I was looking forward to working on this specimen alone...' He beams at me.

Row leaves us, passing down a flight of steps in order to clamber over recently-broken rocks.

But now, after so much wrangling, the unexpected intervenes. There is *movement* in the old rocks. A defect explodes suddenly into a fracture, a long cornice cracks. The beam falls, battering the ground. Of course, Roland springs out of the way, darting along a ledge. The old mason commands in a loud voice, 'Be more careful! Pass closer to the tectonic shelter!' But it is clear Roland is not going to make it. There is a rending crack in the rock and masonry, the whole staircase before him falls into the abyss. But he has retreated towards the gaping entrance to the shelter. Totally ignoring me, Zircon shouts down to Roland, instructing him, telling him what he has to do. Far from appearing upset, there is a look of resignation on Row's face.

He shouts back to me, 'It's all right! This won't make any difference!' Zircon gazes down to where Row jumps backward into the hardened shelter. As masonry and rock collapses, he is cut from sight.

'Row! You're sure he's going to be all right?'

'Certain. He can pass through the dimly-illuminated gallery, and meet us at the other side.'

'Hmm. Sounds all right.'

'So, now I am your guardian!'

'Uh-huh. Thanks! Hope you won't find me too much trouble.'

'Perhaps it it's better that this has happened...'

'How could you say that Zircon?' Briefly I lose my footing, it has become noticeably darker, shadows lie in unexpected places.

'How did you come to be involved with someone like Roland...?' Hardly am I able to splutter in protest when he interrupts. '...Look, I understand he has already been trying to impress you with unfolding and openings on a greater scale.'

'Much greater... quite unfamiliar.'

'All the same, he is just another member of the secret legislature... His true purpose in this has been to hand you over to me.'

'That cannot be true. We met a special delegation... actually I suspect Roland is a robot.' I almost gasp aloud as Zircon totally ignores me.

'Delegation? *Ah ha, ha*! I'd forget about them... Or her... it was Aza wasn't it?'

'There is no chance I will forget about what happened, to me, in the middle of it all!'

'You were given some story about your presence being needed to witness a collision of worlds.'

'Was *that* what it was? I did witness, er... what ever it was.'

'All right, so they used you... that doesn't change the fact that your journey here... Well, all right it wouldn't be fair to say it hasn't begun...' Again I cannot stifle a splutter of protest. Spittle flies. '...All right, all right, you are stained with this reality, but your journey has not yet climaxed.'

'Are you serious...?' I breathe in deeply. The air is remarkably fresh, bracing even. '...Wait a moment... you said Roland will be able to just carry on.'

'Of course, he will. You think I arranged this collapse to befall him?'

'You did, didn't you?'

'Too many questions, do you hear? Roland is already too far away for short-wave communications. But so is everybody. You and I must descend alone.'

4. Not a Museum

'Descend!'

'To the heart of the labyrinth hidden beneath us.'

This is so extraordinary a place, a reality: here life continues without apparent dependence on the biological functions. These are or have become mere motifs, flourishes provided for amusement only.

'What are you doing?' I have been looking at the backs of my hands, feeling my hair, eyeballs. The stuff of life requires sustenance. Yet everything within feels totally familiar, despite our long continuation without a break.

'Oh, nothing. Just wondering how we can go on so long without even, say a drink of water.'

'Look. There is business to hand. You can have a drink of water any time, if you must...' Indeed a drinking-fountain appears not far away. It is true: there's not a vestige of thirst, any more than there are feelings of being unwell. We pass the faucet without even looking at it.

'Earlier, Row showed me the foundations under an immense floor.'

'What? The man's an anarchist! That's not been cleared of hazards. You could both have been de-natured!'

'We'll have to share the blame equally. I'd not have missed that excursion for anything.'

'This descent will be deeper.' At one point, my awareness of the timbre of his voice surpasses the grip of his words, words for us alone. No one overhears us. Our foot-falls on the planed flagstones produce remarkable recurrent echoes, feather-like but often quite loud.

'Do you use computers?'

'Use what? Sorry. Those haven't been seen since the discovery of time-crystals.'

'What's the difference?' Our voices are strange! Yet this is nothing to do with speech: it is the silence, so perfect it gives every sound a distinct edge.

'Difference? In functioning. The crystals do not take any time at all. They can be and often are bundled together into huge mainframes, if that's any comfort to you!'

Before, I'd assumed the lighting here came from outside. Now, after having taken a series of turns, there is the feeling not so much of leaving illumination behind, rather of entering a region of gradually less explicable lighting. In the dusk-like pallor, he resumes the discourse, 'The Orthogonal Maze, as the Vault is also known, is seldom visited. There are professions bodies, learned societies which include this journey in their conditions of entry. To have passed through the Asymmetric Vestibule is an unusual distinction!'

'These names... they refer to the same maze?'

'Yes! All refer to the Deep Central Labyrinth.'

Our voices are strange! Yet this is nothing to do with speech: it is the silence, so perfect it gives every sound a distinct edge.

'"Zircon". I've heard it before. How did you come by that name?'

'I earned it! "Zircon" is a hard, colourless, refractory gemstone. The mineral often occurs with impurities such as hafnia, though, which give it a range of colours.'

'Are you doing any work in the place where we're going?'

'No. Have done in the past; but not for a long time.'

Surely pleased to grab an opportunity to discuss his work, the designated mason says, 'You may be surprised, or perhaps not...' He looks me in the eye. '...but much of my work in sculpture, bas-relief and so forth is done in deserted cities, where there is a real possibility no-one may ever see it! The last job was in a city *always* in bright, orange Sunlight. The work involved carving and polishing of a frieze, at some considerable altitude...'

The labyrinth has for some distance now comprised a warren of interconnected rooms, often richly decorated, always windowless, obscurely illuminated. We take one passage in near pitch-darkness, sound assumes added priority; all that can be heard are our voices, our footfalls and unlimited echoes.

'So you were working in a place, now have I got this right... in a place where the Sun takes a fixed, never-moving place in the sky.'

'Yes! That's right. This figure, no-one might ever see: a contribution, only a detail for a structure, a tower so huge its styling and mood vary with height; and itself by no means the biggest in the block. Anyway, somewhere near the top an arch spans before a wall. The relief was cut from the supporting lintel. A dangerous project, to carve the work I had to lean over the abyss, over the silent concrete and steel canyon below, to aim my chisel!'

'So you were not disheartened by this prospect?'

'Of course not! The *architectural* effect of the Sun's light there is so striking: the remote, steadfast arch, the fixedness, the silence of the inexhaustible light.'

He stands still, to look at me, to prise out a response, 'Well, wasteful perhaps, but it is said nature is wasteful...' My words trail off, as a large painting fleetingly appears hanging on one wall of a room to the right. It looks fine, dramatic, but:

'Zircon! This work! It is famous! What's it doing here?' He walks over to it, looks at me then back at the brushwork.

'The canvas you've seen in a gallery... it's a forgery!'

Now for once the illumination is adequate; we pass a door, it stands half open. The room beyond is in darkness, however some light falls inwards: hair on the back of my neck prickles as it rises.

'Zircon! It looks like a person! There's someone in there!'

'This way...!' He gestures, ignoring the question. '...You'll fall behind!' With barely a glance to check that his companion is still following, the crystallographer strides through and down corridors, galleries and staircases. Rooms are decorated with protected displays of minerals: a circle of blue spinels set in a cluster crystal of bismuth metal; a massive black tourmaline is surrounded by coloured tourmalines. As I catch up, he says, 'Yes, there are fewer than 4000 mineral species known worldwide. Varieties such as griphite, botryogen, lilac charoite, dioptase, coccolite…'

'Stop! Enough!'

'…sodic oligoclase…' he adds, with a restrained smile.

'Zircon… it occurred to me once in a museum, that unlike many other treasures, the actual gems there now may still be on display in thousands of years!'

'This is not a museum… but look out for what is on display!'

We encounter disturbing, uninvestigated objects: one is marked with a tablet in Gothic lettering, it can be read without the least difficulty. 'Organ built specially for Khzareuffschleisser.' Really? It is hard to stifle a snigger. An armchair has been neatly cut down the middle: the right side rests inside the complex machine. But to the left the soft furnishing has contours designed to accommodate foreign, preter-human shapes.

Again! No doubt about it! There is a slight tremor in the rock. Nowhere near as violent as before, but the sensation is unmistakable. Indeed, as we pass the organ, a part happens to drop to the floor, rolling before coming to rest. Not far beyond hangs a framed, untitled painting, painted long ago, the surface is cracked. It depicts… the "Organ"! It takes an effort to avoid snatching at his sleeve… In the painting, the loose part is clearly rendered, on the floor.

5. The Staircase

'We must choose…' Like a coin on edge, the very old man spins a full revolution and a quarter, before violently pointing. '...This way. It is still important to confuse the misleading forces. Even those which have only an outside chance of misdirecting us.'

Walking through galleries, chambers still at successively deeper levels, he has many questions:

'Were you an orphan? Have you ever had a serious illness? What is your sexual orientation? Are you a murderer?'

'Stuff you! Of course not... although often enough...'

But he is not listening: with scarcely a nod, he says, 'The staircase is close.' Still with the wall to our left, and a considerable drop to be seen through the balusters, the far side of the room is becoming apparent.

We pass an open doorway. Without him noticing, I slip in to have a look. There's an unaccountable mystery to this apartment or suite. It is a bedroom perhaps, and giving the firm impression that this is not my first visit. On the back of a Chippendale table rests a swivel-mounted, bevelled mirror. Still moving into the room, I turn to look into it. Behind the image of my head is what appears to be daylight. It is as if the Sun is appearing as it would wallowing in very bright cloud. But on looking away from the mirror nothing is to be found in the room which could account for this reflection. I strive to find again the image by looking from just the same position, into the mirror.

'What are you doing? Come on! We are nearly at the end of this mezzanine! You can all but see the Eastern Staircase!' Turning away from the passage with its fine balustrade, and thus out of the huge irregular room, he motions to access stairs.

'You know, for a moment it seemed possible to see outdoors back there!'

'No. Not at this depth.' We take the flight; it runs down into an empty, polished landing, quite long in proportion but with only three walls. Marble facing is black.

'This is it...!' he announces. '...The landing vestibule of... the Staircase!' Evidently, I'm not as impressed as he expected.

'This? Another huge staircase?'

'I'm forgetting! You've already done a descent with whatshisname.'

'With Row!'

'This time you will be passing away altogether from the superficial, more or less dead realm which you explored with him.'

'By walking down steps? Not that I mind steps of course.'

'For these steps you will have a natural affinity, they will acclimatise you for what lies below.'

'All right.' We have been following the landing to nearly the halfway point.

'There are only two things I have to show you, or explain to you...' Ahead and to the left are mural features. He continues, there's not a vestige of a smile.

'...You're familiar with volcanic activity... perhaps you've done some touring?'

'Oh yes, I've been up a few volcanoes.'

'...Ah. Well, what you have to grasp is that down here we encounter control over the lifeless wilderness of the underworld.' I gasp with excitement!

'Seriously? Control?'

'That is what I said! Just as up there on the surface...'
He gestures dismissively, '...out in the open, a building
contrasts with a rocky outcrop. Why? Because rocks have
been cut to shape, dressed and used to build. Here you will
encounter the orderly management of the nuclear fires of
the underworld: rivers of magma channelled along perfectly
straight lines, organised into ornamental lakes, cataracts and
fountains.' He is serious!

'But... but there's only two of us... How can we
survive?'

'By keeping our wits about us. To pass through the
synchronous lattice, which we have to do, involves only one
encounter. That will be enough, even though it will be quite
evident the lattice itself is infinite.'

A low wall stands to the right, at the far end this gives
way to an exceptionally deep staircase. On the way over, a
panel in the main wall to our left becomes evident. Before
taking the steps, we walk over to it.

'It is a vertical map of this region.'

'So, where are we?'

'Let me see...' He peers at the scarcely-visible
tracework. '...Look! Here is the end of the tunnel you
arrived by. There's the room of your cushions...' He can say
no more: the engraving is unfinished, it ends at the point
where we met.

Turning around we are ready to take the flight, and
cautiously move towards the top.

'The steps! Why are the steps so wide?' Zircon touches
me roughly on the shoulder before I can see down.

'Just wait! There are things to know about this flight.
To the left is a continuous, hewn marble or barytes wall. To

the right, an impenetrable void! Beyond the balustrade the drop is unlimited!'

'The void...! OK.' I rush forwards to get the first look, but again he forcefully grasps my shoulder!

'You must not, *must not* gaze into the void!' Our eyes meet.

'Thankyou...! I understand...' We move towards the threshold.

'Zircon!' It is impossible to see anything at the bottom of the flight... the appalling staircase just tumbles into the distance very far below. Worse than that, there is an elemental battle between unlimited visual acuity, and the ever closer neighbourhoods of the vanishing point.

As if with huge piano keys to either side of us, we pass down the middle of the unchanging gradient.

Increasing barometric pressure makes the ears pop. As we descend the flight, a swarming, twisting pattern to our left unfolds, even small detail within it seeming to draw from its ever larger motifs. Zircon gestures with his left arm.

'Look back now!'

With a fleeting glance in his direction, cautiously I turn round to the left. On staring up, it is astounding how many of the wide steps we have already taken. Something he was saying before strikes me: now Roland seems further from here than any distance. As if he is only an idea, a drawing even! It is a shock, to break the spell I involuntarily turn back.

'How can we have covered so many steps?'

'Care! The void...!'

'Ahh!'

'What you perceive down here... well, you should regard it as nominal, sufficient to give you an idea only. For example, how are your ears?'

'Stopped popping! They feel fine now. But we must be at some depth?'

'We are well passed many times the depth of a typical gold mine!'

'Right!'

'But that bears almost no relation to our true depth.'

'Why?'

'You must include the passage of time!'

'We have been walking down these steps for quite a while, hours surely.'

'Much longer. You can take it we have been walking down these steps for days on end. For months, for many years.'

'Uhhhh!'

The polished white stairs suddenly feel inescapable. Narrowly missing the void, I stare straight at him as he speaks, 'Actually, we are well more than halfway down.' This reassurance is hardly enough, I strive to keep the conversation going.

'You mentioned two things Zircon! You said there are two things you have to explain. What is the other?'

'The surface world is just that, the surface only. The place where life begins. Very small, very limited. But it is perfectly possible to conceive of a pyramid standing amongst the stars, say three or four stars making the base and a bright one at the apex. Well that pyramid does not have to be empty space... it could be solid!'

'It would collapse!'

'If it were made of matter. But the structure we are now entering is not.' Unmistakably, far below can be seen the final "piano keys" of the flight.

'This is some kind of pyramid?'

'No, no... that was just a simple example. This place is more like an ornate city in the underworld, with colossal structures, vast entrances and interlocking patterns which go on... without limit.'

Of course, this has been far the longest of our descents. Near the bottom of the flight, it actually occurs to me that the sharpness of cutting, the spotless finish of the steps give the appearance they have never once before been used. The mason exclaims, 'Get ready to look! To the left! The South Staircase!' The wall to our side comes to a razor-sharp end, cut through at right angles by another wall. I follow the edge up, up... Here, at this place an identical staircase comes down to meet ours, at a square marble piazza. This square of course is based exactly on the width of our recent steps. Hurried glances ahead and to the right do not reveal western or northern staircases. On the contrary, in each case we are faced with sheer polished quartz rising into the hanging abyss.

'Zircon! We're stuck now...' The only anodyne to fear is humour. '...We'll have to walk back up!'

'Turn round!' I feel a cold sweat as I obey. There is no sign of our staircase, or of any staircase. We are somewhere else!

6. The Inner Labyrinth

'Follow me!' Intuition prompts another look back: yes indeed, the eastern staircase is no more than a memory.

We've arrived at chambers, passages, occasional downward flights. This is total dependence on my guide. But he takes a wrong turn, it opens into a space near a ceiling. We have to double back and take another door from an earlier room. As before, light is reflected only from adjacent rooms or concourses, never do we pass a direct source. But sometimes the background is much stronger, implying a powerful lamp just round the corner. Now there are fewer junctions, bends, side passages.

'So far we've seen only ante-rooms. But soon we will enter the true maze.' Our passage is featureless, straight, square in section, it extends and vanishes to a point ahead. I snatch round, hardly surprisingly it is the same behind.

His manner has become abrupt, noticeable since we began the long descent: he talks now only intermittently, not encouraging me to speak. The words are exact, to be followed as in a puzzle or calculation, although what he says is obscure.

'We must avoid conjugate passages...! That route requires the braiding of at least three world-lines!' This condition does not ease, what he says gets more serious, onerous.

The groundmass of the chambers is uniform, patternless, in panels or slabs, often from floor to ceiling. Lines only appear where the slabs are different in colour, or of the same but lighter or darker. These vertical and horizontal lines as well make up highly illusory patterns. To make matters worse they often invert: solids collapse, hollows suddenly bulge outwards. His figure vanishes into a doorway. I chase after only to find a chamber apparently filled with corners, there is no sign of him. The main exit seemingly reveals more doorways in the room beyond, but the exit is only an illusion, slabs are combined to look like an open space. My movement proves the doorway next to it is real. But so are one or two others.

'I'm here…!' Standing behind me! '…Come on!' He is very fit, setting the pace. Now, to what he says I pay close attention.

'This maze is not a game. That is, an incorrect choice can mean an opportunity to take the alternative will never arise. The reason is that on retracing your footsteps, the turns which may be remembered, no matter how clearly, may have no relation to those which you will in fact find.'

'That's how it appeared just then, a moment ago!' He seems to feel this matter warrants no further discussion.

'First we must pass through the Figurative Vault… This way…!' He motions down shallow, uncarpeted stairs. '…Mind!' Even the treads have simulated, illusory edges.

The staircase accounts for one wall of a room containing nothing but a table. The remaining three walls each have a series of doorways, all open, all leading into darkness.

'Each door…' He gestures. '…leads to somewhere different!' I walk up to one. It is in shadow, beyond the threshold there is only increasing darkness. No sign of light falling on the floor from adjacent doorways in the room. I lunge to pass through it, but he restrains me with astonishing force.

'Wait! First the correct door has to be selected!'

'Sure! Fine!' I wince humorously, as he releases my shoulder. On the table in the centre of the room rests an opened chessboard, a game is in progress.

'So! Very elaborate pieces.' Some have five or more lathed discs above the base. The biggest reach almost a foot high. Both sides have three rows!

'Chess rules vary from region to region, from epoch to epoch.'

'Let's have a look… mmm… the officers have hardly moved. But the lesser pieces and pawns are well engaged.'

'The pieces are not so big as… those.' He points to one of the doorways, a shadowy outline within is visible.

'What's in there?'

'All the doorways are open. But only some of them are free. Come, look in here, for example. Careful!' I peer into the darkness, then abruptly spring back. A huge ivory chess piece, taller than either of us, imperiously stares back. Beneath it, a floor of chequered tiles passes into inky shadow.

'But how are we going to choose? There are so many doors, four or five per wall. I don't fancy making a mistake!'

'Just gaze at the board!' The ordinary chequer pattern seems to extend outwards like a floor; now the political confinement of the pieces leaves, from so many possibilities, but one way forward. He is already walking toward the door I have selected!

We enter a plain marble corridor which leads to a junction. On the far wall of the intersecting passage is etched a striking pattern. From floor to ceiling it covers the wall, its many motifs are built up from rays ruled on the polished agate. After interpreting the pattern and thus choosing the correct leg of the junction, we advance towards the inner core of the maze.

He seems to advance more cautiously, the streaked marble of the maze becomes darker. Soon only the lightest veins show any hue, the surrounding marble appearing either very dark or black.

Ahead are faint, linear-edged flashes of light. Suddenly, it becomes clear we are facing a heavy door, of black glass. The passage is fairly wide, there is no frame: the barrier itself resembles a square wall. Halting, our eyes strive to adjust to the darkness. The brittle surface is cut in octagons; there is no handle. The panelling is surrounded by strips of tooled glass; the many planes shimmer even in the dim light. Zircon speaks, 'We used the actinic pattern to plan the route. Was there any more to your interpretation of the wall pattern?'

'Well, there was: inevitably, we would come up against this barrier. Also that should we succeed in passing through, there can be no turning back!'

My companion crouches, a knee on the ground. He takes several gemstones from a pocket, and lays them out. After peering at the door, he replaces all but one.

'The lock has a crystalline mechanism. It so happens I have a key…'

He holds up the remaining stone, a rhombohedral crystal, a sapphire.

'…This is it!'

7. The Second Law

Zircon grasps the jewel and holds it in the central depression of the door, a place ringed by an octagon of gemstones, diopsides. Nothing happens for a moment; then a sapphire light spreads from the centre of the door, until the structure brightly bathes the whole scene in a steady, single colour.

'What you see is caused by a match with the gemstone fixed inside the door. The lock has recognised the key.' The glow fades and vanishes, leaving a fine vertical line in front of us. What we've regarded as one door is now revealed to be a pair, which open slowly, away from us. We wait until the rotation of the doors is complete, so they are uniform with the passage beyond, just as they had been with one another.

Beneath the gleaming black ceiling there's a faint orange glow visible in the distance. Zircon rises, thrusts forward. Surely at last this is the inner centre! It seems pretty obvious it must be. Following him, I glimpse minerals set into the walls and floor. The surrounding vitreous matter is as transparent as the purest water. Beneath can be seen interfaces of glasses, crystals in different colours and refractions. Some interfaces are plane; others take the curves of waves and orbits. The orange glow gets brighter as we pace the passage, illuminating it to great depth. Looking straight down, converging patterns of opaque crystals can be seen. They are embedded in an endless cubic lattice. It just goes down and down. Abruptly, my companion stops.

'The material we're standing on: if you were to cut some of it off, that piece would float.'

'It feels hard!'

'True! Cutting a piece off would be difficult. It is harder than diamond!'

'What is it?'

'Degenerate matter, held in the grip of the strange force...' Recesses, carved at regular intervals into each wall contain Corinthian urns, resting on polished granite plinths. He continues, '... The stuff is incapable of conducting heat, and in its reflective form is incapable of penetration by radiant heat.' As he says this, the orange glow can just be felt on the face.

An urn swirls with coloured striations. Zircon approaches and removes its oval lid. Dense, white vapours roll from the opened vessel, down its sides, some cusps even roll away from the plinth. Ripples settle, become still.

'Now look ahead to below the bright area: you'll see that this pavement spreads out into the floor of a room.'

We walk along the passage and through the spacious entrance at one corner of the room: the place is filled with a strong orange-yellow light. Several metres away from where we stand, the floor gives way to a depression, extending into the distance in the two directions from our corner. This forms an apparently rectangular lake, which is filled with clarified volcanic lava, to a level less than a metre below the edge of the depression. The lava throws off a fierce light, which bathes my face, body and arms.

'This basin is filled with molten basalt. Although you can see through the pavement, it shades us from almost all of the surface. Much of the light radiated is absorbed by the ceiling, so you can move nearer the edge to view it. Keep low!'

Taking a pace into the room, I walk down the wide transparent pavement flanking the basin. The glowing magma shines through from many depths, silhouetting the cubic lattice of crystals between the eye and the source of light. Each of them reflects and bends the powerful light according to its colour and index. Their patterns appear open to interpretation, like the mural patterns which led us here.

The pavement of vitreous adamant is quite cold to the touch. Recalling his recent remark, I crouch nearer the edge with one knee on the floor. The great energy in light and soft X-rays thrown from the basalt tears at my face, but it is possible to remain there for a short while. The lava surface is plane as the pavement above it. In the absence of apparent motion, it is only this flatness and visible containment in the crystal adamant basin that suggests the lava is liquid. Above, at a height of several metres, is a roof of polished black material, which both reflects darkly the glowing contents of the basin, and Zircon and myself. His face, his clothes are bright orange in the light. I notice that my companion too has moved nearer the sharp, vitreous edge. He gazes into the orange brilliance, then moves back into the centre of the pavement, and at this I cautiously get up and rejoin him.

We walk along the pavement, now and then passing ample seats cut into semicircular recesses in the stone wall. The interiors are set with patterns of zeolites, fire-opal and beryllonite; and as we walk past each alcove these patterns flash and sparkle.

Taking one recess we sit, and contemplate the scene. In silence, the surface remains quite still, as does its reflection in the gleaming roof.

We discuss the technicalities of the pool of magma and energy.

'Do you see a rectangle in the centre of the ceiling?'

'Oh, yes, just.' The polished black material falls away to a rectangular hole, perfectly black, but not shiny, so that one suddenly perceives it.

'That is an air outlet, maintained at least ten millibars below the ambient pressure. It thus draws away air ionised in this room, ensuring the basin does not affect its surroundings. Nor poison us.'

After a short time, we resume our journey along the pavement. The alcoves give way to a portico, decorated on either side by fluted marble columns. In the darkness beyond opens a high-ceilinged chamber.

Zircon looks up, as if he is going to look at my body, bathed in the orange light; but he gazes right into the centre of the open surface of the basin. I ask, 'Is there any chance we could go all the way round?'

There is a definite pause before he replies. Then, 'Every chance! All right? Let's go!' We walk to the next corner. There is a perceptible increase in the radiant light, as the aperture of lava due to the corner briefly widens. During the further walk, again I look into the pavement, before we approach the corner diagonally opposite that of our entrance. From this place, the entrance can scarcely be made out for the glare above the basin.

After continuing again we pause, at a marble bench positioned exactly opposite our exit. The orange glare of the lava all but obscures what lies beyond.

Continuing the circuit we pass the remaining far corner. To the left a mural drawn with parallel tiles rises to the ceiling. Mineral wafers and jewels achieve the effect. The work is fine as the eye can resolve, only a machine or robot could have created it. The cartoon depicts a city where gravity is less perhaps, slender towers rise into the sky, buildings crowd together to form a distant horizon. Suddenly the exquisiteness is only the image, the tearing light from just behind is the reality.

The pavement approaches our place of entrance: at this corner Zircon walks round; I gaze back along the passage, trying to spot the vapour-laden urn. But it is a different scene altogether. Passing the incandescent basin of lava, I too walk around the corner, my gaze fixed on the sharp orange-yellow vee to my side. And then look up. The sculptor is a few paces ahead. It takes no more than a moment to catch up with him, motioning me to join him on the wall side, he is studying the patterned cornice. Thus we take the pavement, paced already once, which leads up to our exit. Suddenly, it occurs to me that, to my surprise we have walked by the alcove at which we first sat, without noticing it.

Again we reach the tall open portico, decorated on either side by fluted marble columns. Taking it, we leave the room of the brilliant basin, and pass into the final stages of the maze. The glow behind us grows dimmer; and after a while becomes extinguished.

CHAPTER 6
ROW

1. Waterfall, Rainfall

Zircon really suggests that our walk round the lava tank was the minimum required to claim a visit. More advanced visitors would actually see patterned, ornate fountains of lava. They might expect to see the foundations of classical structures charged and pummeled by waves of basalt. It becomes evident that this is territory which follows after, comes after technological advance.

Voice subdued, I ask, 'Would it be correct to say that place... the basin... is the maze-centre?'

'Yes! Certainly. But. No-one else could find it! If we were to return, taking the same entrance, we would not find it!'

Decorative wall patterns give way to tapestries, rugs, the place is opposite to where we have been.

Now he breaks a long silence.

'Not far ahead lies the end of the maze. Of course, we still have to make our way up to the surface.'

His manner has noticeably loosened up, the touch of humour has returned. We pace through passages, enclosures, galleries, libraries even. Fine styling is set off against seemingly endless varieties of granite: hornblende, pegmatite glinting with mica inclusions, luxullianite.

We face a vast entrance hall or concourse, wide certainly, but so deep and long it takes time to enter. Straight ahead, the chamber contains an appalling staircase which rises to an inscrutable, far distant vanishing-point. Wait a moment… to the right there is another flight! Not for the first time, my hackles rise.

This is the Eastern Staircase! The same flight. Yes, the flight of our descent! The pace quickens. Ignoring the paradox, I rush over the threshold and on up the steps at maximum speed.

'Come on! I'll beat you to the top.' He laughs aloud, but the deep, slightly shallow treads allow a pretence of speed for a limited period. Of course effort soon takes its toll. Breathing rapidly, I turn backwards. He is immediately behind me.

'I didn't even hear you.'

'Why have you stopped running?'

'Stuff that!' At walking-pace, we resume the ascent.

'Exercise is healthy.'

'Obviously, this is absurd, we'll never be able to cover the field.'

'Turn around.' Once again I do this.

'Zircon! We're half way up already!' A back step is necessary to avoid losing my footing.

'Optimistic, but perhaps a fair guess.' Overcoming the surprise, I'm compelled to marvel at the stonework:

'Just look at those blades of marble, zooming up to their convergence, completely vanishing… at the vanishing point. And now in both directions!'

What he says is already clear to me.

'We have only so much time left together.'

'So many questions to be left unanswered...' The wall patterns for the ascent lie to the right, sweeping upwards without limit. These, of course, bear no resemblance to those at the foot of the flight. '...You have distracted me again, you must have used hypnosis... hang on... Wait a moment, sir... yes... Roland!' The actual person is arising from the comic book cartoon implanted in my head on the way down.

'Your pal Row...?'

'We will see him before our time runs out?'

'Of course, I'll hand you over to that high-ranking ruffian, if that is sincerely your wish.'

'*Ha-ha*. Of course, it is!'

There is a period of taking the wide steps without comment, without effort, with the swooping murals to the right, the void to our left.

Long ago, as two of us were finding our escape from the outer layer of this reality, we encountered an escutcheon enclosing a small pair of doors. Beyond these were gold-leaf leitmotifs, work which no-one would ever see. Now most explicitly this quality has returned: the mural patterns are too flattened to be comprehended!

The flight ascends unbroken ahead of us; now at last we have distinction from our downward passage. Foundations rising from the void enable further flights made up of much bigger, huge steps, which stand like buildings left and right. Their tops form landings which can be reached from the centre flight. Small gardens thrive on the landings, tendrils of pale, leafy plants hang some distance against the polished walls. There has been recent rainfall.

After some further distance, my legs feel like jelly. Brushing creepers and thorns, we make our way over to a nearby garden, grandly sitting on a speckled porphyry bench.

'There is...' he pauses uncharacteristically.

'Er, yes?'

'You have witnessed the oxidation of history.'

'As terrifying as it was engrossing.'

'There is another little favour we'd ask of you.'

'Another! Little?'

'Pay attention. There is a large-scale destruction, awaiting undertaking, which can only be accomplished via the mediation of a visitor. There may have been others, but you are the first since records began.'

'You expect me to consent? *Ha-ha*! Of course, I consent!' The old arm-twister handles jewellery on his fingers. How could I have missed noticing these rings until now?

'You'll meet quite a few others in the operation.'

'Right. Hmm... Thinking back to the earlier labyrinth, that certainly was no museum.'

'Go on... Why do you say that?'

'At the time I said nothing to you. Most windows in the passages showed very little, some even no more than a brick wall. But one particular window gave the kind of panoramic view one would expect from near the top of a tall city building.'

'Yes. We could have spent more time looking at more paintings, and at furniture designed for shapes far from the human. But it would have delayed us.'

While he speaks, I gaze absently at the marble, geometric mountainside. Waves of his rustic and rather soiled gown roll, as he moves to get up.

Recollections inevitably lead to questions about the incandescent basin. While on the move our eyes meet, I even draw in breath to speak... however, words do not come out. Something has silenced me. He continues, 'Nature is not in command here! Indeed you've had glimpses of places where nature has *never* ruled.'

The remainder of the ascent feels easy, our exchanges resume almost without interruption. He seems to emphasise that time I may have to myself will not last, and should therefore make the most of it. Our chatter becomes less with the physical effort. Despite the flattening, I look at each mural from as far over to the side as possible. Their vast, movement-filled patterns successively reach down to each of the huge steps.

Now the array of gardens hangs below us.

'It's getting brighter!' Daylight filters down from a long skylight. Talking to him has so distracted me: the hike has come to an end.

'...The landing vestibule of... the Staircase!'

'Correct. That's exactly what it is.' We stride over the threshold, defined by the final step of the ascent, and pace into the landing. I snap round, confident of what I will find. Ha! Indeed! There is now no sign of the appalling staircase to the underworld. Directly ahead thunders a waterfall. Clear and transparent, the water twists and knots bright colours, as it crashes onto marbles, translucent weirs.

'We are near the entrance to the outside world.'

Leaving the gleaming floor of the vestibule he points upwards. 'The dome and cupola above span two entrances: one for the river falling in... and... one for us.'

'Oi!'

A familiar voice! Zircon greets Row dryly, 'So you found your way!'

Exchanging accounts, we all step out into dazzling sunshine. There's a warm, late afternoon breeze.

'If you walk down that grove, you'll be able to see beyond these buildings and nearby country. Look for a range of mountains...' I am unable to prevent a sinking feeling as the sculptor speaks. '...In fair conditions of visibility, you'll see a high peak near the middle of the range...' His face is dark, difficult to make out, the Sun is behind. '...In fact, a continent away but about in that direction, lies a grandiose volcano!' He turns to Roland.

'There's a quite racy car here. Yours? Parked in that cave over to the left.' Row chucks a small bunch of keys into the air.

'Yes, sir!' They head over to have a look.

As the voices lessen, I try to get a glimpse of the mountain range. But clusters of carving-inlaid towers on the terraces all around are in the way. Turning back, now there's no sign of him. That's it! Zircon has vanished!

Pessimistically, I look around... from behind a nearby urn... There! Over by one of the towers sunlight catches a figure... only a statue. Slowly pacing a pavement of mosaic, I walk towards the grove. Certain he is gone. I nonetheless look round for any sign, starting once or twice at forms near the edge of vision. More statues, and before them plants growing from widely-fluted urns. Wondering if he has ever reached the summit of this great volcano himself, my head reels with the impact of our long encounter.

Before looking for Row and finding out about the car, I head for the grove. On reaching it, the distant mountains can be seen. The air is hazy however, and I turn to check around the grove. In its trees are oranges and various dark-skinned fruits. Picking one and lying in the grass, I hungrily consume pulp and juice. It goes down very well, soon followed by another. Row appears. But the fruit contains some kind of drug. In the hot sunshine I doze; then after nightfall stagger to a sheltered spot and fall deeply asleep.

2. The Unique Device

There is the rustle of a zephyr in leaves above; the soft sound has wakened me. Without a moon, the sky is filled with bright stars. Where the Milky Way intersects with the zodiac, glitters the pattern of Gemini.

Visible in silhouette, the distant mountains form an irregular horizon against stars of low altitude. Suddenly the fixed constellations seem to drop, as a meteor slices through the stars. It is quickly chased by another.

'You awake at last?' He has returned after getting fuel and supplies for the car.

'Morning!'

'Ready for a fast desert crossing?' After long sleep the air is chill.

'Maybe. I mean, of course.' We decide to wait awhile until it feels warmer. To one side there is the yellow-pink of approaching dawn. He finds some music on a tiny radio, but tries to get a News broadcast. Reception is poor. It is possible to guess the distance of objects around from their outline. In fact the star-light is just sufficient to weakly illuminate the ground. We head for the cave with his glinting pink and violet car. There are coffee, maps and stuff on the back seats.

Blue-white sparks in the sky herald the passage of another, much lower meteor. While it is causing objects to cast moving shadows on the ground, the particle breaks up: a brilliant, smaller piece branches away from the slightly deflected, larger part.

'…Ahh!' But he ignores it.

'I'll be chauffeur! Hop in.' Jumping in, I relish the comfort of the front passenger seat. With a throaty crackle we set off north, the mountains to the right.

Threading through a series of rocky tracks, the way is open. Moving slightly west of north, Row enters a fine highway; to our right the Sun will surely soon rise.

'So that old fixer managed to persuade you to go on another operation?'

'How could I possibly have turned him down?'

'You realise this will mean another industrial site. Then zig-zagging from one place to another.' We're eating some of the fruits on the move. The last stars have vanished. The Sun casts its first light, edging peaks of the distant range with orange. And the whopping volcano, the climax of operations, is a quarter of a world beyond the mountains.

'You'll have me with you this time, if that doesn't put you off.'

'*Ha-ha*… Now hang on: are you saying this next stage will amount to a re-visitation of the blast cone?'

'It's understandable that you should think that. But look at it like this: you've taken the Eastern staircase, far down. And then, after your sojourn, back up. The pairing principle is much the same. One important difference is that we will be walking towards, rather than fleeing from the trouble. Another is that we will be actively seeking enablement, rather than you passively witnessing.'

'Oh, er... Fully understood... Hmm...'

The sky fills with the approaching sunrise. He continues, 'I have been entrusted with a certain relic or artefact.'

'You? What is it?'

'Don't ask what it is or who gave it to me. It's on the back seat. We have to destroy it.'

'Let's do it now!'

'Breaking it into pieces, flattening it with a hammer, or throwing it in the fire would all be of no use.'

'Why?'

'Because materials leave a trace, and scattered ashes leave no trace. A middle or forensic state is required: there has to be proof it is destroyed, yet it must not be in any way reconstitutable from the articles of proof.'

'Is that it, the case on the back seat?'

'That is a shielded briefcase with a fire-resistant lining. It contains a digitally locked photovoltaic module, which holds the artefact.'

'Are you saying that this other industrial site has to be visited, in order to destroy the artefact?'

'That's about it. The location is in a dreary place by the name of Greyscar. Very interesting up to a point. You'll approve of the site itself.'

Although the single carriageway is wide, in perfect condition, there's no other traffic. We discuss the nature of the operation, the second part of which will apparently be more tricky. The Sun rises, encountering cirrus.

Discussion turns to the motive for destroying the relic or fragment.

'In a phrase, obliterative demolition!'

'What's that? That's surely on a different scale altogether.'

'No, no. It's not the artefact which has to be razed. We're talking about vast, invariably very ugly stone structures. When it comes to really major long-overdue demolitions, a special type of engine is required. It is not for use in the underworld. It does not fly. Therefore it is called a Land Engine. There are very few of these Gestalt Devices.'

'Gestalt...? Few... how many?'

'You could count them on one hand... but...' Row affects a gloating smile. '...Zircon has talked you into a larger picture. The present operation is so heavy it cannot be undertaken by a Land Engine alone. Instead it will be used to control a grander machine. There is only one such device in the world, the Unique Device, Udev for short.'

'Amazing! How many other shocks have you got ready to spring?'

'Just want to lay out the facts straight away. Anyway, that's about it.'

'Well, all right. So... This one and only machine, for what is it to be used?'

'Forensic decimation.'

'Sounds like a daunting challenge. Obviously, I won't be able to help.'

'Just carry on. No more is expected. Anyway, an Engine capable of gestalt-demolition or shock razing of the largest and oldest structures has to be switched on with a special key.'

'Why can this not be manufactured?'

'For nearly every key in the world that would be a fair question. But this particular key can only be made by destroying a certain artefact.'

'You're saying the tools for making the key are in the case on the back seat?'

'Yes…' He fleetingly looks away from the road. '…The whole procedure of summoning and starting up the Device is called the disentrammelment.' Roland drives very fast: aside from occasional gentle curves the road is straight. He's doing well over 200mph. I try to focus on business as he speaks:

3. Greyscar

'It's imperative that it is understood that…'

'Come on, that's not you talking, it's Zircon!'

'It's just that I'm at the disposal, if that's the right word, of the people organising the chain of control. We will be facing much uncertainty.' The Sun has now risen high in the sky, to a place above the mountains.

'Say! There's a TV in the car.'

Row reaches to a worn push-button. An image swims to life, seemingly endless channels can be called up just by turning a knob. Just as I am getting interested in a documentary on stockpiles of dangerous drugs seized by police, he explains, 'You can get all previous broadcasts from anywhere, going back to the dawn of television. Just choose a channel, then wind the time keys back.' Hardly seconds are required to get the hang of it. There's an unlimited range of News, drama, comedy, movies. The early black-and white programmes seems to have an extraordinary authority. It becomes so absorbing I forget the car, even my companion. His jokes at my expense fall on deaf ears.

It is noon; cloud is now more in evidence. After a while we slow down, lose a lot of speed. Suddenly where the highway swings off to the left, he continues onto a desert track. The sand surface has a stony basis; there's no difficulty with the vehicle.

It is a partly blue sky: in one place cirrus can be seen over a distant table-formation. We are throwing up a large dust-plume.

'Arghhh... Would you like to drive for bit?' Row suddenly asks.

'Yeah, OK.' After pulling up for a coffee from the flask and a move round we carry on along the track. Neither is in the mood for conversation. He flips on the TV, watches it for about two seconds then switches off.

The dashboard is so familiar it looks out of date. There are one or two controls however, for which I cannot account. This chrome knob here for example, definitely not a cigarette lighter. My right hand strays towards it.

'Hey! Don't touch that! Do you want to get us both killed?'

'Oh no! I'm sorry, let's change…' I swerve to the side while braking.

But:

'No! Carry on.' After persuading me to continue Row explains at length about this, and other, unforeseen capabilities of the car.

The track is hard, straight, wide: it's possible to drive quite fast. Deep blue-green-tinting and UV filtering cut glare from the windscreen, the air-conditioner thunders. For hours we've had no company but the Sun. It is no effort to concentrate and from time to time as well take in topographic features to either side.

Low altitude tundra is getting evident. Now he discusses practicalities.

'Before we can fulfil Zircon's assignment, the first key has to be obtained from a peculiar museum-like mill, at the centre of the industrial site. The key is one of two which will be needed to start the Engine.'

'And to stop the Engine?'

'Just like your TV at home. It switches itself off after a while. All right. Let me tell you a bit about the area first. We are making for terrain quite different from what we've been travelling though so far today. Firstly, we're gradually entering a cooler climate. And secondly we have to reach a built-up zone, an abandoned town, Greyscar… Hey! Do you want a break?'

'Oh, yes, sure.'

Again we change places, before he resumes, 'Land in these parts is plentiful: food, textiles, etc. are manufactured directly from the rocks, there is no such thing as arable land. So houses, factories, buildings generally are seldom demolished. Indeed... the structures are carefully restored, preserved!'

'Hmmm.' Now and then signs of habitation occur, often ruined.

'Visits aren't always encouraged, danger warnings are posted outside disused sites, but otherwise no great effort is made to keep out the curious, who are regarded as ramblers, not trespassers. But in this case nearby towns are all deserted, the huge complex is located in a remote, desolate region...'

There are some mountains in the distance; the more widespread vegetation of a cooler climate is becoming apparent. The sky is filling with fluffy clouds.

'Can you take the car? I've got some navigating to do.'

'Sure.' There's a short break. Larger clouds are joining up before we resume. He rummages in a glove box, flicks out an old, folding map.

'OK. This road has a branch coming up, we must take a left.' After a further drive, one or two factory buildings appear. We drive along isolated streets then through a suburb of houses, business premises. Some have small gardens, many of the properties are deserted. We are approaching the city environment of Greyscar.

Further in, the more desolate it becomes. Other vehicles are only occasional, there are no people at all. Various styles of building have been left, maintained even, rather than being abandoned. There are shops and commercial buildings which have not been used for generations. Red brick terraces are commonplace, wrought iron wind-vanes and lightning conductors claw the sky.

In the greater distance apartment blocks rise, well above those of estates behind the street. We pass a silent, double-decker bus left at the side of the road. He comments, 'We could have arrived by a VTOL device, but we'll need the car later.'

'A jet?'

'Indeed. Coming in and leaving on such a flight, it would have been possible to study the disused factory plant... from near the horizon, say twenty-five kilometres away. That lost view will just have to be left to the imagination... in fact... there is the plant!'

Along streets there are glimpses of a major industrial complex. Cooling towers appear to have been left uncleaned, streaked with soot. Nearer the plant land use is sparse, open areas let us see into the distance.

'We're getting there.'

'Don't forget, we've got to get in!'

None of the stubble of chimneys at the site ahead produce any smoke. With one exception. Just one stack seems to have come to life! In the middle, in the centre, it looks like the biggest. And this tower releases a far-reaching, dense black cloud, very slow to disperse. Obviously some process is still going on, or has recently started there. Now the release stops, but the plume holds together as it drifts away. We're now not so far from the site, driving through one of the rotting suburbs.

The team pulls up, parking the car around an unobtrusive corner. Roland reaches back and takes the briefcase. Piling out of the vehicle, our explorations continue on foot.

It is overcast and rather windy, as if from nowhere a forceful gust will noisily flap the clothes. After deciding which direction is north, we take a road leading towards the site, the site to be explored tomorrow. There is no traffic.

Frontages are classic, usually in bright gold signwriting on black glass, sometimes cracked: off-licences, ironmongers, upholsterers, grocers, haberdashers. All out of date, none of the retailers is still in business; the odd car drives past.

'Wow! See how late it is. How time has passed!'

'What are we going to do for the night?'

'We'll find somewhere.'

Weeds are growing from cracks in the paving stones, we look around: no occupied homes. None, not one!

'We'll just check door to door, find a cosy retreat for the night.' An unaccountable silence falls over us. As Row speaks you could hear a pin drop.

'Where's our car? Did you keep track? Eh? I did!'

4. Pallid Rays

It is easy to find a place, the house is fairly large, filled with old, stale furniture. Drawing up chairs, we make a cuppa in one of the downstairs rooms. Soon we are well conversing.

'You know, on the descent, at one point Zircon lost his way.'

'Did he? *Ha, ha,* what an amateur. The trouble is he has a monopoly. No one else knows the way.'

'The incident was scary enough.' Row is still laughing.

'Zircon, the Received Architect. Well, go on, what happened?'

'We had to back-track!'

Row asks, 'This was after you'd taken the Eastern staircase?' As we talk wind rattles the panes, Greyscar is a windy town.

'Yes. He said something like, "I think we have to turn off here, through that little door." It was almost too small, ghastly, we both had to crouch and push to get through. It lead to a disturbing, different place. Some light came from afar, but did not reach up to the ceiling or whatever was above us. Also illumination was fitful: sometimes the shadows moved.'

'Fire perhaps,' Row suggests.

'No, I don't think so. I said, "Zircon! Are you sure we are in a room? This feels more like being down a mine!" He paid no attention, thrusting forward, losing his footing once or twice. The place had a dry, powdery smell.'

'You both were groping in un-cleared ground.'

'Sure. Clouds of dust rose as we passed. Above us was only the solid, black sky.' Again the wind rattles.

'Sometimes an architectural flourish faintly flickered before vanishing.' There is the noise of a vehicle passing in the distance, the first we've heard for some hours.

'Hold it! What did I do with the case? Ah, there it is!' He gets up, has a quick look inside. 'Sorry about that. So, was he looking after you?'

'Oh yes. Ahead on the left, was a silhouette: the razor outline of a huge, dust-laden urn. Shafts of illumination beyond the urn seem to slant upwards from a place hidden far to the left. The goblet's massive plinth marked a corner: one way leading along the ledge to us, the other towards the light. To the right away from the rocky wall, the ground fell away steepening into a black precipice.'

'Dangerous, then,' Row comments.

'He said, "Careful! Stay here!" The ground gave under him as he made forwards, at one point the Artist seemed to stagger into a pool of ink. After he gained the corner, I watched Zircon turn and face directly into the light. He did not appear to be looking at any particular thing in the far perspective; instead simply bathing in the pallid rays. The profile, his eyes, hair stood out with dramatic clarity. Abruptly he wheeled round.'

Row gloats, 'U-turn I bet.'

'Hey! Cut it out, the Designated Surveyor got it right a thousand times... Oh, all right it was a U-turn. He said, "Quick! Go back! We've come the wrong way! Hurry!" I waited for him, but he roughly shoved me in the direction of the little door.'

'Must have seen something nasty!'

'Anyway we had to abandon his short-cut or whatever it was.'

It has got very late. We've a choice of sleeping rooms. Too tired, I collapse on a bed, the last memory is of him making another cuppa downstairs.

After many hours, sleep is now not so deep. Pushing away a vivid dream, I awaken. Daybreak! It is very early.

The first up, I make the tea. After looking in a couple of rooms, I can't find him, and give a shout. Row appears.

'Morning! Oh yes, tea. Great! Do you know last night I brought you up some, but you were gone.'

The day ahead of us, we set off, he carries the case. Wallpaper and fireplaces hang in cliffs; everywhere lies a rust-coloured oxide. Housing straggles to nothing. The sky is a sullen grey, clouds shifting all the time, it is dark even in early morning.

'Earlier we saw a monumental smokestack, from the car. What's happened to it? It's been swallowed by these nearby buildings!'

But ahead, waste areas have been cleared, it looks as if a life-size street map has been printed on the ground. The view is unobstructed. We pass onto a wider, concrete road which confronts the huge technical complex.

The road is blocked by the wire mesh gate of a main security entrance. What lies beyond is of acute interest, we walk so briskly forwards that it feels warmer. There resides the object of curiosity, the mystery. Enclosed by its rigid mesh perimeter fence, is a vast and imposing industrial area, free of domestic buildings, quite deserted.

5. Diffuse, Inert

To the left of the mesh barrier is a glasswork gate-house. The disc of the Sun rides briefly through cloud, causing a weak light to sparkle from inside.

Yes! Row has a card which releases the gate. Before it's a quarter open we have slipped through. He pushes the gate shut, we walk to the deserted post. A ribbed bottle stands against the window, perhaps the lens which had caught the Sun.

'We've some distance to cover.'

'Why, if I may ask, was this place not thrown open to you, for our purposes?'

'Fair question, I suppose. But the answer is that to pull off the *fait accompli,* those in the know have to be kept to the absolute minimum.'

Very much compelled, driven... we walk forwards into the site. Even at this early stage, there is an awareness of a core power located somewhere, ahead perhaps, surrounded by the dead complex.

'Is there any sign of anyone else?'

'No sign anyone has been in the vicinity, at a guess no one at all for a long time.'

'We will find irreparable decay?'

'No! On the contrary! The place may have been abandoned long ago, but there are no signs of decay. Nor of vandalism for that matter...' He glances down at the handle of the case. '...We're in for an interesting walk.'

The approach road passes downwards while veering slightly to the right, against a backdrop of imposing industrial installations. If anything, these have served to hide the extent of the plant. The wind carries no leaves, no litter, gusting emptily. Row says, 'This place was covertly warmed up specially for us. The reason we have to use it to destroy the artefact is to do with what some call the moods of the Vehicle.'

'The Gestalt Engine is a machine presumably. No genuine machine has moods!'

'Just a turn of phrase. Using the Engine is a matter of opportunity. For example in the course of a major demolition, it becomes heavier, more massive. It tends to sink, its operation gets more sluggish. It can even grind to a halt.'

After the approach, there seem to be unlimited avenues of offices, laboratories, service bridges, factory plant, warehouses. Overhead gantries, conduits, wide-bore aluminised manifolds often run between buildings. Ventilator fans flicker in the wind.

No workers, people of any age. No animals either. You might expect the odd cat. No overflying birds, come to think of it. Who could tell whether this plant will function again? Even ever be visited again? By now we've reached enormous installations, inscrutable, breathtaking, the noise of the wind striking them is so loud, an unending howl.

'Turning the key so to speak is only the final stage...'

'Sorry, final stage of what?'

'...Disentrammelment of the Land Engine. Raising the Device out of the ground is the basic problem. Then starting it up, the key is not needed for this. The key enables use of its vast armoury of weapons.'

Behind foundries, reactors, ball mills... the distant chimney suddenly comes into sight. Other stacks may appear taller, but only because these silent, inert towers are nearer: one or two we walk past. The far column is our objective, this was what has to be reached. It alone is alive: although discharging no smoke, above it there plays a heat haze, resembling a turbulent stream.

'We are approaching one of the largest industrial exhausts ever constructed?'

'Well one of, you could say that.'

The objective lies ahead, a little to our left. But further along this convenient road ends, making a junction with an avenue. We look across: extending far in each direction are adamant grey factory buildings, blocking our way. To turn right would actually take us further away. Thus we've no choice but to turn left. So we are walking, but not much approaching the tall stack.

'This is the problem!' Large, forbidding doors, often padlocked, are set in the ferro-concrete walls bordering the route. The whole area is overlaid with intersecting, rusted railways. These run along the avenue, or pass into the factories, sometimes crossing our path. There are no locomotives or rolling stock; but one pair of rails shows bright lines through the rust.

These we follow as they curve right, into a cavernous building with high iron-frame, corrugated roof. The track weaves through interior doorways, perhaps better described as gaps in huge baffles across the width of the building. After taking one or two of these, we realise there is no longer a direct line of sight to the avenue outside. The gloom, from the dark sky, is now compounded by the absence of lighting, even of openings which can let in light. All the same Roland seems focussed on the operation.

'The vast stack is not our goal in itself. Just next to it is a facility where the functions of the entire plant can be concentrated onto the piece, in order to destroy it.'

'Row! This is the second time we've made this mistake. We didn't think to bring a lamp of any kind!'

'Too much planning is a give-away. We've just got to get through.'

As the entrance recedes, the rails sink lower into the concrete floor, they hardly protrude at all. From that region comes no more than a weak glare. If you've got no light, then you have to do without light. But not in this case: thus arises an old, nightmarish question. How can what little light there is be collected, concentrated? With a challenge, there is invariably an answer, a way that turns the tables. But in this particular predicament you are left hopelessly reaching for a way out, a means of proving to yourself that you are not in a fix. To see a little hint of light, not only not enough for use, for guidance; but as well not even enough for some lesser purpose, aesthetic perhaps, or familiarising: in some ways that's worse than none, than no light at all.

He pulls off a glove, and feels the steel ribbons with the fingers: smoothness edged by concrete. Then we put our heads down, ears pressed against the cold steel. The mineral, inorganic silence everywhere enables a far reaching search for very faint sounds. This is profound listening, catching sounds *miles* away. Nothing.

'Sensory deprivation!'

'Hold it!' There is a tiny reciprocating sound, lasting a few seconds. It is repeated several times, followed by a louder yet still faint ringing sound.

'Everything is live. This whole installation is just waiting to pounce!'

To the sound we listen for a while; then stand up and walk on into the darkness. At a certain place the track branches; there we take the track leading straight inwards. Twin reflections of the line can just be made out. Behind lies a diffuse pall of light, and aside from that there's no sign of the entrance. Then the reflections seem to come to an end. We have slowed to nearly a halt before touching what can only be... buffers!

Treading carefully, groping about just beyond the buffers, there is the feel of a metal wall, then some kind of wheel. But as it happens we return to the buffers, and lean on the rear plate, looking back toward the distant pall. From the ground arises the smell of discarded machine oil. Hopeless; we will just have to go back. After getting ready to do this, one of us remembers the handle. Perhaps it can be turned!

Reaching with bare hands, we touch the oval rim of a steel door, fitted with a steering-wheel handle on our side. After a couple of tugs, the wheel swings though a revolution or so, then stops with a click. An oval strip of light proclaims the hatch open, all it needs is a shove

'That was braving the dark!'

'Better dark than heights, wouldn't you say?'

'Well... maybe.'

It is a relief to have found the door. We've penetrated the interior! It takes a moment for awareness of the scene to take hold...

6. Needle Vent

A grey factory panorama, relieved by occasional patches of colour. displays before us. Mighty chains hang motionless. There are rails, more buffers, mineral wagons; we climb through and sit on the sill of the oval door. Dense mineral waste is heaped everywhere. In the metallic light wagons with their gimballed hoppers can be seen coupled in line; others further away are visible through the gaps. The rails pass between vertical, bolt-studded stanchions.

As to direction, the active flue is straight ahead. But considering the size of the site in front of us, still some way off. But not beyond reasonable walking distance.

The gleaming rails span forward, starting down a slight incline. A nearby mineral wagon is hitched to a buffer. We pass round to look at the rear coupling, this is fitted with a lever pin-release. Grasping it, we give the lever a wrench. No use.

'Tough!'

'Can't make it move!' However, lying on two hooks on the chassis is a metal tube, some type of tool, but it fits over the release handle. With so much leverage it is easy to withdraw the pin: immediately the wagon begins to slide forward. Slinging the tube back onto its hooks, we jump onto the moving chassis. The wagon picks up speed, as we make our way over the grey oxide load, and climb down onto the front buffers.

Moving over unjointed, continuous rail, the wagon makes very little noise – sometimes less than the soft whistle of the air. By the time it's on the level, the wagon is travelling pretty fast. Too fast to jump off comfortably, even after managing to land on a cushion of the bland dust. At one place, we fear the wagon might enter an automatic tipping-station. But shortly we slow and come to rest and clamber off.

Amongst the sidings it's not difficult to find a track-inspection wagon. Row places the briefcase in a recess. Powerful batteries are fully charged, we get the car running and move forwards, soon travelling quite fast.

The route runs past condensers, furnace flues, chemical, perhaps even nuclear reactors. At last being transported towards the distant objective, we can visualise the fixed orifice of the tower: the gases peacefully escaping from it in a folding, dancing heat haze.

Roland slows the wagon to less than walking-pace. It is at this point that faint background noises seem to float within the great silence. Not easy to describe... like the jangling of suspended glass tubing. Locking the brakes, we jump off.

'Bit more walking!'

Sidings lie ahead, several occupied with shunted wagons, but most empty. A set of points lie between us and the sidings, so we run ahead up to the manual setting lever, and swing it. The points clank as they change position, and thus shortly after ease our wagon through a smooth, ogival curve to an empty siding.

Watching it slowly roll down towards the buffers, our attention is grabbed by the sound of traffic on the through line, possibly another wagon. From far behind, it is approaching rapidly. Racing back, we hurriedly reset the points. Pulled by a diesel loco, this wagon comes into view, charged with a full load of mineral ore. It rattles over the junction, following the curve of the line to a distant entrance. By the time it passes into the daylight, our inspection-car has come to rest at the buffers.

'So, the noises we've been hearing... do they amount to anything?'

'Certainly. It is a case of tiny beginnings gradually surpassing everything.'

'Well, what are these noises?'

'Noises caused by activity close to our objective.'

The jangling background has become loud enough to get the direction: the disturbance is coming from outside one wall of the covered shunting-yard. This wall contains a small door, set into a much bigger pair of folding doors mounted on rollers. Unlocked. Opening it, for the first time since following a pair of rails into the cavernous enclosure, we step outside.

About a kilometre away towers the colossal vent, the view unobstructed from the ground upwards. Much wider of course, it rises like a needle. From its tip, the source of the noises, curls a pigtail of black smoke widening with distance into an enormous plume. Every few seconds at the root of the pigtail, flashes yellow fire.

We glance at the ground, at the platform supporting this vicinity of the complex. There is no road to the base, simply an open passage across the platform as wide as an airport runway. Thus, although factory buildings lie to either side, the way to the chimney is unobstructed; we walk towards it.

The plume discharged from the chimney-mouth is blown in a direction away from us, the dense smoke fights with the wind. Widening, the plume becomes a black funnel dominating the sky.

'The prevailing wind seems to be from almost directly behind. The plume fluctuates all right, but hasn't been blowing towards us!'

'We'll need more time to be sure of that!'

The tower is not brick, perhaps so tall a structure could not be built from brick. The Sun briefly shines through dark, silver-edged cloud, casting an unreal light on the dirty concrete surface.

Halfway or more to the tower, on the right, stands a curious old mill building. Covering the ground, we pace up to it. This it turns out is the place where the artefact has to be destroyed. The building has a curious bearing and distinction; its front door is shut but not locked.

'We have to work in here while keeping an eye on the fire plume!'

'Yes. There's clearly been a build-up!'

'For now the danger is reasonably far away.'

7. Impaled

Aside from its dignified bearing, the mill is utilitarian, industrial. The panelling is slightly ornate, two floors each have high ceilings. Turning the handle, opening the door, we can see reasonably well; tall windows helping to make up for poor daylight. With the howling wind, with the distant roar of the flame we enter.

An industrial citadel! This small place stands in defiance of the more recent world. A community of superseded artisans has been overwhelmed by the huge plant. The mill has preserved the last, concentrated residue of the epoch. Their artefacts have been arranged with ironic pride, as if to shame advance.

Disposed around a raised centre-piece, the objects are clearly if incompletely marked:

"The result of an early application of imitation intelligence to the biochemistry of..." Another is: *"The above is all that remains of the final attempt to..."* A piece on a plinth dominates the ground floor. According to a plaque, this was exhibited at the *"27th International Congress on the Pornography of Machines"*. Some kind of interactive device, it clearly has not been touched, let alone

used for a long time. But we decide to ignore it, noting the noises coming from outside.

A metal staircase leads to the upper floor. There's some kind of machine or engine upstairs.

'I vote we go up!'

'Yes, we've come all this way. Let's...'

Both of us chase up the staircase. There is an old, monstrously large wheel. The spindle is mounted on a massive device of unknown purpose. The wheel starts turning! Slowly but ever faster.

'Come on! We've got to get out.'

We're again on the ground floor.

'Do you mean to say that the whole of this unparalleled industrial emplacement is concentrated, into this little place, just for the purpose of...' Row nods as I speak. '...irreversibly destroying the artefact?'

'Indeed, exactly. This operation is so critical, there's no knowing what will happen here after the job is done. We'll no doubt see for ourselves!'

Row swings the shielded briefcase onto a table and slips out the box containing the artefact. 'Hang on: I've got to remember the release code!'

'Come on! Even indoors the noise of the flare is getting intimidating.'

'Only kidding!' Snap! The artefact awaiting destruction has to be introduced into the lathe impaled on a refractory pallet. We perform this step, using the tools and blank rivets available.

The lathe makes quite a lot of noise, and operates frustratingly slowly. But very soon after the jaws are fully open, the pallet is snatched into it, and the cast metal wheel starts rotating. Through a window in the side of the device, it is possible to view and witness the destruction. Cutting planes repeatedly strike from various directions, there is an extraordinary impression of precision patterns being fought back by the artefact. But suddenly a deep rending occurs, resistance apparently without foundation shatters without limit. The manifestly broken artefact is expelled from the lathe on its pallet.

'Hurry up! The noises are terrible.'

'The remains of the destroyed article have to be set in glass.'

'There's not time!' But Row is already doing it. The pieces are coated in black, heat-resistant matter. A blowtorch strikes, heating a slab of glass. He layers this over the remains, the mass is turned over, the operation is repeated. The orange-pink of hot glass rapidly falls away, but further he applies a magnetic cooling device, so that in seconds it is possible to lift the ingot with calipers and drop it into the shielded briefcase.

'We've got to get out of here.' We can hear the old, monstrously large wheel upstairs turning faster than ever.

Grabbing the case, abandoning the mill, we rush for the entrance, to be arrested by fearsome noises. The sound coming down is punctuated with explosive crackling, following a second or so after sudden brightenings of the flare. Flames can be seen at the meetings of bulges in the smoke.

'C'mon! The whole thing is about to blow up!'

'You're right.' We beat a hasty retreat. More deadly crepitations come down from the tower. A continuous flare plays at the base of the plume. There is a small but definite shaking movement of surrounding buildings. We sprint back toward the railway shed, quite a distance.

'The outcome for all concerned must be in doubt!'

'Well, yes, we'll have to see how it turns out.' Soon burning pellets of bituminous matter are reaching half-way down the chimney. The outside of the structure gives off a dull heat, it can surely be felt on the cheeks. Pursued by thundering and crashing, we fly through the opening into the folding doors on rollers. There is a distinct impression that just the pair of us alone will witness the final paroxysm of the complex.

Collapsing against the railway shed, we brace to get a proper view. The amount of smoke and fire above violently increases, hurling aside the tapering smoke plume. Frenzied gases charge straight upwards from the vent, mushrooming out and becoming indistinguishable from the clouds. With a continuous roar from the orifice, cascades of boiling slime tip down the outer surface from the overloaded, furious vent. Intermittent, muffled explosions seem to occur inside it.

Amazingly, an intuition speaks: it's all over, this is no more than a futile display, a meaningless reaction to your success with the forensic destruction. Surely, our predicament is resolved! He too has heard it this voice… we exchange a smile.

The absurdity of the display is endorsed by extraordinary changes in the discharge. There is a gritty sound, like a vacuum cleaner sucking up broken light-bulb bits. Grey-brown dust shoots out of the tower.

'The process has worked itself out?'

'Sure. Something like that.'

'Why did we have to set the remains in glass?'

'Just let me check. Yes, they're OK. Why? Because instruments in the Gestalt Engine have to perform an atom-for atom scan of the coating. This process is liable to burn out the mainframe, and perhaps even the on-board replacement. But once it is confirmed that the artefact has been forensically destroyed, then the full destructive power of the Gestalt Engine is liberated from all restraint.'

Returning to the track-inspection wagon in the sidings, Row slings the briefcase on board. We start it up, and thus travel back to the covered yard filled with mineral wagons. Exhausted, passing through the oval metal door, we re-trace our route, carrying the key to the Land Engine all the way back to the gate-house. After a final look at the complex, after checking on the car we seek out again our comfortable, dusty refuge.

Falling asleep very early, again I am beset by strange dreams.

In the morning, we find some fuel for ourselves and for the car.

After a general tidy up, we bid farewell to Greyscar and set off with the glass entity, the route taking us into rocky desert.

CHAPTER 7
ONE DEFINITION OF THE GESTALT

1. The Vehicle

'Did you bring any souvenirs of Greyscar?'

'I did not... *ha-ha*!'

Occasionally stratified rocks in buff, sandy colours are exposed by artesian springs.

'Hey, look at that...!' Row has to slow down to get through a rocky, windy corner. Fleetingly, linguistic, symbolic carvings can be glimpsed, cut onto a nearly flat surface. '...Let's get a photo!' But he races on through the dust. After a while we reach a metalled road. Clumps of date trees of all ages grow where there is water. On the horizon flat-topped formations gradually pass.

A distant dust funnel appears. Not a vortex... Yes, another vehicle approaches, it's moving fast. We slow down, pull right over, revving to make for the scrub if necessary. But the pick-up cuts past, well over to his side but otherwise totally ignoring us.

Arid zone vegetation is fascinating, when there is any. A second vehicle coming the other way approaches.

'What have we here...? Looks like a police car. One at least. Let me handle this...' He grins. '...Or maybe this sort of thing is your kind of stuff?'

'What? *Ha, ha*. No, sir.' The approaching vehicles brake as fast as they have been moving, all coming to a precision halt. Huge shades glint as two officers get out of the nearest car. Row manages a smile as one towers over the now-lowered window.

'Afternoon. l/d please.' Roland flashes forward a semi-transparent card, like a conjuror, there was no seeing where it came from. An almost gloating expression fills the officer's face as a third gets out of the squad car.

'Very sorry to have taken up your time, sir. You...'

He squints in at me and the contents. '...You are carrying something?'

Roland points to the briefcase. 'There!'

'You are both expected at your accommodation. It's not so far to go. You're actually due at the front desk in an hour.'

'We'll get cracking.'

'Please take care, sir. Observe the restrictions.' The officers stand by their vehicles as we zoom away. The territory is arid savanna; occasional woody shrubs grow in the ochre soil.

Row explains, 'Nothing is left to chance. Every step we take is observed and noted.'

'Really?'

Dwellings of mud-brick pass. Without comment, he continues, 'The Device has moods, it can take a vicious turn if not ruthlessly, brutally controlled. The men call it the "the dog". Flattering term, some would say. That reminds me, the organisers of the operational chain of command...'

'Come off it, Row...!'

'Stop making me laugh. I nearly drove into that rock...! Now what was I saying... These planners allow just enough time for each sub-operation, each individual part. And no more. We are no exception, the rules apply equally to us.'

'All right. Fair enough.'

What can be seen, simply by looking is mesmeric. Progressions of impressions fall reassuringly into place. The boundary between sleep and waking slips away. Relaxation is the priority. There's no need to interpret the scene. Yes, there is! I almost shout aloud, 'Row! Where's this?' All around are buildings.

'You were snoring!'

'You mean we've arrived...' We're at a railway station hotel. Handing the case to me, Row wastes no time getting the car into a lock-up. We check into the quiet, dimly-lit guest house, possibly the only clients.

'Don't get too comfortable. First thing tomorrow we take the maglev.'

'Maglev? Frictionless.'

'Almost...' Evidently, he takes pleasure in discussing the system. '...It travels at nearly 1000 mph, slower in built-up areas. There are quieter times, when the service is not so frequent. But on busy days the main line conveys two thousand passengers per transit.'

Before taking our rooms, there's a comfortable lounge for us.

'There'll be times when it's imperative that we move quickly. After getting to one of the main stations, crew members will transport us to the current location of the Device. You and I will need to actually board the Device.'

'From what you said while we were on the road, we'll be lucky to survive inside this Engine.'

'Have no fear, *ha-ha*. It'll be much safer inside than out.'

'Did you say, you've done this before...'

'Yes. Look, I hope you feel fully complicit in all this. There is a certain amount of danger. The crew are dolts and incompetents in almost everything but their work. The procedures are very well established. Very occasionally, the system takes a spill, but it's an outside chance.'

'It'll have to be truly dire to rival wandering the ash-laden escarpment. Er, yes, Row, of course I do.'

'There are two stages ahead. First we have to seek out a long overdue demolition, and then get on with it, just to get the Machine fully warmed up.'

'Warmed up! Why is this necessary?'

'One reason is the Device is so unwieldy. It's mass is variable. Often it gets so heavy it actually sinks into the ground.'

'So full control of it is by no means guaranteed.'

'You've got the idea... Beginning this first phase involves a very destructive process. Over time, cities at this latitude have merged into an endless conurbation. The Device will have to plough its way through several miles of this, to reach the doomed structure.'

Suddenly tiredness takes over, bedding in the rooms assures long, dreamless sleep. At the crack of dawn we are on the platform; Roland carries the case.

'I'm sorry it's going to be a dash until we're on board. It has to do with the *modus* of the device.' I turn from him.

'*Arhhhh!*' There's a train that feels like it's six inches from my nose!

'Quiet isn't it?' We get in, the monorail races over sidings and into a tunnel. There's not even a slight buzz from the lighting.

'It will be a rush after we've got into the actual Engine as well.' I look down at what's in his hand.

'When will this be handed over?'

'Straight away. It will be used immediately.'

The very fast train decelerates and halts at a big-city underground complex. As we get out a squad of paramilitaries all but arrests us.

'This way, sir Hurry!'

Both of us are bundled into an armoured personnel carrier. Two officers hastily introduce themselves. They've been assigned to do no more than oversee the two of us and the case. From corner seats it's possible to see a crowd being pushed back as the exhausts throw up a dirty plume. The vehicle thrusts forward from the Maglev station, swinging round a bend and into a boulevard from which vehicles are still being cleared. The street is wide, but we seem to be too near an urban centre to get a glimpse individual buildings.

'We're on the way to near the site of a previous demolition. The entire Device has sunk well below ground level, besides it has undergone considerable lateral movement. Yes! To where we are now! Once the Monster surfaces, we'll have to get inside it straight way, and travel to where the work is waiting to be done, another site.'

Thus we are forcefully taken to an extensive area, which begins to suffer upheaval even as we arrive. Everyone piles out of the carrier. There are alarming vibrations, buildings fall sideways as a dome of ground splits to reveal the tungsten of a monstrously potent-looking device. After some while it stops rising, the surface is hot.

He glances at me, obviously knowing what's coming. We are pushed forwards.

'That door! It's essential you board immediately!' Still more crew are waiting to urge and shove us up a metal staircase, where we are met by a member of the command crew.

'Can't use the lift yet!'

Via more flights of stairs we are conducted to the top of the vehicle and shown into a huge room with seats and a wrap-around window. No less than the Commander himself addresses us, 'Roland! How are you? An honour to meet you, sir.'

'Likewise, Commander.'

'And... This is our visitor.' We shake hands. Row passes to him the refractory briefcase.

'The fragmented artefact! Thank you both very much.' Securing the case with a wrist bracelet, the master steps backward, and is gone.

2. Sacrifice

We are taken to numbered seats near the middle. Deep padding makes them particularly comfortable; but the safety-harnesses are rather intimidating. Something in a hold immediately below us is dropped. There are shouts.

'Have you ever driven a bulldozer?'

'Er, no...' Row snatches at the air. '...Wait. Did do something like that... But no.' Occasionally, there is a minute sound, accompanied by the sensation of loss of support, as cavities beneath the Land Engine collapse.

'I have, as a student. Expensive piece of plant. A bulldozer is worth its weight in silver!'

Large, the room is packed with optic trunks, readouts, displays, consoles, fire-fighting equipment, all in a fairly greasy condition. Cans tilt over a valve, hazardous fumes roll around the room. Footsteps, crashes can be heard through the ceiling, the walls, from below; the noise of general activity is louder than ever.

'They're tightening up for today's trip.'

'Has the engine itself started?'

'It has not. You'll know all about that...' He is rudely broken into by a dull scraping noise: a steel hook is lowered through a ring anchored to the hull of the stationary Gestalt Vehicle. '...The auxiliary engine wakes up a powerful intermediate motor, which they're testing now. It runs on fuel from the main tanks, two floors below us.'

'And then that gets the main motor going!'

'Exactly... the noise of the prime mover starting up is ground-shaking. It's the exhaust system backfiring, they don't bother with silencers... definitely part of the fun!'

A crew-member tells us, 'First the Vehicle has to be oriented.' Using a distant windlass mounted on a squat concrete tower, the Engine is to be rotated by wire until it faces forwards. Loose, mainly hidden from view, the super-strong wire threads through intervening streets.

A plume of smoke pushes up from the tower; the cable snaps straight, flicking a curtain of concrete and bricks upwards. There is the sound of discarded appliances being compacted, sunglasses being stepped on, the point of a nail being drawn across glass, as the metal bulk of the Land Engine is rotated on its belly. The operation halts before the Machine points in the direction of the windlass, to avoid the obstruction.

The auxiliary engine kicks. The team drawing charge from enormous batteries jump back as the engine revs up. The switchgear is basic; from the arcing carbon brushes an oily, electrical smell rises.

Several attempts are made to engage the intermediate motor; success is signalled by a deep, throbbing vibration.

'What's the next step?'

'Safety checks. Looks like we're going to make a move!'

Activity. Seat-belts rattle. We listen. Each of us tenses. A harsh, metallic voice comes over the public address, 'Attention! Final checks! Departure imminent!'

'Air-conditioning to internal! Ventilation channels sealed!'

Another, louder voice, 'Fire detail to emergency exit stations! Power doors closing! Standby for start routine! Armature engaged!'

'Uhhh!' Piercing noise from the Prime Mover! Fists covering ears! Uncontrollable vibration. Things drop, bones shake. We are both shocked forward and to one side. The intermediate motor has engaged the main driving force! Even seasoned operatives wince at the repeated backfiring, which subsides after a minute or two. The throbbing of the mighty motor remains, however. The rock stratum itself seems in danger of cracking as the Device again backfires. But soon everyone is immersed in the pulsing of the mighty motor.

'And now... are you ready for a violent journey in the Land Engine?'

'No! I mean, yes!'

The terrible sound of the motor rises, the Land Engine thunders forward. The even force due to acceleration acts on us: a petrol station and hotel seem to be consumed in one gulp, the former throwing up a brief sheet of fire. Streets and avenues of the city open all around, to the ear-splitting progress of the Engine.

The speed passes 200 kph: there is a sighing from the storm of bricks, girders, concrete slabs, glass, plastic and chrome thrown into a quasi-liquid by our passage. All around are the shouts of the crew, 'Hydraulic legs! On! On!' Change in engine whine.

'Pressure up, still rising, full... NOW!' Suddenly, we rise seventy metres. Wheels and tracks have been replaced by great jointed legs, whose arachnidian forms flick at the lower field of the viewing screen. But we lose height, as the feet sink into the street like a road drill into a wedding cake. Soon we are low enough for the whirring tracks and wheels to re-engage the buildings below.

'This is the extent of the sacrifice the city must make, to enable what should have been done long ago.'

The hastily-erected windlass block appears on the opposite side, that too zips out of sight. Suddenly, someone puts music on over the public address. Very loud. Rhythmic stuff, strongly backed by trills and screeches. The view out is breathtaking.

Now the Vehicle has to greatly slow down, as it passes a still-inhabited area.

3. Preliminary

'Oh... Right!' Row says to a junior officer. Then to me, 'Come on, you may find this interesting...'

'*Ha-ha*!'

'...It is reckoned safe enough for us to get out of the seats and pass to another level. The laboratory is there, where they're looking at what's in the case: you remember, the glass ingot containing the destroyed artefact.'

In the experiments suite, untidy, bulky cable trunks converge on what appears to be a battered hospital scanner. An industrial robot slips the vial out of its case. The object is sucked into a cavity, where it is suspended in space.

'This is the precise part.' Pale light from the apparatus falls on the faces all around.

'Wow! That moved quickly.'

'Affine, three-axis orientation.' The glass snaps into a series of different positions, as it is scrutinised by visible and X-ray lasers.

'This'll take ages. Right, let's get back.' We are shown back to the same seats.

Now the speed builds up. Cameras point to either side, backwards.

'Row! Look what's happening... See in those screens!' Roofs crackle like shells. Occasionally we unseat a factory chimney, even smack straight into one. The Machine dislocates and rips open a five-thousand-litre flask of industrial perfume. From the entertainment speakers a loud wash of white sound fills the air, then flutters away.

Roland casually remarks, 'Technically, we've done our work... we're no longer needed.'

'So, we'll miss out on the climax? Worse than murder!'

'You can rest assured they'll find a way to let us see whether or not our efforts have culminated in success.'

A crew-member comes over, to brief Row on how the operation is progressing. For a few moments they speak in low voices, then he turns to me. 'I'm sorry, but a newly-installed main-frame has failed.'

'Has it damaged the piece? Presumably, we can have another try?'

'Indeed. The back-up has already been connected. The results should come in any minute.'

'Let's hope there's no problem.'

'Unlikely. All the readings looked OK. In fact...' Someone near the door gives the thumbs-up. Shortly, Row is handed written confirmation that the artefact was genuine, and has been forensically destroyed.

'Right. We can forget about that.'

Covering my eyes, blacking everything out, I try to grapple with the present situation.

'So right now we're in just the first phase.'

'That's it. The practice phase if you like.'

'Surely, demolition is a straightforward process?'

'Root demolition is not so straightforward. You may be surprised to learn that there are notorious, long overdue demolitions still waiting, because earlier attempts have failed. In each case the abominable landmarks have resisted such measures as being subsidated, demolished using gelignite or even vibrated to collapse.'

'Did you say subsidated?'

'Deliberately undermined.'

'How could this resistance be possible? Once demolished, always demolished!'

'Wrong I'm afraid. For the really old, centrally-located and most enormous structures, invariably granite, what you say is just not true. Following a botched attempt to terminate a structure, any of a range of means of recovery may occur. Anything from replacement with more recent, stronger materials, all the way to complete re-erection from rubble, relying on records, plans, drawings and photos.'

'And perhaps by repurposing of dressed stones?'

'In many cases, yes. We are talking about buildings liable to be re-created from their reflection in a window, from their shadow even. It sounds far-fetched, but the range of regeneration techniques extends to plywood mock-ups which from a distance resemble the original.'

'You mean people are taken in by these?'

'Long enough for the replicas to hide the restoration going on inside.'

'When's the demonstration demolition going to actually start?'

'Soon. Any moment.'

The Engine rises over an urban ridge, just as it shifts to the right. Enormities of the city are becoming visible, the clouds seem to be involved. But he snaps, 'Don't look in that direction! You'll get carried away… Look over there, that's what we're after.' An oppressive, appallingly ugly building fills one of the telescopic screens. It seems to have every kind of decoration crammed into its architecture at once.

'In terms of the status of this urban region, all the enormities you were just looking at come to nought, because buildings such as this have not been got rid of.'

'So what's the problem?'

'As surely you will see, some structures stubbornly resist demolition.'

'Surely, the whole art must be to minimise damage nearby to the site.'

'Certainly. But when it comes to it, city authorities are invariably willing to allow considerable damage in order to get rid of the hardest structures. By the way… the window! It's made of Trylar, the stuff has been toughened in a neutron furnace. Anything less would be like using cardboard against what's coming.'

At last the bulky structure heaves into view, we are more or less making straight towards it. It stands before us, we thunder towards it. The Land Engine rises to higher ground. Yet the objective towers above us as we approach. Surrounding buildings collapse sideways as the Engine drives straight into it. We are all concussed by the impact, the Device has to reverse.

'Are you sure there's nobody about?'

'Not completely. The area has been very thoroughly cleared.'

'Ah. OK then.'

'Look! Over there. No, at the top of the broken concrete slab.'

'Several figures, climbing over!'

'Not supposed to be there. Nothing we can do. Demolition chasers!'

Suddenly, our land Engine strikes at the building with hydraulic hammers. Tremendous battering attacks with the 25-ton iron fists cause such local vibration that all remaining nearby buildings collapse. But as to the objective structure itself, massive, very hard components that have long rested on one the other take considerable softening up.

The resistance of the building is astonishing, as if at first it is no more than marked. Fire starts, quickly engulfing the entire roof, yet this seems no more than a draught against and through the solid structure.

The machine is relentless, even if those at the controls were to become discouraged, its program and purpose is to devour all obstruction. The entire machine repeatedly rises and retreats, in this way butting its quarry. Hydraulic screws are deployed. A crack opens in one of the stone corner foundations. A noise loud enough to reach all of us accompanies the fall of all that it supports. Ton-weight blocks, tumbling down and outwards batter the glass screen. Some are so heavy as to jerk everyone on board.

There is something demented about the Machine: auxiliary hammers are deployed, the heavy steel balls strike at segments of falling masonry, even at individual stones, breaking them further before they hit the ground.

All this time the midday Sun shines down on the proceedings as if nothing is happening.

The power of the blows can be gauged by the dull glow of heat becoming visible on the grit-caked, scored surfaces. Huge single blocks are exploding to powder. We hear a major part of the building fall directly onto our roof. The whine of the engine rises as most of the building collapses.

Frenzied battering brings down two more large walls, the machine pounces forward, springs backwards.

Now dust, black smoke belches and billows upwards as there is decisive collapse directly above the foundations. The Device strikes a final, downward blow with sudden and tremendous violence: anyone not wearing a seatbelt is liable to have been injured.

Thus is completed the first phase, whetting the appetite of the Device. There is a feeling of bodily exhaustion. The action has knocked the breath out of us; it is a while before talk resumes, 'What was that about the Udev? This is to be used for our second phase?'

'Indeed, it will be indispensable. Let me explain bit by bit. This Gestalt Engine is one of several variable mass devices. But some demolitions it cannot undertake.'

'So, that's when the Unique Device becomes necessary?'

'Yes. For our use of it during this current project, control from the ground is of key importance.'

'What is the U-device?'

'A robot so large it carries a sizeable nuclear power station. When its tripod is fully extended, the UDev reaches above the clouds!'

'How is such a huge thing used?'

'The work is so messy, unweildy, it will have to perform its demolition via excavation.'

'Grading, some kind of traction?'

'Yes, maybe. The work is far too hazardous for manned operation. The extraction has to be controlled from the ground, and for the culmination of the second phase followed by a gestalt device like ours to take over control during igneous disposal.'

'Engrossing!'

'We are undertaking the front-line work. Afterwards mopping-up teams will arrive with what is in effect a giant vacuum cleaner, and draw off the rubble into a container. The debris can then be transported by rail to a geologically active landfill.'

'Well, perhaps I can guess what one of those is...'

'You'll see! After that the "socket" left by the foundations will be decontaminated, then levelled with synthetic crustal material.'

Again a messenger confers with Row, who smiles, thanking him.

'Apparently, we're welcome to these seats for a day or so. But we'll be in the way after that. So they've arranged a diversion for us. We're invited to rejoin the Machine and its compliment for the climax.'

4. Gently Librating

The huge window is such a bonus. This sky is the sort you'd expect for early June: the chill of spring still brings wind and cloud, to an otherwise clean and brilliantly blue sky. There are few high altitude clouds, those lower, confined to the horizon are whipped into flat-bottomed, curly shapes. Looking around, such odd shapes can be found. There's a square cloud, blue-white it is so far away.

'You're looking at the UDev!'

'Such a nice day. What...?' How many times have I seen that gloating smile? '...That?'

'It's travelling at 500mph. Towards us…' The gaze of the entire complement is locked in the same direction. The tripod is becoming visible. The chimera now is close enough to lose its cloud-like colours. '…It's slowing down.'

'Just as well!'

'*Ha, ha.*'

'There's something else dangerous on it. The grab has to get hold of a cube of ground one quarter of a kilometre on a side and lift it upwards reasonably quickly. Not even a nuclear power-plant can generate that much energy fast enough. The tripod has an energy capacitor. The power-plant is now operating at full belt, the control rods are right out, in order to charge it up. You can see a steam plume rising to one side. Of course, if the capacitor became damaged, there could be a devastating explosion.'

'A tripod, yet it can walk?'

'It actually has four legs, see… The spare is called the ranging leg, it can be any one of them. At all times, UDev has three widely-spaced points of contact with the ground. The ranging leg is swapping round all the time the system is on the move.'

Hypnotised by the approach, it's been easy to miss that the tripod has greatly retracted its legs. The installation at the summit can be studied in detail. The whole system has slowed and come to a halt over a fixed position. Our own demolition engine thunders into action, the wheels and racks grinding us along an approach route. This gives a series of glimpses of a blackened, lamentably hideous objective structure. It towers and spreads on a shocking scale.

Certainly this is the tripod's objective. It is an extraordinarily tall, ancient building. It is dark, worn with time, obscenely ugly.

'That's the job! See what you mean. Too big for us alone.'

'Yes. For untold centuries it has cast a dark shadow over an entire continent!' Momentarily, it looks as if even the UDev could not lift such a load, but that feeling passes. Obviously it is possible.

Plasma torches bite into the ground, refractory piping draws off molten rock, soon there is a square trench of considerable width and depth around the building, over a quarter of a kilometre on a side. The immense grapnel, about the size of the nuclear power station carried by the robot, darkens the sky above the building. It widens, hardened steel grinders at the tips of its fingers and hands plunge into the channels, passing far down until the screws are switched on. The explanations go on and on, but hardly can they keep up with the pace of the work.

'Wait for it... Yes! It's actually cutting the ground from under the building.'

'Now comes the test of the power delivery system!' Everything tensions. A searing blast of steam and vapor reaches into the sky. All are hit with a thunderous yet high-pitched noise.

'There's no-one on board. We are controlling it... That up there at the back is the reactor.'

Huge gears can be heard flying round, as a dark cube of ground is elevated into the sky. So precise is the move, so slight the acceleration that the extraordinarily tall, ancient structure rises intact on the cube.

Soon the material accretion is elevated with the summit of the tripod itself, as the legs are extended. The ranging leg is now deployed, it seems to probe dangerously near us, and suddenly crashes into the ground. It makes vibrating punches into the ground to ensure it is stable enough to take the enormous weight. Now it exchanges place with one of the tripod legs, which becomes the ranging leg, all the while the three load-bearing legs are telescoping out at different rates. Carrying its catch, the UDev has taken a step.

Our Device noisily wheels round to follow it, amid one or two shouts there is a hubub of conversation. Suddenly, the Commander is leaning over us.

'They tell me the load is secure.'

'What a relief. Well done!'

'You may know the UDev has to proceed very slowly wherever a step is liable to be uncertain.'

'Such as this urban area?'

'Of course. But also over the nearby low-lying territory. Some of it is swampy. This is a journey of thousands of miles.'

'It's going to take ages!'

'This is the point. Months. A month anyway. Everything will greatly speed up of course on higher ground, once the UDev reaches the rocks.'

It is impossible to avoid taking a sneak look at what is going on outside as Row says, 'So we are just going to get in your way!'

'No, no. We can find work for you both in the galley. Long hours of course… But I had a better idea.' I listen with alarm.

'May I ask about that?'

'There are motorbikes in the hold for special purposes. The abandoned city of Tenatis lies not far from the route the UDev will be taking.'

'Oh… Sure!'

'You can take our visitor there!'

'So can we do this?'

'Yes. I have to leave you now. The first Officer will show you to the hold when you've got ready.'

'Thankyou.' Everywhere there is the hustle building up to the activity of supervising and controlling the advance of the UDev. We waste no time in making arrangements to get out of the way.

Along with many crew members, we are gripped by the very spectacular image of the dark structure, so enormous, so tall and yet so dwarfed by the Tripod, gently librating in the sky. All of us follow details through strong binoculars. It is very interesting, but eventually he taps me on the shoulder.

'Come on. We've got to find our way out of this urban agglomeration, don't forget.'

A senior officer speaks, 'You ready already?'

'Howdy! Er, give us two more minutes.' The officer leads us to the hold, we are shown two battered but powerful motorbikes. Technicians help to get the machines out of the Device and onto the road. The bikes are fuelled and started up. Jackets and helmets are passed to us and checked.

'Hold it. You might need these!' A technician fixes a pair of field glasses inside a pannier on one of the bikes.

'Great! I love binoculars.'

'So do I.' Soon we are on the way.

5. Sun and the Hurricane

A number of times I cannot keep up with Row, he is faster on bends. Most roads are jammed with traffic. Here I am on a huge bike lost in a strange megalopolis. But each time he thunders up from behind having looped round. After a lot of work, we finally reach a fast and spectacular arterial road leading straight out the built-up region. After passing far ahead of much traffic, Roland flags me down, we pull off at a flyover for a brief look back at the distant urban agglomeration. Then at high speed we travel into wild territory, holding in the same direction for several hours.

The journey to Tenatis takes several days, during this time traffic on the intercontinental trunk road gradually becomes less. Taking a break along a wild road, we encounter gaggle of people.

Welcoming the company we join them, the motorbikes idling at walking-pace. Judging by their clothes these could be working people on a holiday ramble. An older man by the name of Weyn motions to a distant cloud bank moving up. The air stays clear, but soon the sky is overcast. It remains warm.

Interest in the bikes is evident: two at a time, ramblers in the group take turns riding with us. In single file we pass through a wide, sparse wood; chatter ricochets from the trees. The ground is not everywhere level, mountains are in evidence to the south-east. As the group passes through a clearing, low cloud pushes and thrusts into what has been an open sky. Trees thin out to bushes and bracken, making what lies above more present, darker, actually oppressive. Curling, fuming clouds race overhead, always in one direction. The mountains... are no longer visible! Someone shouts, 'Look at that!' A branch or small tree is being carried in the sky by the wind. More pieces follow. All are perplexed.

'Surely, there's the danger it might fall!'

'Oh, yes...' Over the talk there is in the trees, a sudden howl.

'We must shelter somewhere!' I speak with emphasis, the wind snaps one or two decaying branches above us. The weather and the desolation of this place go hand in hand, vying for peculiarity. It becomes noticeable how many trees around us are dead.

Someone yells, 'Aghhh! It's supposed to be day and I can hardly see properly!' A darker grey cloud, lower than the rest rides faster, climbing under the backs of others already moving quite rapidly. It is chased by another. The wind takes the same direction; but occasionally there is a lull, it drops to nothing, the clouds pass noiselessly. Often the company glances upwards.

Barbed wire fencing! It's quite high, but long neglected; in places there are openings. We move over ash and stones then pavement, onto a concrete road. The wind does not die down, heaving cloud remains.

The weed-infested blocks lead, after a further walk to a deserted airfield: there is another group waiting. One or two parked motorbikes and cars are in evidence. Most seem to know the others; undoubtedly some people have not met for a long time.

With hasty glances at the sky, the merged group sets off along the paved road. After walking not very far, most stop to look up: there is no doubt this cloud belt is lowering. The wind picks up, gusting alarmingly. It goes on getting stronger, the sound of chatter is abruptly quashed. An authoritative voice shouts, 'The airfield! We'll take cover in the old pre-fabs!' The group beats a retreat. The vaporous cover is undoubtedly lowering, the surfaces are not at all diffuse, the clouds seem very near as we run. High ground to either side of the road has disappeared. Here and there small groups pause to view the spectacle, anxious hands urge them to join the general rush.

Several have already sprinted through the dilapidated entrance to the airfield buildings. They are followed very quickly by others, keen to shelter behind the concrete.

Doors have long since rotted, there is a smell of urine. We drive the bikes inside. The extensive warren of bare concrete is very welcome. Most rush far inside, a few pause at the entrance look upwards.

'Wind's getting harder... look out! Get back!' Huge dark, objects fly just above the ground, then with a crash an oil-drum is blown in through one entrance. It strikes the wall violently, two or three jump back as it bounces to rest.

'C'mon! We've got to fill the doorways!' Breeze-blocks, concrete and steel lengths are piled up, as the howling pitch of the wind rises still further.

Soon, despite the din, there is a quite cosy atmosphere; a fire has been started near a slit opening, tea is brewing. But the noise of the wind and of whole trees battering the shelter is very loud and violent, people look at each other. The outer structure is impacted repeatedly, there are heavy crashes perhaps caused by stones. Scarcely a drop of rain falls from the dark, yellowish clouds: yet often lightning strikes. Magenta-blue shafts fall across the broken floor, as light from close-by discharges cuts into our shelter through the rubble.

We fall into conversation.

'That was some driving back there!' I stage a lunge at Row, as if to land a massive blow to the heart. 'A robot! You're a bloody robot, aren't you?'

He smiles. 'Well... yes, to a certain extent!' Two or three of the crowd take an interest in what is said, but without themselves contributing a word. Uncertainty, ambiguity far outweigh what is said. If a robot, then Roland has descended from the future, not arisen from the past.

Through remaining still, we are cut by the cold and decay of the shelter. Despite the dark it is possible to just see colour green on damp concrete where colonies of moss and lichens thrive. People are gathering near one of the entrances.

It has been clear all along that there was no possibility of the concrete yielding to the hurricane. Suddenly, the wind drops. It is over.

After settling in so nicely no one feels like making a move; but eventually we say our goodbyes, and the group sets off.

The wind, which but for our recent experience would no doubt pass unnoticed, is still strong, still falling. Sometimes it carries packets of rain. The bikes start easily; we return to the super-highway.

After two further days of travel at high speed, there is a return to arid climate. The highway is all but deserted; repeatedly the rocks demand a pause for picture-taking, for grabbing the binoculars. In a high pass we gain a vantage point, through rolling mountainous terrain. A grey anomaly appears in the distance: the city of Tenatis.

CHAPTER 8
THE PATTERNED ABYSS

1. Tenatis

Ahead appears the sprawling city of Tenatis. The dried-up remains of it, anyway. After a long journey, this part of which has been by motorbike, we reach the place.

After travelling an abandoned road, early in the still, cloudless afternoon we enter. Far into the torrid desert, the city is large, modern-epoch, of past wealth. Amid its still-vertical towers the route leads along wide, silent boulevards. We glean that the abandonment is permanent, never again will this place be occupied. Date, coconut palms still grow where they have been planted, in the company of bladder cacti, tree thistles and grasses that have found their way in uninvited. Few buildings have collapsed, most of the window glass, often coppered against the Sun, remains in place. But there clearly have been explosions, some very violent, throwing rubble across the widest avenues.

Threading through rubble-free streets, it becomes clear that what we have taken to be a huge, dead city springing from Sun-baked rocks is in fact only a facade. There is urban development from eras long past, streets of houses as they would have been for generations long forgotten.

Impressions built up as we probe successive streets can be compared one against the other. There is rivalry when it comes to choosing.

'Let's have a look in here!'

'Mmmm... maybe more interesting if we go further. That street is clear. What do you say?'

The bikes have to be parked, GPS positioning adjusted, we agree to continue on foot. Now the weather appears to be conforming to the locale! The Sun has gone in, unprepossessing clouds rule. There is no rain.

We are bumped by a coincidence: together, at the same instant, we pick, we make for the same building, an ordinary house with its own garden.

'Come on, let's try to get in.'

'There's another door round the side, but... may as well try the front door first.' Ready to give it a shove, we find it unlocked, easy to open.

'Uhh... this is really strange!' The first impression is of an extended suburban house, whose content forms a carefully-arranged display. Furniture, wallpaper, ornaments are all unspoiled, dust free. It seems likely that no-one has ever actually lived in the house. What else is to be found further in?

Thus comes a shock moment when the broken, ossified city turns the tables on us. No longer are we trespassers gazing down on prone, helpless ruins. No longer indulging ourselves to our full and complete satisfaction.

This is the moment at which we are arraigned, frozen by an unknown, unprecedented influence. Our sense of purpose is humbled by the realisation that this city is a different entity altogether. Lifeless, dead yes, but these are mere conditions which had to have been met, to provide the base or rostrum upon which this influence rests. The very frills of death await our inspection, having been sewn into a world of form recognisable to neither of us. There is an extraordinary feeling of even danger itself being a minor consideration, placed beside the compulsion to play our part, to progress the investigation.

The glass panel in the front door lets in light, plenty for a dull day. The hall is jammed with bizarre decorations! There's a range of artifacts: antique dental equipment, a biscuit-making machine, the control box from a urinal, down to a pile of loose piano keys. Some of these are plastered with toothpaste, molasses, ink. Such articles are positioned in the hall, corridors, staircases in every room nearby.

The interior lighting is fortunate for us, although it proves to be inexplicable. Only under the rather jerky guidance of Row did I encounter anything like this. Initially, illumination seems to be coming from a room or two away from or on our path. Daylight, not artificial light. But when we get there, again we cannot find the source. It is only whatever lies beyond, out of our direct line of sight, appears to be the source of illumination. It feels as if there must be windows somewhere, yet we find only further rooms, closets, cabinets, cupboards.

The house suggests no particular sequence, the doorways usually just lead further into the building. A large room or two might be followed by a small connecting room, by a staircase leading to a dead end, by a meeting of corridors.

Before exploring further, we have to devise a workable escape plan, a way to get out of the place in a hurry. A simple procedure achieves this: repeatedly trying a new route, then returning to somewhere reasonably familiar.

The tour includes arches, glass doors, side doors, doors long obstructed by furniture, trap doors, imitation doors leading nowhere, swing doors.

The electrical supply is cut of course, but there are occasional skylights. Through these filter some illumination from the lower parts of the roof. With regular pauses, it is just about possible to avoid getting lost in the maze of passages, steps, cellars, corridors, basements.

It is thus possible to reach well beyond the first house; the apparently cultivated degradation everywhere makes the houses appear as one building, if not a street or more of buildings accreted into a single, dilapidated labyrinth. After one of our returns, in fact not far from the hall, a shut door can be made out in the faint, stagnant light.

Unlocked; it yields only a few centimetres. Something seems to be blocking it. We apply more force. A scratching sound accompanies a series of crashes. The door slowly opens, with more noises; it has to be really forced. As soon as there is space, one of us pushes their head and shoulders through the gap.

2. The Fallen City

Now we take turns leaning through the partly-blocked door. As eyes adjust to the gloom a wealth of detail becomes visible, earthenware flagons, carboys, jars, bottles, flasks. There are various buckets, galvanised, enamel, plastic, not all empty. Stacks of plates, collapsed venetian blinds, vacuum cleaners, garden accessories cover the floor and reach up the walls. These things obstructed the door, our earlier efforts have shattered a couple of the bottles. Beyond precarious heaps of atlases, soda-siphons, brass band pieces, stands another door.

In turn, we shove through the now-opened door, having to kick aside boxes of soiled hospital equipment. There are hazards: pieces of broken glass are stuck onto the pale olive screen of a truly obsolete television set. Each outfacing point is tipped with a dark, spiky, paste. Memories of biology lessons floated back, as we examine the crooked bristles. Setiferous. In some cases the paste looks damp. There are old clothes, laundered, folded and skillfully mutilated. Floor stain from a tin spills over tasselled silk cushions, thickly scattered with vacuum cleaner fluff. The items are carefully, almost professionally arranged, some are topped with spray paint like delicacies in a bakery!

The ceiling is papered over with newsprint. Partial, smudged headlines can be seen, the light insufficient to make much sense of them. There appears to be something else bulging through the newspapers, surely not the original ceiling, it is by no means level.

But the mockery is not superficial: it applies to places that would never normally be looked at. Lift one article up, and below find items out of sight, but no less carefully arranged. Break open an axed mobile phone, and find inside that battery, circuitry, switches have been cracked into pieces, rearranged, crazily glued together and brightly painted! The objects have something in common with the natural world. The apparent deliberateness can only be an illusion.

A skylight lets in a weak pallor; under it we make our way. Jumbled amongst the glassware are bulk packing cases, enough of these can be stacked to reach the skylight. Shifting one box, we accidentally knock a bottle onto several beneath it. As it cracks the jar releases a kind of molasses, this oozes over the shattered lower bottles. Froth starts rising, there is a smell of vinegar.

The honours are left to me: careful balance is needed while climbing up, the boxes tend to give a little. Something rests on the skylight, at first resisting an upward push, but then sliding off as the window opens. The space above is in effect a chimney rising through an otherwise solid pile of discarded possessions and fittings. Amongst these we can even see a disused lavatory. And above this is another skylight. As we stare upwards, the glass front of a picture frame, poked by heavy objects behind it, suddenly jumps out of the frame, and tilts unsteadily forward. I drop the inside skylight, and make downwards for a firmer base.

Satisfied a cascade of rubbish is unlikely to come crashing through the skylight, at last we worm our way over to the far door. Objects have to be cleared from in front of it, they have to be crammed into any space that can be found. The door of painted, panelled wood is stuck, but one firm pull is all that is needed to make it swing towards us.

What lies beyond the second door? After stepping backwards onto the piled, obsolete effects to allow the panelling to swing towards us… the investigators advance. We behold a room a fair bit larger than the present one, almost completely without shape, every corner lost, overwhelmed by mounds of forgotten, abandoned, worn-out, discarded belongings. For instance, the wall on the hinged side of the door props up heaps of dented, clockwork models. Out of date, miniature steam packet boats can be seen; or pressed steel articles enamelled with faces, windows, drawings of machinery, their seams rusting. Archaic objects not manufactured for generations.

But before us proudly thrusts a single outstanding feature, baffling, riveting. The room's unique treasure. Like a half-finished statue appearing from a featureless block of marble, there towers within: the full-size cockpit section, part of one wing and an underslung gas-turbofan engine of a wide-bodied jet airliner! A double-decker giant, of the type taken out of service then brought back by popular demand. It is impossible to do anything but freeze and contemplate the offering, as if in a gallery. "This is not art": the words seemed to form by themselves. In its setting the object seems to go beyond even a colossal sculpture or canvas. At last we climb down a precarious bank of paintboxes, gramophone records, discarded speedometers to a spot under the cockpit cabin. A rope ladder hangs out of the hatch, after giving slightly it bears our weight. The risk-takers climb up and in through the aluminium door-frame.

Inside, it is just about possible to see. Barely half the instrumentation in the control panel has been left untouched. Behind many glass windows of dials have been slipped photos of dials with needles at a certain setting; behind others are ink drawings. Self-adhesive paper has been stuck in front of phosphor screens, again depicting instrument readings. Printed circuit boards have been split, and the pieces glued in patterns onto the inside of the window canopy. Some of the wire trunks from behind the instrument panel have been pulled out and plaited, one of the thicker plaits leading to a flowerpot filled with dry, brittle earth. A number of bent coat-hangers have been tied together with string. One end has been bound with yards of adhesive tape to the frame of the first pilot's seat; the other end is wired through the stiff cover of a flight manual, so as to form a precarious coffee-cup rest. In fact the cover supports at an angle cup and saucer, showing a dark residue!

Stop! No more!

That ends our foray. We've seen enough! How do we get out?

Give or take a couple of wrong turns, the escape plan works. The rot, the degradation has spread like fungus, through the insides of entire streets of ordinary domestic residences. Now, climbing over the detritus we reverse the earlier course. Getting out into the open is relatively easy.

3. Body vs. Stone

'So! Our so-called ruined city has had a go at us. It might even be said that the adversary has gained the advantage. No doubt that was only a first swipe at us.'

'Row, you're right of course. Especially as we'd had our fill before exploring further.'

'Perhaps we should have stayed in the cockpit and relaxed over a coffee. Tricky to get two cups on the tray though!'

'Snort!'

With no sign whatever of people, nor of animal life, we find our means of transport waiting exactly where we left the bikes.

'Come on. Let's see what we can find beyond suburbia.' After some travel, the weather becomes a pre-occupation:

'It's hours before sunset... but getting so dark.' But even in the absence of strong light, there is a feeling that the place where we currently are needs to be thoroughly checked and examined. Indeed entrances nearby are so shadowy that it it's almost impossible to discern where they lead. The first which I try is simply blocked by a wall. Row finds the same, another false entrance. All the while, there's not a drop of rain.

'Wait a sec! This one leads somewhere.' Obviously, there is something very different further down the passage, but we double back first as a precaution against getting lost. Where does it lead? This is evidently a new lesson in the geometry of reality. The passage leads into a series of stone chambers. The last of these opens into a location or scene of incommensurable scale. Of this there was not any indication, back at the entrance. The place stalls the formation of a general impression: it is filled with successive features which steal the attention before it as a whole can be apprehended.

The prospect before us is dominated by tall, bulky colonnades. The platforms supported by these themselves support lesser colonnades, further back. This feature is repeated, the result is a hierarchy of distant, retreating mezzanines. Every now and then the series of columns breaks, giving the appearance of frontages of buildings cut through by streets. The upward shafts are disproportionately wide, even taking into consideration the mass which they have to support. Distant rays of light graze past various obstacles to reach us. Far above, the ceiling is powdery, patchy, dark; the lighting uncertain. Dry dusts rise as we progress down towards the first street. But these impressions are put aside by the sheer width of the stout columns. Tall, yes; but disproportionately bulky, they're surely too close together. The ground behind the front columns supports many more. Just visible in the colourless light, these almost hidden columns are even wider, even closer together: the space between them is actually less than the width.

We progress down to and past the first "break". It is so like being outside, although we are inside. The perspective of columns leads not to a wall, but another decking of colonnades. Similar edifices stand on the other side of the room, just visible in the uncertain light. All is grey or dark grey. Row speaks:

'Really, I don't think we'll find much here. Tenatis contains within it this featureless place, the city has proved the subtleties of the interior are not to be dismissed. Time to move on, I'd say.'

'Hang on. The stonework is at body heat. I wonder what's further inside the mezzanines.' After carefully peering inwards, I turn... only to find Row gone! So. Why not have a quick look myself? Naturally, the light gets weaker further in. After getting through a few layers of columns, it becomes clear that the gaps between them are well less than the widths. I stuff myself between two hefty, otherwise formless pillars. After easily passing through, I am now confronted by plump, shadowy columns almost in contact with one another. After passing in front of successive pairs, checking that the gaps are equal, I attempt to squeeze past two of the shapeless pillars.

What do I think I am going? The next layer is liable to present pillars actually touching, an impenetrable stockade of stone. Now one pillar presses flat against my back, there's not going to be room. The plump, smooth pillars offer no yield. They are stone! After diving in, getting out is not going to be so easy. But breathing and wriggling combined produce a small slip, this releases me into what limited space there is. Suddenly, I stand stock still: it is a trick of the light, one of the previous rows appear to have moved. Anyway, all remains motionless as I stare. There is still some available light, shadows have not merged into total blackness as might have been expected. But now there's the problem of funding my way to the front. No particular direction looks at all promising. Something pulls at my arm.

'What are you doing?' Row's voice is sharp as ever, he's close by, but I can hardly see him.

'*Ha-ha*! What kept you?'

'I found a rule for getting out. Come on! We must go back, retrace our steps!'

4. Tempus Edax Rerum

We are agreed and compelled to get on to the next stage: to enter one of the grander buildings! To strive to apprehend the deepest secret of Tenatis!

Outside, the city is a warm orange, the shadows lengthening, the Sun low in the sky. It takes less than an hour to find our way back to the parked motorbikes. After lying awhile star-gazing, we bed down, not so comfortably, for the night.

At about fifteen degrees above the horizon the Sun awakens us, cold and rather stiff. The sky is again cloudless; the city rapidly heats up. The bikes are prepared, fuelled. But obviously the abandonment means overcoming near-impassable obstacles. Only the widest boulevards marked on the map can provide access. Thus we drive through the forgotten city, getting further into its centre. Over the trees can be seen several sweeping towers, one of the tallest being tipped with a vaulting glass pinnacle. Rising behind these on one side is a wide peacock-blue dome, set among tall cedar trees and laced with twisting spirals and geodesics of gold. This is architecture cut off at a certain phase, to be left exposed to destruction.

Thus we're able to drive almost unchallenged through the abandoned city; along suspension bridges and through tunnels, through shadows of arches and curved towers, through leafy, overgrown streets. Here, each side of the way is flanked by waist-high grass, interspersed with palm trees, leading to denser trees further back.

At the perimeter of a park grow clumps of bushes. Roland exclaims, 'Look!'

I catch my breath at the sight of what appears to be the shadowy outline of a man standing in them. Several other figures appear; a family of gorillas. They seem to have been watching our progress for some time, it has interrupted their roaming of the deserted city.

By late morning the following day, it feels like time to leave. After preparing, fuelling the bikes, we aim for the

most open roads, pausing for a last look before departing…
But! There among the sun-bleached ruins is an anomaly!
Even in the ruined state architecture is revelatory. Now in
contrast we have found a glass pavilion, new, unspoiled as
the day it was completed!

'Come on!' We swing the bikes round and turn back.
The adventurers are after something, without even knowing
what it is.

The grounds of the pavilion have an unexpected
dampness, and give a curious feeling of being somewhere
else, of no longer being in the ruined city.

It contains a windowless marble block, several metres
in height, flanked by white steps. These spill out from
bronze doors and frame, the entrance extending almost to
the roof. Despite the size, this place feels like the objective.
Jumping the bikes onto the stands, grabbing the binoculars,
we walk up the steps. Requiring hardly a touch on the
handles, the two doors travel noiselessly inwards from the
centre.

Without waiting for the heavy bronze barriers to swing
fully open, we pace forward, out of the dazzling morning
and into subdued light. The space inside appears far greater,
banishing all evidence of a world only a few steps behind!

There rises an elliptical stairwell, making an entrance-
hall; faint, sulphurous light comes from far inside.

All around is proof that the beauty of the city is only
skin-deep. Items of property lie abandoned: a coffee-
vending machine lies flat on its back; turnstiles leading
nowhere rest against a wall. Bird dung runs down exquisite
oil paintings. In the more distant past ornaments have
shattered, lintels have fallen. The hall surely leads to an

enormous, perhaps unlimited interior: all of it likely to be in a state of ruin.

Once finely carpeted, the elegant staircase is cut from marble; its balustrade has long gone. Making only one circuit, it curves up through several floors and adjoining corridors.

Why not ascend? Evidently animals have, areas of carpets are worn bare by successive trotting. We take the shallow stairs; a corridor filled with mirrors leads into pure blackness. Further up we almost trip over a metal box trailing wires: a pay-phone fitting, raided and dumped. The ornate top landing is blackened in several places where visitors have lit fires. At that level are two littered corridors, opposed in direction and seemingly endless.

'Roller! We've been here before.'

'Not here.'

'Yes here, in a different epoch maybe, but here.'

'Hang on... yes... I see what you mean... you're right. That was when we took one of the straight corridors.'

'We had to. Don't you remember, we could not take the middle passage. It led only to darkness. We've been here already, we actually walked down, er... let's see... that passage before it got piled with litter. You chose it Roland!' We appear to have entered the same place in a much later epoch.

Indeed between the littered corridors there is another passage. The difference is that now the sulphurous light passes towards us reflected from beyond. All but blocked with rubble, parts of the ceiling have fallen in.

The way ahead looks reasonably safe though, despite the damage. There is an irresistible compulsion to press on:

feeling our way carefully, we clamber over the loose surface. This third corridor eventually becomes replaced by gaps between fallen marble blocks. Small fragments are still falling! Finding our way between the blocks leads us out onto a balcony.

Oh! What a room! The scale of it beggars belief. It opens below us, the balcony looks down from near the ceiling.

It takes more than several moments to grasp the scene below. Deeply covering its floor, and often reaching far up the walls are the remains of classical buildings. These appear to have been dropped, as single whole objects, wherever there was space. Those which have fallen far have exploded to fine particles. But some have been dropped on top of others, not falling so far and still retaining something of their form.

In size the room is arresting, imposing; but then comes another shock: it is just an upper gallery or mezzanine of a still larger room. This too is filled with architectural wreckage, wreckage which prevents that in the first room tumbling into the second. Following cornices into the distance, we both gasp on realising this process repeats... apparently without end.

Part of the balustrade has long fallen, smashing to powder on the debris below. A section still in place seems to be secure. Dust falls as each of us leans on it. Looking forwards, we gaze into the chasm. It seems to have a soft incandescence: although without direct light, the interior grows slightly brighter, more pastel further in.

Clearly, the only possible route lies between the wall on one side, and the balustrade on the other. At one time this would have been a magnificent path of polished crystalline limestone. The dislocated marble underfoot feels reasonably solid, so with gaze glued to the ground, we progress, sometimes dislodging falls of rock. One of these set off a minor avalanche, a pair of boulders crashing onto the top of an architrave of ethereal size far below.

Within the grand succession of rooms and their majestic, striking decor, everywhere the keynote is ruin, chaos. They appear to be architectural filing cabinets, waste-bins. Yet used incidentally for the purpose of creating breathtaking displays, exhibits even.

It becomes evident that another viewpoint can be gained by going to one end of the balcony, and walking out onto a wide ledge of fractured marble. Like the balcony, this forms part of the cornice near the ceiling of the first room. To our side, fluted recesses and pilasters alternate with broken rock, debris and dust. All the material shows a white or bleached yellow.

This first room, no doubt as with its successors, is a vast cube, the width of which has to be traversed. Pausing for a moment to check on one another's willingness to accept the challenge, we set out. After covering considerable distance, and after treading one or two quite narrow tongues of marble ledge, we arrive at the opposite corner. It gives a dizzying view down from the ceiling into this first room.

Dizzying! Straight away the gaze is drawn onto ancient marble ruins, near the centre of the floor. They bear curious parallel patterns which have been fused through the stone, as if by shadowing with a template from enormously powerful rays: the structures may have been cleared from a site stricken by a nuclear device. We negotiate the corner, and after a spell gazing at the far wall, continue along the cornice-ledge.

At a stretch where the debris reaches up as high as the cornice, more than once each of us slips on the crumbly surface. With the feeling that to go further would be risky, we look round then climb down onto a natural bench of broken masonry.

From here it is easy to see into the second chamber, which of course opens from an entire wall of the first. Dominating one side is the instantly recognisable Greek key. But the stately engraving, the wall itself is impacted and penetrated by a vast metal object, perhaps stainless steel, lying skew across the width of this larger room. Upon the pile of objects filling it, in places nearly to the ceiling, lie whole skyscrapers dropped like toys. Most are fractured; some still rigid, straight, but lying at a drunken angle. One or two look familiar. Almost lost in one corner, lies an airport building.

Now erupts the madness of fighting over who has the binoculars.

'Thanks…!' I take hold of the very lightweight glasses.

'They self-adjust for your eyes. The zoom is up to you.'

'Sod! These glasses are powerful. So sharp. You can go on and on seeing further and further.' The effect is extraordinary, like pointing a mirror at a mirror. But this is only a comparison, the shockingly vast rooms spilling downwards evidently stand alone, each with their extraordinary contents.

Putting the accessory away to get the general view, we try to guess what actually lies in the further rooms. It is just possible to gaze with naked eye into the next room, the third, indeed to glimpse even further. But at the thought of having to find the way out, we surrender the sheltered platform.

Back-stepping, cavorting about above the appalling drop, we gingerly withdraw. The greatest hazard comes with sliding and falling on the back, jerkily spreading out both arms to take hold of the ground, dislodging falls of masonry.

The corner is familiar territory, we even throw stones into the abyss. There are muted noises, from impacts, echoes. The glasses are passed back and forth, the long remaining course providing opportunities for rests and surveillance. After one or two panicky spills, we gain the place of our entry. And so on into the middle corridor. Step-by-step all is reversed. The bronze doors! As we approach, they silently swing open.

Waiting in the gardens, just as they have been left, are the motorbikes. They start at first kick. To the thunder of the machines and stretchy, trailing echoes from the ruins, we edge out. Along the rock-strewn, crevassed roads, there is no comment on any other thing which the deserted city might have to offer.

5. Convulsion

Taking an eastbound super-highway, we ride carefully: there's rubble aplenty leaving Tenatis, even plants growing through the metalling. But the road is totally deserted. Further away there are still occasional treacherous obstructions. Roland glances at an instrument, and waves an arm south.

Thus we leave the road and travel over smooth, bare rock for ten or more miles. There is no need for a return journey of many hours! And thus also, late in the afternoon, it comes into view: the dark, immense form of the electro-thermodynamic entity. It has halted near a limestone precipice, waiting for us. The quasi-pyramid has a toothless gap at the open entry hatch. Its brow wrinkles with activity as a few of the group move behind the viewing screen. Some are yet wandering around outside as we approach.

A ground-level door opens, the bikes are taken from us and hoisted in. We pile into a room called the motor bay, and then on to the viewing bay. Work is in progress to prepare the Vehicle for the remainder of the operation, which will include the final ascent. For us, our numbered seats have been kept vacant. Outside crew-members joke and shout, although through the reinforced screen they appear to be miming.

'How about a communal place to relax while we're waiting?' I put to Row.

'Yes. Great... the mess isn't too bad... it'll only be emergency lighting, though.'

'Sounds OK!' The lounge is quite large, one or two others are talking at a table. We find a snug, quiet corner. Memories of recent risks and discoveries are still subsiding. Row remarks that not once did either of us look back at Tenatis, as we sink into the padded, aircraft-type seats.

Grey and pale orange decor helps to break the stark lines of the windowless mess-room. Permanent emergency lighting has been uncovered, and this is supplemented by hidden strip-lights.

'Does everyone here know everybody else?' I ask him.

'Yes. That's maybe fair comment. For such a mixed bunch. By now they probably, do, anyway. It's the luck of the draw. The job has to be done, we're the pattern of people who fell into place. There are at least three service robots roaming about in the Land Engine. But I've not seen any of them.'

'Service robots can be mighty. Very heavily built and strong.'

'They are probably not even anthropomorphic. But more than just the self-levitating platforms in use everywhere.'

He is interrupted by a movement of the whole Land Engine. In a series of crunchy steps, it settles downwards by as much as a metre.

'Don't worry! That was normal. It would feel different if there was a large cavity under us.'

'Has a fairground feel to it.'

'We'd better go up to the motor bay, to see what's happening!'

During the seemingly endless preparations, Row suddenly says, 'Fancy having a look round? It'll be menacing, but safe enough if you're careful. It's definitely interesting.'

'Uhh... yes, yes!'

'We'll have to be quick!' Stepping through a door in a bulkhead, we walk into the bowels of the machine. Metal studs in my shoes ring on the catwalks. There is the hot, mineral atmosphere of a marine engine room; but also an extraordinarily powerful sense of contained pressure and energy. We travel for some while; big as it already is, the Vehicle actually seems larger inside than out.

'Down that way are wash-rooms, showers; and not to forget the communal bath. There's a fully-equipped laundry somewhere. And... In here you can get a close view of the intermediate motor!' Row motions to a hatch, through which we pass, onto a long inspection bay. Below, to some distance either side and to our front, extend rows of levers and tappets, each lever usually rock-still, but now and then suddenly snapping up and down in no apparent pattern.

'The main motor hasn't started. We would have heard it, been assaulted by it!' says Row, sitting down on the catwalk. I sit down not far way; indeed do as he has done, stretch out on the scored metal gridway.

Vibrations soothingly batter every bone. Sleep is coming, should really not let this happen now, better to stay awake, dreams are playing, these shouldn't be spoiled. Many fantastic, daft dreams, some vividly clear. *Arrghhh!* A klaxon or alarm of some kind suddenly goes off.

'Get up! The main engine will be firing soon!' We bolt for somewhere quieter. Chasing out of the vibrating tappet platform, we clank our way back to the motor bay. At entrance level there are only two, a man and an older woman, standing over the instruments: Row heads us up a helical stairway.

'Through here is the control deck.' He indicates an unmarked backup door. We enter, the suite is very busy. But despite the discretion, one or two unoccupied with the consoles give us a glare.

Someone says, 'The countdown has already started!'
'Sure!'

The Commander speaks to my guardian, 'We want to get going, sir.'

'Truly sorry. My fault!' Row says.

'There are adjacent seats here...' We take places at the front of the viewing bay. The system is halted within six or eight hundred metres of a steep scarp.

'Hurry! Strap yourselves in!'

I glance at Row doing up his belt, do up my own. Before us the concave wrap-around viewing screen spans the length of the control suite. In a lowered voice, I ask my companion, 'Is there anything we can do to, er... help, Row?'

'Stay out of the way! If either of us is needed, which we won't be, we'll be the first to know! Just relax, don't ask too many questions, enjoy the ride.'

'How did the Vehicle come to be?'

'There I'm unqualified. Visharakand is Chief Draftsman and standby acting Commander, but you won't get much out of him. It's a mystery, the experts disagree anyway. The main question is the age of the Device. No one knows this, some of the estimates are off the scale. The design is scarcely better accounted for. You'll see the Machine has extraordinary capabilities. Some of these were made possible only recently. And attempts were made to remove a number of so-called obsolete features. These efforts were not altogether successful.'

Leaning forward against the restraint of the belt, I look up and out of the viewing screen: the sky contains not a cloud.

The usual alerts are followed by a rapid start sequence.

6. Prime Mover

There is the most disturbing impression of a greater silence, as the ancient canyons hurl back as echoes the mighty roars of the Designated Engine. Using only tracks the vehicle lunges down a natural, open avenue, we reach a considerable speed. The Machine makes a series of right-angle turns, avoiding a dark, clothy but huge object on the ground which nobody recognises. Soon the second officer nods to one of the others, who transfers the system to walking mode. We rise rapidly: on account of the unyielding ground in place of cavity-riddled broken masonry, the legs are extended much further. Thus the squat nucleus of the Land Engine contributes only a fraction to our total height. Snapping legs rush us along at greatly increased speed. The Device reaches the end of the swathe, cutting across a gravelled moraine, effortlessly scaling huge boulders, and passing far into the wild terrain.

'Soon you will see the Udev, in fact…' The Machine is moving very fast over the rocks. '…There it is!' To be sure, the wispy outline can be picked out amongst clouds near the horizon. The Engine has to lose altitude to catch up with the monster. By that time, the quarry is approaching a wide river.

Controllers decide this is a suitable place to give the UDev a drink. Heavy turbines are lowered to draw off cubic metres per second. The water is filtered then run into the turbines which force it at high pressure up the long climb to the summit installation. There is an immediate plume of water vapour released, no doubt coincidence. But soon the river begins to flow in both directions at once: toward the huge intake. In less than a minute the level sinks to reveal the gaping inlet. With a snorting noise the operation halts, the river begins to recover.

Before the tripod makes a move, the clogged filter has to be emptied. It has dredged so much clay and stone that this material has to be compacted then hurled to one side, to avoid blocking the river. The load is checked, soon the Udev is fast shifting, as we run along beside, controlling it.

Row gazes in a trance out of the viewing window. Cumulonimbus cloud cover is evident; the Land Engine is carrying us over temperate forest.

The topography of the place where the engine waited for us has long receded and vanished from memory. We are far into very different territory: the entirely wild domain of this continent, its greater part, devoid of organised human life. The skies contain no aircraft; aside from two trans-continental arteries, we encounter no roads at all. The legs are extended a final time, I learn that the Vehicle is designed for travel over unspoiled land.

The second officer calls me to his control console, and after brief explanation hands over and, under his watchful scrutiny, I steer and set the speed of the Land Engine. There is a superb view of the terrain from high-definition television screens, as well as out of the window: to our west rises the now more distant mountain range. I spend a long time by him, occasionally joined by Row. At other times, I hear my friend in conversation.

Now we are disturbed by raised voices. A weather chart has just been printed, the barometric pressure is falling rapidly.

We wade across a major river, swollen with ice-melt. Near the middle, two of the legs of the Engine suddenly and rapidly sink. I really can't see how we can recover, forgetting the ease with which the legs can be retracted, as they are automatically, so the steel ball sinks down towards the water, until we are back on the level. Special webbed feet are deployed, the Machine extricates itself. The crew regards this as so routine, that no one complains that I'm at the controls.

The second officer throws a double-shafted steel toggle, which cuts in some kind of supercharger, there is a thrust of extra velocity. Shortly after, I return the console to him.

Row abruptly awakens from a nap.

'Oh! Soddit!'

'What's up?'

'Want a leak!' Row sways over to the control-deck unisex facility, marked in plain letters, 'TOILET.'

With one or two others, I gaze out at the wind-eroded rock stretching to the horizon. It is as if the Vehicle glides noiselessly over the hard surface; yet there is the ever-present murmur from the prime mover. It is somehow unsettling, disconcerting. Not that it is too loud, the soundproofing is very advanced; but for the engine to be so big, to be so close to it.

He stumbles as the Vehicle lurches as he returns. 'Whoops! Thought you were going to cop it there!'

The door behind us bangs open as two crew go down to the mess room. Looking at one another, we get up and join them for a few refreshments. In the rugged facility it is easy to forget how fast the system is travelling. Taking trays to a table, we chat with a couple of strangers then return.

Visibility around the Land Engine has steadily fallen. Large clouds pass so low that on our fully-extended legs, the screen is occasionally swamped.

'Look at those!' The heaving forms begin to resemble laundry, fighting our progress; but according to the radar the speed over land is unaltered. The sky has turned a putty colour.

'Looks thundery!' Suddenly, there is the unmistakable blue-pink illumination of lightning. It happens again, instantly all the lights go out. From behind us the operational safety officer, Ron, allays our concerns:

'Don't worry! The blackout... it's just standard procedure, with any electrical disturbance in the atmosphere. We are now insulated...!' Cut short: two imposing pillars of lightning stab across the front of the viewing-screen, the faces of all start in the darkness. With hardly any delay, a third bolt strikes the roof and centre bulkhead of the Engine smack-on, with a deafening crash. We look at each other, our ears ringing.

'...we are now insulated from the outside world. Also, a lightning conductor has been automatically lowered to drag along the ground. It's a chain, made of a special alloy. That strike would have been earthed by the chain, rather than damaging one of the legs. After a while, it will be retracted...' Fluorescent strips snap on again.

'Whow! It's got into the air. You can smell that lightning!'

Rain no longer strikes the viewing-screen. Soon the weather clears: the Gestalt Vehicle disturbs a herd of impala far below. Moving as a living dusting-cloth over the terrain, the ragged edges of the swarm draw in, keeping a definite boundary. Through the curved window the passengers look down absently, the image hardly seeming to reach them. More than an hour passes, the movements and vibrations of the Engine are deeply hypnotic.

CHAPTER 9
FLOATING IN THE SKY

1. The Horizon

Our progress through the vast, legally-protected wilderness is so rapid, that sign of civilisation comes as a shock. Cutting across a plain ahead of us is an unquestionably linear form, it glints in the Sun like a scalpel cut through reality.

'Levitation! The intercontinental maglev railway!'

We join the rush to the viewing screen. A loud message is put out over the speakers, 'Stand by! Stand by! Prepare for maximum-alert manoeuvre. Actions urgent! Code red!'

'What does that mean?'

Jake, an engineer in filthy overalls, speaks to us, 'We have to cross the railway. It is easy of course, but we have to make sure we don't hit anything!' Suddenly, I visualise the implications of hitting a train, a full train!

'We could cause a horrible accident! Surely, it is too dangerous!'

'Dangerous for us, you mean squire. If we get too close to a train!'

'Why, particularly?'

'The next train has been informed that we are waiting. But like all maglev's, it carries nuclear plasma-weapons. It would vaporise a plane of the Land Engine, cutting us in half before we could strike it!' This all sinks in.

'So what's the procedure?'

Jake lowers his voice. 'Because of its size, the Tripod is no problem. It's already on the far side and programmed to keep going. We have to wait stock-still by the track, until the maglev passes, then make it across. The line itself has defences. We'll be OK as long as we don't clip it!'

I turn to Row. Neither of us says anything. We are fast approaching the track. More people than I realised the Gestalt Vehicle holds swarm around the control deck. Deftly, the machine is brought to a halt, swaying very slightly on its fully extended legs, about half a kilometre from the elevated track. The powerful Engine, all drive systems are cut.

From that height, there is the most spectacular view of the endless progression of polished fibre-metal segments, supporting dark grey magnetic levitation pads. We endure a tense wait. Someone brushes against a small box of disks, which tumble to the floor. Everyone ignores the crash. In the taut silence the second officer, Emerson, lifts a finger into the air and turns towards us. Something rattles. Again there is a wild rush to the viewing-screen. Several of the crew are on the roof.

Jake: 'Here it comes!' The vibrations go on increasing. 'It is travelling at well over 1,000 kph. There's no friction to speak of, but the magnetic fields have to support the weight of the train... probably has 2000 passengers. The whole track and its supporting rock bend a bit, very fast, under the weight, causing supersonic waves to travel ahead through the ground, hence the noise!' Ear-muffs are being hurriedly handed around. 'Quick! The shock-wave could damage your ears!' We look at one another. Suddenly! There is a punch in the chest, an explosion, and it is gone.

The relief in the air is almost solid. Very deep, low vibrations fall to nothing. There is buzz of conversation, as the legs of the Land Engine begin to retract, imparting mechanical energy to the main motor: by sinking downwards, we dispense with the noisy start routine. Now it is necessary to rise up again on the legs: in terms of driving skill, pulling up close to the track was not as difficult, as stepping over without touching it will be; but the real tension has passed. We get over the super-conducting barrier easily, and push on into the plain.

But there is an unaccountable feeling that although we are over the rails, some problem still haunts us. Just why everyone was so anxious is suddenly revealed: Em pulls out a small communicator, and points it at a wall screen. He shouts, 'Look at this. There's a train approaching from the other direction!'

'Impossible! The geo-passing points are hundreds of miles away!'

'See for yourself!' He passes the handset, then snatches it back. We are ignored. No-one explains a thing.

'It's some kind of unscheduled train. Ministry of secret intelligence. Matey! Look at the speed it's travelling!'

There is uproar: we all watch the needle zip from horizon to horizon. Taking a pace back he passes the handset to me. It reads, "Your position accurately plotted. You are in no danger". Seems we dodged the bullet. Soon the general feeling of great relief is swamped by getting on with business.

Row remarks, 'This was quite an old maglev line.'

'Really? Looked new.'

'Actually, I mean in terms of the protection. Repeated hammering from the trains damages the ground. The newer levitation channels are laid in an elastic trench. Much quieter.'

'Shame. Like the passing of Bessemer's converter.'

'For making steel? Yes, I know what you mean.'

The plain ahead appears endless, but its soft ground slows our progress. To port the Sun is sinking fast, almost suddenly turning yellow and then deep orange, before touching the horizon as an oblate orb. The crew attend to their work, the impassive faces raked by very bright orange shafts of Sunset. As light glints in their eyes they seem to pay no attention: all the same there is a deep sense of communal rumination. Atmospheric distortion breaks up the disc into turbulent strata, the final blob is as deep orange can be without actually being red... and... it is no more.

Word is passed that the Engine will press on through the night but at a reduced rate, relying on radar and lasers. We try to get some sleep in the resilient, velvety seats: but are abruptly woken by huge impacts caused by heavy rocks striking the hull. The Machine is negotiating very difficult territory, and occasionally has to reverse and try again. After two more heavy impacts the noise settles, but we get up and head for an array of bunks.

With a last shout to Row I fall onto what is again soft, relaxing bedding. And, guided by the fundamental vibrations of the Engine, plunge into just about the deepest sleep I can remember.

2. The Secret of the Engine

It is as if the instant of falling asleep coincides with that of awakening. A brilliant shaft of morning Sun has found its way past a series of barriers, raking my face, forcing the eyes to open. Where is he? Next door. I siphon in the Sun's light, which is occasionally interrupted as movements of the Vehicle cut it off.

We stagger up after breakfast from the noisy, crowded cafeteria. *Burp! Gwerk!*

'Oh! Forgive me!' *Burp!*

'I noticed you eat almost as fast as the average crew member!'

'"Almost as fast"? What sort of backhanded compliment is that?'

Daytime is there, before us. There's one sure way to make best use of it, but after our earlier gaffe, it is a struggle to get round to speaking out: I suggest a visit inside and below, to see the main motor.

'Mmm. Sounds like a perfect fit. We will, we will. Actually, I was planning nothing more exciting than reading more of my book. Where is it?'

'Just let's try to get a look at the main drive!'

'OK, OK, sure. Ah! There it is…!' Pulling out his battered novel, he looks around for a moment then hurls it down. '…We are ready and able… all right, this time we'll take a more thorough look… You won't forget this. Let's go.' On leaving, it occurs to me I've never thought to ask him about the author or to look at the book's title.

Taking a rear hatch while no-one is looking, we descend in the direction of the loudest noise. The few people about do not notice us, they happen to be moving away. Freedom to roam the mighty Engine of Destruction. What an opportunity! The feeling overtakes curiosity itself.

'Shame they seem to get shirty when passengers try to explore the works!'

The atmosphere is warm, oppressive, laced with exhaust fumes. There are air ducts, but the smell of machines cannot be flushed away. Many things about the sounds of the powerful Gestalt Device are odd, deliberately we slow down. In the course of just a few paces, the noises vary from very loud as if coming from immediately behind an impenetrable metal wall; to quite faint, yet significant, coming from far below. In places the resonances have an everyday quality: traffic in an underpass, a police helicopter, vacuum-cleaner. But a quality which can feel out-of-date, as with a steamroller or a sewing-machine.

Steel doors are hung on massive, well-greased hinges, but so heavy... they are stiff to open. No door is locked; there are numerous stockrooms. Sometimes holding onto a metal handrail, we pass through a series of them. Fitted metal wall-cabinets hold spares. Even used parts, blunt, worn tools have been collected and sorted according application and age. One recess is neatly stacked with antique components, the primitive steels deeply rusted. A couple of these I turn in my fingers, thinking that they cannot have been manufactured for generations. Some of the designs are truly archaic, they seem to antedate the age of powered machines. Further along, Row suddenly lets the metal handrail go. It is finely tooled with cursive, braided patterns.

Nearby stockrooms reveal overly well-represented types of spares, not even put in drawers; there are mounds of them, one room is so full the door cannot be shut. And yet the work is incomplete, in many places a tool or sundry has been snatched away for immediate use, not to be returned; whole drawers are missing. A corridor wall-cabinet is not closed properly. The Vehicle lurches for some reason, an unlocked drawer slides out before us, its contents crash onto the floor.

A succession of hatches, of bulkhead doors, brings us no nearer to the goal: if anything, the throbbing of the main engine is getting less as we progress. Now there is access only to another gallery of riveted metal doors. It's necessary to peer, the lights are barely adequate as if not really needed, they vary and flicker with the overall movements of the huge Vehicle. By now it cannot be denied: the Gestalt Engine is larger inside than out.

After Roland happens to open one of the riveted steel doors, we enter a spacious room. Here long-conserved machinery is stored, no longer used. A catwalk leads over a colossal, silent engine, bulging with inlets, manifolds, auxiliary devices. This perhaps has not run in living memory.

Over in one corner are files or manuals, one or two reference books. Standing under the nearest light, we flick through various soiled documents. Then he pulls one volume down, turning the heavy kaolin paper. So many diagrams. Horizontal sections of machines, safety and maintenance protocols, spares, identification codes, any amount of detail in fine print. However not one of these installations is familiar! It is not possible to even guess the purpose of the equipment.

We are like twins: into our heads pass the same thoughts at the same time.

'Maybe many outsiders, like us, have sneaked in here.'

'To try to learn the secret of the Engine?'

'Yes. Are we so different?'

'Surely not.'

'Quite. Looks like we too have failed in the quest!'

Suddenly! From behind a thickly-painted bulkhead there's an appalling rending, very near. It sounds as if a crank has broken free from a flywheel, there are deafening battering noises, sounds of other machines revving out of control, the wall itself visibly vibrates. There's no sign of an emergency alarm or intercom system. It is pointless looking round for a crew member to come and shut down the installation: there's been no-one to be seen for a long time. Now even as the loose crank thrashes about, another device on the floor below starts up, surely without human intervention, to take up the function of the stricken installation.

'Hey! What are you two doing down here?' The safety officer has caught us trespassing.

'Ron! Really great to see you! There's something wrong back there!' He urges us away.

'There is nothing you can do. Nor I. It will be contained... Anyway, if it is not the Engine is doomed!'

'We were trying to get a glimpse of the main motor!'

'OK...' The crew-member urges us from behind. '...Keep going, your seats are fairly near! Through that hatch... up the steps... then bear to the left...'

Back in the Control Suite, we sheepishly sink onto the synthetic padding, without saying a word.

3. The South Face

After passing over scrub-land and pine forest, the Land Engine loses altitude, sweeping into a region of dense jungle. The passage of the Machine seems to cause almost no disturbance, most especially by comparison with its devastating course through the city.

'Nice here, eh? Let's stop!'

'Short break, then!' It is a coincidence: the huge LED read-out has just clocked noon. There is the hiss of hydraulics, as its jointed legs cause the Engine to sink after the motor is cut. And after this, there is again a slight sinking towards the ground, which ceases after a short while; the unretracted legs however hold us far above the dark green carpet. Also, there is a slight lateral swinging, reminiscent of the play in the cable when a lift car is hanging at the bottom of a long shaft. To the clatter of coffee-cups in the galley, of hob-nail boots on the metal rungs of the roof ladder, we join the swarm upwards to the roof hatch, and out into the hot, high Sun. The crowd spreads across the flat top of our vehicle. We stand against a stout perimeter rail. By us stands the petroleum resources officer, Sid, who gazes into the distance, seemingly unmoved. He discusses recently-developed fuel additives now being tested. Also:

'The main motor cannot breathe so well at high altitude. We are already taking on oxygen which is stored chemically, to blast straight into the cylinders while we are going up!' Absorbing as what he is saying is, my attention is distracted by the vital spectacle. So energetic and diverse, it is made the more impressive by snow-capped peaks now visible on the horizon. Row leans over one of the rails. Birds call; insects swarm; we stare into the wealth of life.

'You remember, before leaving the urban mass, just after we strapped in, you were asking about the Machine?' He gazes ahead while speaking. '…Well, I know very little about it!'

'What sort of things would you expect to know?'

'How safe it is, what the range is… But where is it going? There's always secrecy about that. We might not learn much from watching it depart; but the event will be spectacular, that's for sure!'

We are joined by a crew-member, who gazes upwards.

'This volcano is continuously monitored from space. According to seismic reports, we have no reason to expect any unusual activity.'

'So everything is OK for go?'

'Exactly.'

'Hey…!' Almost before it has started, the break is over. '…They're returning to the control suite!' With a last look at the naked, green environment, we climb back into shock-absorbent seats. In the open wild, the crew make no effort to subdue the raucous noises of the start-up sequence, the throaty roar from the Engine and the crackling blasts from the exhaust cowls seem to be preparing to do battle with the gradient ahead.

It's immense frame has never been out of view. The ground may be inhospitable, but all we have to do is chase the Tripod.

Below, the colour of jungle has been replaced the darker greens of tundra. Almost half of the crew are watching a porno movie, their laughs and yells cannot be escaped. Again I am invited to take a turn at the controls. After having been attending closely to the Vehicle's operation, suddenly I notice we are travelling over rock-strewn mountainous terrain, and evidently gaining altitude. Truly is the Land Engine so called. We speed across valleys and dust-bowls, rivers and gorges. The visibility is good, with a little ice-cloud at high altitude. The Vehicle scuttles up a dusty ridge, over the top, and there, seeming to float in the sky above ranges of lesser mountains, is the grandiose volcano.

'Not bad, eh?'

'But the size of it... it's a monster.' The mysterious upper cones and precipices are dazzlingly white with snow, and almost without movement, a widening white plume drifts horizontally from its summit. The vision disappears and reappears once or twice before we reach a place after which it remains in sight most of the time.

The Gestalt Engine flashes forward. The terrain changes, and after several detours along and over volcanic rilles, we make palpable progress towards the white giant.

There is a drop in talk as the Commander enters, coming to the front of the viewing-bay. He makes for Roland, who rises from the couches.

'Commander! We seem to be doing all right.'

'Oh, yes. The climax is still ahead of us, of course. I have to advise you we have received orders in the last half-hour.' With a word to me, Row fully leaves the seating and the two confer in lowered voices.

Shortly, I overhear, 'Thank you very much, Commander!'

'It has been a privilege, sir.'

With a glance to me, the Helmsman leaves. And settling in again, Row explains, 'They've been summoned to a priority operation. The device will have to use its special properties to in effect roll down the mountainside. We are to be left here, and…'

'Left here!'

'…transported away by hover-jet.'

'*Ha-ha*! Sounds terrifying, Roland!'

A crew-member who happens to be a geologist now comes over, saying to Row, 'I've been asked to advise you on the time you'll be spending outside.'

'Uh. Thank you.'

'The met, report seems to be OK. This is a continuously active, alkaline volcano. Have you had experience before with such mountains?'

I throw in, 'Yes… Mount Etna, Catania, Sicily.'

'Then you should be able to negotiate this one. We've assembled two sets of warm clothing, and light survival kits. Bear in mind your rendezvous will be well within a few hours.'

'I'll be looking for a few rocks to keep.'

'Right. Sure… But don't take any risks picking sulphur crystals from the fumaroles. Will you…?' He looks at him then back to me. '…Those fissures can be silent one second, explosive the next!' He then adds, 'Yes, we're getting near the summit, but the going is getting more difficult. We've retracted the vehicle legs a fair bit, so it may seem that we haven't slowed down. But we have!'

No life of any kind is visible beneath us, and in many of the grooves and trenches winding through the ash lies bright snow. Occasionally we pass through patches of mist. A dormant crater, lipped with jagged, spalled rock passes on one side. We thank the geologist as he moves back from the viewing screen.

Although we are now much closer to it, the Tripod retains an ethereal, cloud-like appearance. After a very spectacular ascent; during which the upper sky assumes a deeper, more purple hue; we come to rest, several hundred metres below the caldera rim. Although supported well behind and below us, the apex of the UDev is far above, as is its load.

Detailed, up-to-date images of the volcanic surface are sent to the Engine from space. From these engineers calculate the best position for the grapnel. At the same time the crew chart out various passes into the caldera for the ascent teams. Cameras are to be located on the slopes, to relay images to controllers.

Precision control brings the tripod to near its final position. Only when this is confirmed will the Engine apply a lock. We are assigned for ascent. Issued with protective clothing and powerful binoculars, now it is for us to disembark, and attempt the final climb and breach of the caldera wall.

Numbers of crew are already swarming onto the icy surface. We each speak:

'C'mon! The top! Let's go and get a look!'

'Let's get going!'

Even with a volcano ahead, it is impossible to avoid noticing the thickness of steel apparent at the main entry hatch. We pile down metal steps onto crunchy ash and rock. Ours is a small party, still we have been assigned two high-definition cameras to fix in place. The equipment is very light, but crew-members insist on carrying it.

The Sun, now evidently well past its zenith, still appears a cutting blue-white. The sky is clear, rising from peacock at the shimmering horizon, to a near-purple directly above us. The prevailing wind carries a gently expanding belt of water vapour, dust and sulphur dioxide into the troposphere, as well as down the mountainside. The clothing we've been given is thermally efficient, but cold wind tears at our faces. Breath water vapour condenses in my beard, and soon the droplets freeze to beads of ice. We've donned mirror-surfaced crash-helmets, to keep the freezing vapour from condensing in the hair.

'Look at the size of that!' The Tripod is so vast its nearest foot is down the mountainside, well below our Vehicle.

'Yes… the other walking-pads, and the ranger pad are out of sight.' These feet are behind rocks or on the far side. The Tripod straddles one of the largest calderas in the world! It takes some effort, at first anyway talking through the wind.

'How thin and spidery the legs are. Wouldn't have thought they could support the load.'

'Very strong. You'd be surprised.'

The colourful, partly-uniformed figures move against either dazzling brightness or dark blue sky. In the present conditions, the last few hundred metres seem like a mountain ascent in itself. Underfoot, the overall impression is of greys; however more vivid colours in the cinders suggest fantastic forms, ejected from deep in the underworld: a delicate, shattered antique; the severed hand of some monster; a fragment of inhuman pottery.

Rather than pausing for rests, in single file we pace upwards slowly but continuously.

'How are you? Warm? Out of breath?'

'How did you guess…? Great…! Wow! Look at that… the distances behind us!'

'Keep going! Don't stop!'

'I wasn't…! Ahh!'

'What is it?'

'I couldn't get my breath then!'

'Same here…! Slow down. There's less oxygen up here. Your heart can't beat so fast when you're exerting. and it works faster than usual when you're resting!'

'That's how it feels!'

'The air up here is fine, but mighty thin.'

The team leader confers with a couple of the others, then says to us, 'The pass is over there! Quite near, reasonably low. Some of the team have to get over to the other side. Should be there soon.' He moves forward to the front. Suddenly, I get a whiff of sulphurous fumes and start making choking noises.

Row says, 'We've got to keep out of the fumes… it's easy to do that: the air currents up here hardly change direction, all we have to do is keep moving on the windward quarter of the summit, so! This looks safe! Let's take this path!'

'OK!' Often the surface is extraordinarily hard, despite assuming a hollow, contorted form. But in many places it gives way with noisy crepitations. Dust thrown up by our progress is snatched away instantly by the wind.

One of the crew swings a load onto one shoulder, without allowing either of us to carry it. The wind is so strong. My companion says, 'Detailed images will have been sent down already. Look! The system is almost right over the middle!' Even the mighty frame seems to have been pulled to a wider angle to reach across.

'One more slight move should do it.'

Experts in the control bay prepare for this final manoeuvre. Very great extension of one leg is needed on account of the steep volcanic slopes. The ranging leg falls on the far inside of the caldera. It probes and retracts a number times before hitting stable rock. Now the ranging leg is exchanged and becomes load-bearing. The vast structure swings over, directly above the lava lake. There is a nuclear power station hovering over the middle of an active volcano! Row glances upwards. 'We are now very near the highest point on the South face of the volcano Pschachimboraxz.'

Our party approaches the lip of the main caldera, which itself is a complex of smaller blast craters and ash cones. Eddies in the air-stream occasionally swirl choking fumes around us. The regular, thunderous blasts each produce an acoustic thump in the chest. We are at the top edge of the caldera, gazing at the primordial fire of the mountain.

'Fantastic!'

Five or six hundred metres within the caldera, two adjacent active cones hurl frothy magma upwards, in cyclic, viscid pulses. The incandescent rock resolves itself into orange stones and boulders which crash onto cinders already fallen. Occasionally, there is a pause, followed by an exceptionally vigorous burst of glowing magma. Greenish fumes unbundle from the cones. Fascinated, we watch the activity for considerable time, from several different vantage points. One of these is a higher point further from the active cones, but affording an excellent view, well beyond the range of the treacherous fumes. We sit in a cleft out of the wind. I drag his head next to my mouth, so it's easy to be heard over the howling wind.

'It's so powerful! What can you say? What can you think?'

'I love it up here!'

Our team secures its cameras on a rocky foundation, cables run to a dish pointed at the Vehicle. Through the glasses it is possible to see teams descending inside distant ramparts of the caldera. Soon it will be possible to lock the Tripod.

4. The Distant Ocean

Indeed now we watch the last manoeuvre. This does not require repositioning of the pads; the frame is moved by precisely drawing in or extending the supporting legs. The UDev is locked in place.

No time is lost: already the grapnel with its unstable load is lowering towards the glowing lava-lake. One or two sounds from it can just be heard. Pieces of ground, broken masonry from other buildings fall in. Now the cube is swung round like a sling, the path it takes calculated to make it possible to turn the cube upside down. Suddenly all support is removed.

'What about the splash effect?'

'Well, they reckon we'll be safe, if that's what's worrying you. There'll be a big splash all right!'

Having been inverted in a deft curve, the structure remains intact, its cube of attached ground now above it. Steel hands violently flick the cube aside, it falls on a distant beach of the lava lake.

Thus does the enormous structure fall free, almost upside down, what was its highest point races towards the plane surface of lava. Everything is relative! Fleetingly the vast stone shadow looks small! From it there is a ruddy reflection as the ancient and dark building plunges in.

'Row! Zircon already showed me this!'

'I don't think so.'

'In a painting…'

There is a paroxysm from the molten rock, it is as if no more terrible wound could have been inflicted by the UDev on the volcano. But this is for show, for us. After making way, walls of red-hot molten rock charge back and crush the dark silhouette. In hardly two seconds the whole thing has vanished.

With an effort it is possible to make out slow-moving waves. These soon pass. No one speaks. Suddenly a huge bubble rises and bursts out of the lava lake, making a sickening, revolting noise. The sound is no more than a signal of digestive processes, after a fine meal. Movement occurs on the surface elsewhere, besides one or two bubbles around the point of impact. There is silence.

Descent to the Land Engine is relatively easy. He asks, 'What was that you were saying?'

'It was in one of Zircon's oil-paintings, hanging on a wall.'

We enter the Machine for the last time. From the window the complement watches as the enormous Tripod is unlocked and released. Now obeying a control centre thousands of miles away, the legs range, extend, retract. The entire system is soon below the Engine. Now it accelerates, leaving us so rapidly that in a couple of minutes the UDev has vanished.

'We must get our things together for the volcano.' There is a rising bustle around us. 'Great! Look! The equipment manager has got our packs! Now... let's go!' On saying farewell to the instruments officer, Wilf, I hand him an ancient coin.

Rhythmic thunder from the upper craters jars the viewing bay. The helmsman himself guides us down to the entry hatch, and leads the way onto the crisp cinders. He points to a suitable place for us to watch their departure, and returns to his Command. From behind the closing hatch, he bows in farewell.

The clotted sulphur vapours are sharply cold, and we pull on SO_2-resistant anoraks. From the designated place, we see the Land Engine twitch briefly on its studded tungsten tracks then crash forward, ripping an obliterating chord through a small crater. Soon the Gestalt Machine is hundreds of metres below us: the legs are extended firstly to take over from the tracks, then to increasing length. The grinding of its motor is still audible in the thin air, as it races towards a ridge.

On the mountain side this falters and rises, providing an uneven, irregular road of solid rock. On the free side, it twists downwards to a jagged precipice.

But the way is blocked by a squarish, vertical cliff. After taking a deeper than usual breath, I turn to Row. 'See that square formation? Won't they crash straight into it?' Pause.

'Only if they expect to, I should think.'

Resembling a tiny grey spider, the Device pounces onto the ridge, which supports it up to the vertical cliff. But within the obstruction, a shadowy aperture opens; and into this vanishes the Land Engine! Again I turn to my companion, but he says, 'Look!' A dense, steamy cloud rises from above the cliff. Several seconds later the noise of a metallic impact or explosion reaches us. This falls to echoes which merge with the thunder of volcanic activity.

As we watch, the cliff has detached as a rigid body! Material below tumbles in clouds of dust, as the huge boulder shifts forward from its place on the ridge, before crashing downwards. Despite the great steepness, the boulder rides the margins of the precipice without overturning, lubricated in its descent by broken rocks and stones. It moves with gathering speed down the cones and trenches of the mountain. Many seconds after we can still see it rising and falling over ridges and parasitic volcanoes. Eventually it plunges, a black dot, into the upper surface of a pearly cloud belt.

'It's gone...!' My exclamation reveals a sudden, stabbing feeling of loss. '...Did you know they were going to depart like that?'

The Gestalt Machine, although a frightening monster, a terrible Engine of destruction, at the same time provided the most secure, comfortable vehicle any passenger could have desired. Alone with Row and both of us safely insulated from an unfriendly environment, it takes grappling with to accept that the Machine is already far gone... along with its Captain and huge crew. After a pause, he replies, 'No. It was as much of a surprise to me as to you. They knew I expected to get off here, they didn't consult me about the course to be taken by the Land Engine... just as they didn't consult you.'

The gap in the mountainside left by the departed cube-like mass rapidly loses its sharp edges, which give way to dusty landslides, watched musingly by each of us.

From the high mountain vantage point, we look down to the incomparable whiteness beneath. Dense cloud is attracted by the massif, further away the bank breaks up into scattered, buoyant forms, all at the same altitude. The horizon is cloudless, below it appear lakes and minor seas. Near the limits of visibility gleams the cyan surface of the ocean.

There's a short while before transportation is scheduled to arrive. I rotate a volcanic bomb in my hands, then set it on the ground. Some distance own the slope, Row strikes a crystalline mass with a steel piton; I look at the shifting cloud bank and beyond to the peacock mantle which wraps this planet, contemplating distantly images which spring from the dome. The Sun is fast sinking, but at the high altitude can only begin to assume a true orange radiance when a width or so from setting. Curling shadows of varying densities cluster and expand within the furnace-light of the cloud, giving a new impression of the depth of the bank, and indeed of our distance above it. Again feeling the cold, I get up to take a parting look at the thundering ash cones; then make my way over the scoria cinder slope down to Row. But pause after a few metres, to look back at the bomb. Several lie nearby. Unsure now which one it was, with the cold closing in rapidly, I move down to my companion. Amid swirling fumes, he says, 'Look at this needle. Just lying on the ground. Monoclinic sulphur. Take it, for the collection!'

'Sure. Thanks.'

'Time we were going, I think. The VTOL will be here soon. Have you been on one of these before?'

'Nothing like. No, never!'

He explains, 'It's an auto-pilot Vertical Take-Off and Landing jet. It comes and goes at about 2000 kph, so it won't take us long.'

'Surely, there will be a problem, landing on the broken ground of the mountain?'

'Nope. We can wait over here, where it's a bit flatter, if you like!'

The Sun is up to its neck in the horizon, departing from a yellow sky. Mist hangs between successive ridges of volcanic ejecta. Row: 'The VTOL craft is powered by a compact nuclear reactor, shielded by condensed matter foil. The stuff is unbelievably heavy, but a metal plate supporting a shield less than a micron thick is enough to cut all radiation! Look! Here it is! Three O'clock to the pinnacle of that cloud!'

The incoming craft swells to a dark triangle, moving in a wide curve towards us. It passes above the vanishing Sun, and with a rising whistle moves up to and hovers over a fairly flat stretch of ground about a hundred and fifty metres in front. Three legs extend and sink into the ground as the motors are stilled. A powerful searchlight snaps on, illuminating a small hoist which settles on the ground.

'Right!'

We sprint for the hoist and climb in. There is a button marked "UP" which Row presses. The hoist takes us to a small window-surrounded stateroom containing five seats fitted with belts. It incorporates a wash-facility, first-aid closet; and some viewing screens for entertainment and communication with the ground. We are full of excitement in the sudden warmth, taking the comfortable g-seats. No sooner are both belts hitched, than a stentorian voice barks a "Keep Clear" message to the freezing mountain-side. The nuclear jet engines whine, fast increasing in pitch and loudness. Scarcely visible, rotating ground falls away below, there is little vibration. Gaining altitude and velocity, we are allowed a startling view of the erupting ash-cones. The brighter stars glint above us.

CHAPTER 10
THE HORNED SPHERE

1. Continent

After two turns at about 500 metres above the lava beds, the craft accelerates away from the volcano in a direction about perpendicular to our approach. The stars are clotted together, pieces of burning magnesium in the sky. Suddenly I turn to Row, it was as if I was somewhere else for a moment.

Following the initial manoeuvre, we enter a linear flight path, holding at the cruising speed in the upper atmosphere. Knowing how long it will take, it's not difficult to work out that we are travelling about the same distance as covered by the Land Engine, but now moving along another side of a square, taking the volcano as one corner.

Neither of us sleeps; but again I gaze dreamily out through the passenger canopy, thinking of how it is, that all the countless distances which one travels add up; a pace taken backwards in a room, a long journey the through the sky; every millimetre is there. Yet one could pass through a door or entrance, perhaps a sculptural arch, a precarious breach in the wall of a ruin, a gleaming laboratory aperture; from one reality to another, from one set-up to an entirely different one. Not only that... think of Zircon's maze...! An attempt to go back may lead anywhere, a return being only one possibility.

My co-traveller points forward. In the twilight, and in the far distance a bright patch can clearly be seen. Low-lying or on a plateau, it is very flat: an appallingly vast metropolis, home to nearly a billion people. Occasionally, brilliant bluish points of light twist and vanish within it. Evidently we are rapidly approaching. And, after a journey of two hours, the craft decelerates. Shortly a seemingly endless network of lights appears; it has not yet grown fully dark. The vertical thrusters of the machine thunder below us, as again we turn a couple of times in the queue above the unusually advanced, extensively-developed metropolis. Everywhere there are lights, independent activities, functions on functions.

A bold, dominant structure displays the identification Continental Aerospace and Rapid Transit Terminus. An upper platform near the main control tower is marked in fluorescent triangles; onto one of these our jet settles. The hoist takes us to the reception lounge, decorated with inflected stainless steel and red, veined rance. Through a passing window there's a huge, alarmingly fast-turning radar. But the view soon changes: the travelators operate at various speeds, they are very fast. We join a queue being herded through the entrance to a scanner. I take in some details. The device seems to be hooked up to surprisingly heavy gear: NMR spectrometer, X-ray laser.

'What's this for?'

'Health. It reads off from your immune system exactly what it does not like, viruses, prions etc., then the beam moves in for the kill. You won't feel a thing! Really!' As I breathe in, he continues 'It's quite old, this facility... Look! You can see... it's been in use for a long time. They're supposed to be introducing much more compact equipment soon.' We go through.

'I definitely felt something!'

'Sissy...! Right...!' He catches my eye. '...I don't know about you, ancient mariner, whoever you may be, but I'm cracked! We want to get round to the flat while there's strength still left.'

'I'm in solemn agreement with you there... flat 59! Your residence and place!'

'Yes! Well, actually the apartment is in house 59: we were talking about it during that time in the mess room, you remember, before moving off in the Machine.'

'Sure I remember, Row. Thankyou!'

'It's very ordinary! You'll be surprised how ordinary. Lived there for awhile, quite some time actually. With several others, there's space. It'll be OK for you though!' Our eyes meet, by gaze again I thank him.

Still in our protective clothing we stand on the platform by the magnetic monorail. Only a few people wait, taking little interest in us. The spectacularly streamlined train arrives and comes to rest, without any sound whatever. Already the doors have swung open; a slight ozone whiff escapes.

'Why is everyone strapping themselves in?' I ask, doing the same.

'This train has to cover a considerable distance, you know!' The system lifts half a metre off its levitating pads, already gently moving forwards. Soon it is rapidly accelerating, then taking enormous bends, we are travelling upside down, still closely hugging the grey support structure. We slice through the sky, magnetically locked only half a metre from the gleaming rail.

Row gives a wink, turning to look at the garish, plain LED speedometer. Amazingly, it is the hypnotic violet colour with a mauve halo which I notice, only then: a *thousand* mph! Just over!

Beyond the middle distance, the journey gives successive glimpses of the towering centre. Soon we are passing in amongst buildings which appear to have arrived from centuries into the distant future. After a series of corkscrew turns, the system comes to rest. Already people are moving to leave before it has noiselessly settled on the receiving springs.

2. The Flat

On getting out at an area designated the Lower Metropolitan Transit Terminal, there is a tremendous urge to pause; he has to yank my sleeve as I gaze around, to get me aboard a fast-link bus. This journey is followed by another, rather longer one. It takes us to a leafy stop, some distance outside the centre of the exceptionally populous city.

After a walk turning down a couple of tree-lined residential streets, we enter a well-maintained but quite old building. The wide staircase reverberates to the sounds of a stereo played loud; we head up to the third and top flight, the sounds getting closer. With a glance at me, he flicks out an analogue key. This opens the door of an entrance facing us.

Tertiary exhaustion sets in. There is dim awareness of meeting new people, they seem enthusiastic, kind, but preoccupied. There is a geniality to the company, as if taking an interest in me, yet far too preoccupied to actually break away from what is being said.

After living in this place for a few days, weeks actually, trips out alone for me become a regular occurrence. Thus do I come to be accosted by a stocky gentleman in a blue-black pullover. His manner is as if he knows me well.

'Come with me! Watts! Yeah, that's me! Hurry up, you're needed in a big way.' It's difficult to avoid smiling as I look closely at him, examine him.

'The car's over there.' With a wink, with irrefutable body language he communicates that it is very important, that I would be unthinkably letting the side down were I not to comply. He shows the greatest gratification at seeing me smile, while remaining serious, deeply preoccupied himself: We exchange a few words, he pulls out a crumpled drawing and shows it to me.

'Seen one of these before?'

'Er yes... believe I have. What is it?' The question is ignored.

'This way, sir, yes get in the front with me. I'll explain as we get over to the arcade! It's not so far!' Dark-shirt has turned round his car, the engine is revving. I jump in beside him at the front, he leaves the kerb while the door is shutting. The car is large, with very wide bench seats, and looks new. He throws it around with speed and skill, and soon we are accelerating up a ramp onto an overhead five-lane orbital. The man hardly appears the worrying kind, and he is desperately worried now. With a stupefied gaze into the traffic, I struggle to think of a way out of this. There is none. Live with it! It'll be OK. His conversation is in short bursts, his attention clearly distracted.

'You'll meet the doctor. The big rush was to bring you. You are a visitor, aren't you?'

'Yes, sir.'

'There has not been a proven case of a visit for centuries. I'm not an expert. The doctor will tell you... not for many centuries.'

'So you'll want me to do something?'

3. Overhead Orbital

'How did you guess? *Ha-ha*...!' Anxiety cuts short his laugh as he continues, '...You all right, there? Switch the radio on if you want. Or record. That button. There's car-sat TV.' Older than me, I notice he has a scar below the eye, and one or two about the neck.

'Mr Watts?'

'No! Watts. I run a couple of amusement arcades. Well, several. We're going to where I live, over one of them. Where my brother and his pal have got themselves into a fix. Have you studied electronics?'

'What! Is that why you've abducted me?' He turns, briefly smiling, as if flattered by this angle, but immediately becomes serious again.

'No, of course not. Never mind. It's just that's Ramon's, my brother's speciality. And with another guy, Sham. It's how they met. Awhile back Sham got hold of special head-sets, like gold motorcycle crash-hats, with cables leading into them. Apparently these went missing from a secret government establishment. These domes produce, quote, altered states of consciousness. Together they've experimented many times with the head-domes, never with any problems.' Tail lights are a ruby blaze before us.

'In fact, they've been round a few times to try out the domes at my place. That's what happened earlier this evening, they called round to show off using the domes to Rita, a lady friend of mine. But this time they got into difficulties, or at least it became impossible to get through to them. After a while, with the two of them just sitting there, we got really worried. Sham has repeatedly warned that switching off, or pulling out the leads is very dangerous. What could I do? I had to make an emergency call… And then drop off Rita on the way over to rescuing you.'

'Rescuing?' Although we are in the fast lane, an accelerating car approaches from behind. We pull over as it passes; then speed up ourselves, holding the outer lane.

'Well, you know what I mean… your belt feel OK?'

'It does.' Watts seems not to hear, his driving remains fixed on what is happening.

At last, he comments, 'Don't worry! The car knows what I want!' For a short stretch, we take the super-orbital.

'We'll get across the city much sooner going this way, this is the most convenient route.' My hair stands on end as Watts races up the ramp to traffic travelling at hundreds of mph. His vehicle goes on and on accelerating, we are doing two hundred and fifty mph. He goes considerably faster than this, after entering a sheaf of lanes designated the fastest.

It is surprising that his powerful streamlined car is rather... rickety. Occasionally, there is the snarl of gears somewhere. The murmuring air conditioner is fine, very strong, but Watts has to raise his voice against the noise of wind blasting behind the passenger door panelling.

The scene at his place is now carefully described.

'Police arrived first, acting as bodyguards then the doctor, a specialist who brought in cases of instruments, he's there now with the head domes connected up to some kind of screen.'

'What was that drawing you showed me in the street?'

'The horned space whatever... "The Horned Sphere"... well it's something to do with what's happened to Ramon and his pal. Better wait to hear what the expert has to say. One thing: he's keen that we avoid the front entrance, and arrive via the repository at the back of the arcade. Don't know why, but that's what he wants! He knows what he's talking about, or I'd never have found you!'

There is a sinking feeling in more ways than one as he slows to leave the super-orbital, pulling over to an exit slip. This we descend at well over a hundred mph, to take an ordinary motorway.

The curvature of the road is sometimes surprising. Before us rises a vast structure largely in darkness; it accommodates the entire highway. We power through, then rapidly lose height. Dead ahead in the far distance is the luminous central metropolis. With a bend well to the east, the centre snaps out of sight occulted by tall local buildings. Only once or twice does it re-appear, between buildings to the north. Watts mentions, 'You can use my mobile if you like!'

'Sure!' Without glancing from the road, he reaches to a custom recess, something drops into his hand, he gives it to me. Unlike his car the mobile is worn, it looks like it has been in the family for generations. The unit has a pleasant feel, it swings around as if made of dense metal; yet... it is not at all heavy. I key in the number.

'Oh! Watts! Er... I'm sorry... Seems to have gone dead!'

Watts snatches it from me, not slowing down, then begins to mutter, 'Oh, yes...' Without warning the man brakes hard, taking a ramp down to a dimly-lit street. He slows right down, almost to a crawl, he is winding down the window as we pull into a dark alley. 'Look out!' To my astonishment, the handset is slightly giving off smoke. The thing appears to be going soft: Watts throws it forcefully out of the window. I watch the set splat against a factory wall, trailing smoking gum.

'Not the first time that's happened. Brought the wrong one! Would you believe, there are drawers full of them at home. Sorry.'

'It's OK!'

'...The car-phone's out too. It's working, but... I got a shock off it yesterday, you'd better not use it. You'll have to wait!' Pulling back onto the overhead carriageway, we speed along in silence. The windscreen has a variable sky and Sun filter. This reduces the hard, unremitting glare from oncoming mercury headlights. The cars often have skylite roofs. Across town, there are some big supermarkets. On several floors, the lighting is so bright as to be a health hazard. Their enormous signs can be seen miles away.

4. Watts

Watts swings off the orbital, driving through wide, silent streets lined with warehouses, factories, advertisement hoardings, garages. The car turns at a floodlit traffic island. Shops pass, then a cinema. He pulls up at a set of lights.

'There it is. Just down from the Chinese restaurant!'

Go. The sedan swerves across the street to a halt. A pink cast falls on the car from a bright street-sign, which I read aloud: '*ROWL.*'

'Yeah. The name… it's an, er, acronym. Ramon and a couple of others are with me as sleeping partners running the arcades!' We get out. 'Right. Follow me…! We have to enter from the back.'

The proprietor pushes through the facility, which is filled with people, and music above the blipping and warbling of the machines. We make straight for the rear of the arcade, allowing only a glimpse the hardware: there are some special amusement-boxes with names like *The Man with Two Bodies; Invisible Psycho; Terrorist University.* But interspersed among the newer units are antique pinball machines, almost childishly painted, lit with bare filament bulbs. They make a lot of noise, are very popular.

'Come on!'

'Right behind you!'

A door at the back opens to a flight of stairs, my host holds it with his foot, seemingly resisting an urge to spoon me through.

'Up here!' At this interface, the bright commercial fittings are swapped for household ornaments, conflicting signs of neglect, tidiness, and different personal influences.

From him there is also a sense of relief, he's got his catch, he's got home with it. A passage from the landing opens into a large room, a hall big enough to have several doors. Set across one corner is a wide African mahogany desk, laden with papers, books, some office devices; the top has built into it a number of light-bulbs and switches. He notices me glance over to it.

'You wanted to use the phone?' At the desk, as I reach for the phone, his hand closes round my arm. 'Wait a moment! I've got a better idea. Since this is a special case. Why don't you write a note? I can have it delivered. There's a courier.'

'OK! Thanks!'

With a pencil, I dash off a note to Row on a leaf of paper, fold and staple it, hand it to him. This Watts folds again and stuffs into a shirt pocket. He says, 'Right! This building... I share part of it with the Telephone Administration. They let me store out-of-use machines on vacant floor space in their archives. In this room here!'

'Wow! It's huge! The building must be bigger than it looks!' We pass rows of silent electronic card-tables, pinball machines, wall-mounted coin-op amusements; some under dust sheets, some gleaming faintly in the dim light. Surprisingly many. Now he takes time to explain a few things.

'Some of the stuff is theirs. All along those racks they keep five copies of every issue of the local directories. Everything is there, goes back untold generations. I only use this room, but the side door behind us, you may have noticed it when we came in... yes... the one with the brass handle, well it leads to larger rooms that are also full of directories and... other things...'

'Businesslike! But odd that they should be so thorough.' The lighting level is low, uneven.

'I'm not saying you're wrong. And maybe you don't know the lengths they go to. Not many do. Numerical Archaeology, it's called. The Administration meticulously archives equipment as well as documents. And there are the records. Ever since the digital exchanges, it's been possible to file away every bit of information, anything, voice, text, image, every bit which passes along any line of the entire network. This they tell me is done.'

Watts cuts diagonally through the repository of obsolete juke-boxes and discontinued electronic amusements. There is a feeling of getting further in, of getting further away from all that has gone before. Yet he makes for another door; squinting in the gloom, selecting two keys. This opens the way to several carpeted rooms, the first looks comfortable as a hotel. Glass faintly shines: a photo-portrait of Watts hangs on the wall. But the light is so inadequate: in one of the rooms, several feeble, oddly-shaded bulbs can scarcely hold back the shadows. When are we going to get there? In the next room, the illumination is fitful, appearing to fall steadily only in certain places.

At last voices can be heard ahead.

'C'mon! We're here!'

5. Dr Chandrasekharan

We pause outside. Then he opens the door without knocking: several faces. Police: two uniformed officers, carrying bulky handguns, plus some plainclothes, by the looks of it. One addresses Watts, 'So this is the total stranger? And you came in through the archives?'

Before Watts has time to speak, he adds, 'Congratulations! Well done! Actually, we are ready to start. It is vital we delay no longer!'

He addresses me, 'How are you? I am Dr Chandrasekharan, of the…' His voice has the timbre of a broadcaster or News announcer. After briefly explaining that I was located by a technique called *retrograde causality*, he hurries on to immediate business.

'…Let me tell you what these two have done, or rather about the equipment they have managed to get their hands on. The domes, the power source were constructed as part of secret medical research: the goal was to try to contain the effects of a certain class of psycho-active drugs. The electronic circuitry is designed to allow research and laboratory staff to get up close to patients deeply under the influence of the so-called radiant psychedelics, which intoxicate anyone nearby, besides the taker.'

'Wow! I've heard about these—'

He cuts me off with a gesture. 'Have you indeed! We'll go into that later. The point for us now is that the project backfired in one way, because the same device can be used in reverse to create psychedelic effects electronically!' His words are professional, very lucid… almost reassuring. During this lecture, Watts gazes fixedly across the room at a cactus growing in a glass urn; now and then the nostrils flare as he takes a deep breath. The doctor's tone abruptly sharpens.

Pointing, he says to me, 'Would you please look at the face of Ramon. Yes, the gentleman sitting there. Try to catch his attention!'

I call the name, but the eyes of the gold-dome-wearing figure remains unmoving. His gaze is fixed on something on the table. On the lid of a small stone box, it could be gypsum, alabaster. Ramon's companion also wears a head-dome; but his gaze flits about the room, catching the eyes of others no more than settling on a small bundle of fluff trapped under the television.

'*Ha...*!' snaps Chandrasekharan... 'A case of the difference between looking at the TV set, and watching TV!'

He gives a grin, but I tell the doctor, 'Ramon... I can't catch his eye!'

'None of us can. Please come over here by this screen.' Dr Chandrasekharan turns to a unit connected by snaking cables to a monitor, and idly pulls out a cartridge from a front recess. It is replaced with another. A bright, unstable grating toggles between primary and secondary colours. Gradually, it becomes clear everyone else, not at the table, is expectantly staring at me.

So I ask, 'Is there a spare dome, please?'

This is the moment the doctor appears to have been waiting for. As if purporting to be doing something else, he nonchalantly leans behind one of his instrument cabinets and pulls out a dome.

Inside its polythene wrapper the helmet gleams with curved bars of gold. A sprung-coiled cable with a socket is clicked into the dome, opposite the position of the wearer's atlas vertebra; the other end is plugged into a bulbous socket below the controls of the high-definition screen. A switch is snapped, the screen goes blank: then it displays curves or spiky tessellations as adjustments are made. He twists a little projection in the dome, instantly the screen gives off a shimmering white light, like incandescent steel being poured over a delicate graphite lattice. Almost too bright to look at, it casts heavy, snapping shadows in the room. The doctor says, 'Your dome is ready now!'

'I trust you. After all, you're a doctor!' I settle the almost weightless object over my head; giving it a final glance, he throws another switch.

6. The Archive

There are three heads of liquid gold, one my own; the dome cables stream in golden pigtails. The walls, confines of the room fall away to a Vitruvian terrace: upon wide steps I sit, under a blue sky. Nearby, set in the brilliant white marble is a mural tablet, flanked by pilasters. This has several lines of inscription, I get up and walk over to it. Each line is composed of letters, numerals, strokes and spaces... I am reading the serial number of one of the doctor's cabinets of instruments!

The eminent psycho-radiologist immediately intervenes to re-orient me. Thus it now it appears there are people about; he stands just behind me. Turning, I stare into his eyes. The inky pupils swell, his breathing is noticeable. He moves closer; with his face only a hands-width away from mine, he turns and looks at Ramon; I do likewise. It feels as if the doctor, the spectators have vanished; Ramon straightens his back slightly, without looking up from the little alabaster box before him. The subject rather magnetises my attention, although I remain loosely aware of the presence of his pal.

Now it appears we are in the room which contains Watts' photograph, the room next to the archives which he shares with the Telephone Administration. The box floats about us, remaining visible even through solid objects. Turning from Ramon, his gaze still fixed on it, I try the door to the repository. Twisting the handle, leaning on the door is no use, it is locked. During this brief distraction, my two domed companions have disappeared.

After looking around without finding them, I return alone to the warehouse access-door: now... it is open. Someone can be heard, presumably either Ramon or his pal, moving further down the storeroom; I follow the sounds. The light is too faint to be of much use, but enough can be heard to guide me to an area used for storing larger trial-of-skill machines. These are finished in unsubtle, brazen cartoons; including a ski slope and a drag track. Nearer the wall, the machines become still larger. Single amusement-stalls contain whole sequences of garishly-painted scenes, resembling more a small fairground ride, than an arcade machine.

Footsteps! It is Ramon surely, moving about in the shadows of a nearby stall, one of the largest. I try walking into the machine, but it is too dark, progress is impossible. Perhaps the device can be switched on, that would make it light up. Many leads run from the back of the machine to a distribution board; from this a heavy lead is plugged into the wall. So I throw the main switch. There's a slight pause, then a sudden rush of light and music and the clatter of steel balls against obstacles, some of these give a shrill ring. Of the quarry there is no sign.

The middle of the stall has itself been used as a junk-room: resting on a counter is a fragile, glass-domed barometer. Its metal bellows are linked by fine gears to a long steel needle. I peer inside at the brass cogs for a while, before allowing the region beyond the glass casing to move into focus. In a dark, recessed gallery of the stall, appears the outline of Ramon's face. Moving over, I twist a light-socket round until it shines into the gallery. Inside, displayed prominently among other photographs, is a portrait of Ramon. The man, however, is absent. Leaving the machine, I switch it off. However in the silence immediately following, there is the sound of a door gently opening and shutting at the far end of the repository.

Even in the company of Watts, this place was rather stark: the strong urge now is to rejoin the others. But the fact remains I have lost my man. There's nothing for it but to probe further into the spooky interior.

At the far end of the store-room is a door, the door which leads to the office boasting a mahogany desk. But this turns out to be open, thus leaving only one possibility: I must have heard the door Watts pointed out, with a brass handle, the entrance to the archives. This door is unlocked; I open and take it.

The entrance leads into a dimly-lit corridor, which itself makes a junction with another, transverse corridor. With now a certain detachment, I walk to the junction. The walls and door-frames are finished in a plain, near-colourless decoration, leaving me feeling hugely out of place, in the shimmering golden dome. Both limbs of the corridor running across my path go into areas beyond the storeroom. The lighting is very poor, yet after a while it becomes possible to see from the junction, in detail, all the way along to where each limb turns at a forward-facing bend. On a table there is a book marked 'Telephone Administration: Guide to Reserve Archives, Sedimentary Street, Viton City.'

Walking up to one of a row of doors in the transverse corridor, I find it does indeed open into a room filled and lined with catalogued racks of telephone directories. So returning to the guide-book, I open it. Several pages give a comprehensive plan of the archives, the courses of the two limbs of the corridor can easily be traced with a finger; at various intervals doors leading into the stacks are marked. The bends in each are clearly marked, as are junctions at which the two limbs themselves divide. The new divisions in turn are followed by right-angle bends, compensating for those of the junctions.

The large-scale part of the plan occupies only two pages; however by carefully balancing the book, it is just possible to ensure that enough light falls on it for me to read continuations of the plans, printed to ever smaller scales. I get a shock, as to the extent of the system of corridors: the new limbs themselves lead to sub-divisions and bends. After straining for a long time in the restricted light, I see the whole process is repeated at least once more. By making some extra bends, the corridors form into a succession of distinctive arrowhead patterns.

From the book, I learn two more surprising things. Owing to the considerable lengths of each segment of corridor, by staircases, extra right-angle turns, etc., it is possible for two parallel corridors to pass one under the other, and back over again, and then to carry on, so that the two are in fact intertwined. According to the plan, the intertwining of corridors occurs in many places. Indeed, once after each division, although not immediately after. It is the adjacent limbs produced by two consecutive divisions which are intertwined.

The second surprising thing is the number of rooms accessed by the lengthening stretches of passage. This appears to quadruple after every division, in proportion to the ever-widening system of corridors.

Concluding that to search for Ramon in the archives would be unrealistic if not hopeless, I close the book. After all, the door-shutting which could earlier be heard from the arcade machine might have been somebody else. So, clasping my hand round the rubber helix of cable that leads up to it, I lift off the dome.

7. Chase

Streaks of dried coffee stick to a cup in Dr Chandrasekharan's hand. After the slightest pause, he speaks, 'Well, how did we make out?'

'Ramon, gave me the slip!'

'Mmm. I'm afraid there's nothing for it but to keep trying. OK?'

There is a feeling that my time in the archives was not wasted, almost a feeling that the rest will be easy. 'OK. I'll have another crack at it...' For a moment, no-one speaks. '...Tell me, are the archives really like I just found?'

'Indeed! All you experience while the dome is switched on is illusion, but illusion which contains reality as a special case.'

'… Do you want to ask about anything else?'

'Er, yes, I do actually. Can the alabaster box be opened?'

'Certainly…!' He smiles, glancing around. '…It is a question of finding a way to take off the lid! Now…!' He isn't in the mood to offer me a break. '…Can I help you with your dome?'

'Er, yes.' I resettle it, immediately seeing Ramon's hair stream behind him as he runs away. The quarry tenses at the edge of a pavement, then at the earliest opportunity thrusts himself between cars in busy traffic. I do similarly, and from a pedestrian island see him rush into small ornate gardens. These are totally surrounded by traffic. As he runs between flower beds, the glare given out by a "Pass Either Side" bollard enfeebles his image. He almost slips out of sight in a mist of retinal blood vessels. Again squirming through a gap in the traffic, I see flashing reflections of my consciousness-dome in the car fenders.

After crossing this and a couple more lawns, after thrusting through crowds of people, passing jewellery stalls, pizza houses and side-stepping in front of cars and delivery vans, I see him turn into a very brightly-lit side street. There could be no more important business than catching up with Ramon. Everything happening in this metropolis is a mere backdrop to the chase. Even for example that noise, a police siren which is getting louder. Surely soon I will collar him, the unique pursuit is in its closing stages. Suddenly, it is clear the noise has no part in the present engagement. A warning light stabs with increasing insistency. People are getting out of the way, some retreat up the side street. I get out of the way.

A police car is racing towards us: even speeding cars are nudged aside by it, it is approaching very rapidly. Taking a pace and a half back, I stand rock still, hypnotised by the bright streak of car. Travelling so fast, still accelerating, it manoeuvres very little. The siren is piercing. Cars have mounted the kerb to get out of the way. There is the very audible, stomach-churning load on the motor as it powers past, I see the faces of the officers. It has passed. One or two comments. The siren can be heard until the squad-car hammers into a tunnel.

There is no sign of Ramon below the streetlights, in the neon brilliance, among the mauve panels advertising 'Sauna and Massage.' I pause by a group looking into a tavern, where a couple are performing a remarkable act with a Tesla-coil discharge. Winding blue-violet electric sparks radiate from the girl's nose and hair ends, they jump between her hand and that of her partner.

A few more are pausing to watch; but he is nowhere in the group. There! Ramon appears: seated in a restaurant. The dome can be penetrated! Running a hand through my hair and giving my clothes a flick, I go in to join him.

'Ramon! Howdy! Do you mind if I join you?'

There is no reply, slowly I take a seat opposite. Without looking up Ramon flicks his head with a snap, throwing his hair up and backwards, it's swirling motion freely independent of the dome at its roots. I follow his gaze down to an object on the table: the little alabaster box.

From small cups we take China tea. Not two metres from our table, in the corner of my eye appears a diner: Ramon's friend.

Those at a table further away can, in fact, be overheard. One of the speakers sounds like a man who was nearby shortly after first meeting Watts. There is an overwhelming urge to look round and check. In other words, to look away from my quarry; to succumb to the very urge that could have lost me Zircon in the self-adjoint maze. But as Ramon stares intently at the box, the distant voice becomes indistinguishable from the general background murmur.

I reach for the box; does it after all have a lid? Yes. It won't come off. About to give the lid a tap on a dinner-plate, Ramon make a grab for the box. Our hands touch it simultaneously. At that instant, the lid of the box rises like a stone slab and flies upwards, into the sky. We both gaze into the little alabaster vessel.

It contains a fluid, which, despite the small area, ripples then surges like waves of the sea. The waters charge against the alabaster walls, sending spouts of foam almost to the rim.

Breaking from the sea is an island or land mass. The sea itself heaves and swells, now spreading out to the horizon; while in from the shore, there rises a range of craggy, barren mountains.

High on an otherwise lifeless slope spring two trees: the trunks and branches are angry arteries of fire. The limbs repeatedly divide, always into pairs. A wind rustles, then rapidly gains great velocity. Stones are flung into the air; boulders crash into the sea.

During this time, the trees throw off vortices of sparks as they twist against one another in the eddies and whirlwinds. Shortly the noise falls away; the hurricane subsides and passes. But now the trees are entangled one with the other, so as to form, by intertwining starting at branches of the two trunks, an iridescent, homed sphere.

Ramon laughs aloud, I catch his eye. The little alabaster casket simply rests on the table; beside it, the lid. This he replaces, saying, 'I'd like you to have another tea before we return!' Cups are poured.

We remove the domes. Watts is in conversation with Ramon's earlier companion: this he instantly breaks off. In the middle of asking a series of questions, he gives me an assurance: the courier delivered my note to Row, while the three of us were "away". This was obviously for quite a while: it is late afternoon. Dr Chandrasekharan addresses me, 'You have undone the Gordian knot. All that remains is to return our fragile equipment to the institute. The Authority is ever in your debt!'

I ask him about telepathy.

'Telepathy? No such thing. Gestalt telepathy is certainly possible. And gestalt retro-telepathy. Even control over what's happening with a dome on!' He continues, 'Anyway, thank you...' It is strange, almost startling, hearing him use my name.

Ramon says, 'This gent has er... appointments, so... excuse us while I drive him back.' Watts suddenly reveals how generous a man he is, offering me a piece of gold. His brother ushers me from the room, out to the car. Like Watts', it is wide and fast.

On the way I mention to him, 'The Metro'll be fine. I'd prefer that!'

'OK, fine.' He pulls up. '…This is the station at Cyberia St. Market, you can get to the park at your address with one change. All right?'

'Sure!'

The door opens by itself. As I get out, he says, 'If ever you're in a fix… let me know. Or Watts!' The car jumps away.

CHAPTER 11
DERELICT EMBASSY

1. An Embassy

As I walk from the Metro to the dwelling where Roland is currently to be found, my concern is that there's plenty of explaining to do. On giving the front door a tap, it feels that this is a minor matter, there is the clearest, indeed strongest impression that now is the last time I will enter this building.

It is so pleasant entering, finding greetings, much talk, welcome refreshments.

'OK, Rolo. That's my accounting in full! What have you been up to while I've been away?'

'Trying to survey the damage you have inflicted on all of us, during your brief sojourn in the Aeonic reality.'

'I could have done worse, you know. Let me have another try!'

'No need. We shall never recover from what you have already done!' This daft conversation persists, with others joining in. We resolve to have a walkabout next day. The plan is to have a look at diplomatic architecture which happens to lie within the locale.

***

'There's not much stuff here, these are just ordinary palaces.'

'Not much activity either. Aside from traffic coursing round the gardens. I suppose you'd have to check at night to see just how many buildings are actually occupied.'

We follow a wide approach road, then take a few turnings.

One of these leads into a fine square of cream-painted houses, many with individual front gardens. There are numbers of interesting buildings: embassies, the offices of learned professions, their libraries can be seen through lower-floor windows. Yet the square also contains a few houses in disrepair.

The railings and garden in front of one are particularly seedy. It is next to one corner of the square. Litter has accumulated; weeds grow tall. Surprisingly, only two doors along, video surveillance cameras turn automatically, a couple of limousines are parked, facing away. Visitors call and leave, but using only the distant part of the pavement. It is as if the shadow of neglect falls from the house, onto the paving-stones and street; with time this seems to have become accepted, and now perhaps passes unnoticed. We approach the building.

'Look at that!' Dirt on the pavement does not seem to have been disturbed by people passing: an ice-cream dropped long ago has rotted on the stone to a tough gum. Just inside the railings, a curious metal device rusts among the weeds. From an upper floor, an old, old telephone lead awaits removal, the bulky insulator still evident on its bracket.

Wind rattles a bent wire against the wall. Directly above, I notice heaving, darker cloud taking shape in the sky. Row too looks. Yet away to the south the Sun effulges. Weather divides, in conformity with the buildings! As if shutting a door for the very last time, with extraordinary, involuntary gentleness I lay a hand on his shoulder.

'So! It's been empty for ages!'

'Yes, I happen to know it has. Also...' Row turns to the steps, walks up and gives the front door a shove. '...the door opens.' We walk through, closing it, and setting off inwards.

Loose central heating radiators, litter, damp floorboards abound. We pace through the entrance hall, passing further into the building, through consecutive rooms.

'Have you been in this building before?'

'Not actually inside...' Turning to me, he asks, '...Have you?'

'Be serious!'

The rooms become gradually but steadily larger, their finish now predominantly marble. Indeed walking through them, our talk is interspersed with comments on the size.

'Wow! A *jet* could fly through here!'

'Listen! It's so quiet!' Earlier, there had been the occasional reminder of the city, a muffled yell, car horns, the distant rattle of a road drill. But for some time there's been nothing at all, the transition having been masked by our voices. Nor at this stage is decay evident. These rooms have not been entered for a very long time; so far from the entrance all is dry and dust-free. Our foot-fails vanish into long and often sumptuous carpets. Any noise makes for the nearest cavities, it hides behind mute, outsize furnishings.

'Where does light here come from?'

'I've seen this sort of thing before!' Our speech is distant, lacking in force.

Half-closing the eyes, I slowly lift my gaze until just catching sight of Row. No more than this contact is retained as we drift, each into our individual thoughts.

2. The Corner of the Ocean

Against one wall there's a satin-lined sofa, and drawn up by it a table; furniture is dwarfed by the wall and its enormous, wide-bevelled mirrors. Row walks round to the sofa, on it I sit down. He too sits down, our eyes begin a wordless conversation.

This is the climax of the new and different reality! The summit is at hand! But what about getting down...? Always the difficult part! Now he speaks, 'After the next room is a special region. It contains a port, or gateway to the reality of your birth.'

'Come with me, Row!'

'Thanks! Won't be able to do that!'

'Why? You must!'

'Only after you're back will you know. It is for you to find your way to the world, the society you regard as familiar. There is no rush, you'll have time for a last look round. Remember! Each opportunity to do what has to be done should be grabbed as it arises.'

'But what if I lose my way?'

'No, no. It's far simpler than that!'

One or two occasional ornaments in coloured glass rest on the table. Eventually, I rise from the sofa. Row soon follows.

At some distance, at the corner of the room, are double doors panelled in carved cornelian. Walking down there, I grasp and turn one of the handles; both doors swing silently open. Before us is a profoundly larger room. For the ornate, turquoise ceiling rises up in steps and domes to greater heights, with distance into the chamber. We are near the corner: to the right a tiered and colonnaded wall extends far ahead of us, while a similar wall spans far to the left. From the pavement at our feet, scored with veins of silver, elliptical marble steps reach down to a warm beach of pebbles. And washing these is the blue-green ocean. Its waves break against the marble walls of the room. We stand, meditating the living surface before us.

By themselves, the doors have soundlessly closed. Similar elliptical steps lie to either side. I slowly walk down to and over the convex pebbles, during which time it sinks in that this room *contains the sky*. Behind, there is a feeling that these are doors which could never be re-opened, for beyond them lies only the rock of this place, not the place I have just left. Where is Roland? No sign! Roller! Shouting his name is no use. I knew it. Anything different would have come as a surprise, a disappointment even. Yes... there is no sign of him!

After a short while I sit, handling and tapping some of the pebbles, then lie down. The Sun is not in evidence, in its place feathery swathes of light shine above the oceanic horizon. I am aware of the rolling waves. Suddenly the Sun comes out, a shaft of light reaches down and bathes the scene. Clouds drift before it, as I rise to my feet and walk to the water's edge. Legs folded, back straight, I sit before the green lens. All around is the peaceful sound of incessantly charging waves. Time passes.

Glancing up at the saffron light over the ocean gives a feeling at last of turmoil subsiding. Alone, I stand up, inhaling deeply and stretching my arms far, then turn towards the marble steps.

Ascending the steps, I contemplate the decorations, in the patterned wall ahead. It carries a progression of alcoves, sunk into the aragonite-limestone. Each contains a brass alloy statue, brightly resistant to marine corrosion. One is of a figure surrounded by topaz symbols of oceanic life. My gaze rests fixed for some time on the bright, blank eyes.

Slowly I walk along the marble pavement, that leads up to the corner of the oceanic room. On the way, I pass alternately single and double doors. The two walls of the corner meet, intersecting in a vertical line. Marking the end of the pavement, this line makes a sublime marble perpendicular, at the corner of the ocean. Each of the highly polished planes, to either side of the vertical, is broken by an outstandingly large, single door. These are also distinguished by a few marble steps. Arriving at the corner, I turn, gazing diagonally out across the breakers, waves and heaving swell; gazing all the way out across the ocean. And there resting against the corner, I remain for a long time.

How is the turquoise ceiling supported? It is made I presume from rigid, buoyant elements welded together. But these are only guesses. And the real puzzle is its extent. Fifty metres or more above me, each of the two walls meets its nearby domes at a magnificent cornice. Dappled reflections play above this endlessly. Further away, as it rises over the ocean, the curvature of the ceiling steadily lessens, the shape is hyperboloid. It is the same, familiar Sun that shone... awhile back. Yet appearing in a different world, in a world in which the ocean is perhaps flat, not merely the flat-seeming part of a great ball; and in which the sky appears contained within an unlimited ceiling, an unfamiliar world whose workings I have not begun to fathom.

As if this were not enough, as one passes out in the direction of the water, the ceiling not only vaults to much greater heights, its colours merge with those of the sky. The boundary between ceiling and sky is thus nowhere to be discerned.

Now my gaze recedes to the farthest point of the horizon. Intermittently it is cut by waves near, by waves far, or very far; now it stands aloof from all of them, a perfect horizontal, unreachable even at the speed of sight. What do I care? My indifference is abutted by the weight of the grey infinity of water: it already challenges my power of endless gazing, before the faculty has even arisen. Soon I am studying shipping in extraordinary detail. Rust from countless anchor-weighings shows above the water lines; figures can be seen working on deck. Enormous, even terrifying vessels become discernible in the remote distance. Sometimes they occult one another; at other times there is the feeling of gazing into maritime eras gone by.

From the vantage point, it is of course possible to see along the wide orange and white marble pavement that spans before the alcoves of the remaining wall. This pavement I now take; thereby having negotiated the corner of the ocean itself. Often I pause between passing fluted columns, to stare into the waves. Shoals of glittering fish, bladder seaweed, living corals and sponges are visible in the transparent water. Even a gliding sting-ray. Light ripples on the nearby surface of the ceiling.

The pavement follows a straight path; in places it breaks into steps of composite stone, which ascend a few metres. Thus the level tends to remain above the surge and spray of the largest waves. At these places there is also a widening, and an increase in the size of the columns between myself and the ocean: a reminder of its depth.

Passing again alternating double and single doors, I walk back towards the pebble shore, at the one and only corner of this profound room. The viewpoint makes the wall of my entry appear to lead out into the ocean, while suggesting the wall now close by runs in front of it.

Halting just before reaching the corner, I ascend a few marble steps. There is at their summit a single door, leading into the wall. Having entered through one wall, I now contemplate leaving through its companion. For a long time, I stare at the cut-glass handle, then turn it. There is no resistance, the crystal flashes without at first any other movement. But this action has released some powered or gravity-assisted mechanism; it is perfectly soundless, after a few seconds in the direction away from me the door slowly opens by itself.

CHAPTER 12
THE GARDENS

1. The Secret of Glass

A noisy, buffeting breeze blows through the polished stone aperture, so long as it is open. But above this, and above the peaceful sound of waves breaking on the shore, is a faint singing resonance.

Walking through onto a platform suspended in darkness, I turn for one last look at the corner of the ocean, along the tiered marble pavement, at the doors set into the niched, patterned wall, at its sculptured symbols of oceanic life. For a last look out across the waves and heaving swell; before I brace myself and push closed the door. Made from polished and tooled stone, it has to be pushed hard, against the wind. On unseen hinges the massive beam moves noiselessly, picking up speed as it swings toward the frame.

An impression of the reverberating crash seems to reach me, before the actual impact: there is no handle, no means by which I could slow down or ever reopen it. The cushioned recess is designed to receive the door resiliently; yet the crash, in part due to the locking mechanism, is rending, thunderous. Widening, booming echoes charge through the room or whatever it is that now contains me.

Darkness closes with unexpected ferocity, like a knife cutting away the last light. A tremendous battle ensues between darkness and brilliance, to the setting of sweet, pure mirages of sound. As the shock from the door passes upwards, beneath, along the walls, so does it liberate and bring about total illumination. Contrast, shade, line, muted colour can be seen reaching into the very far distance.

Inundated by quantities of sound, I enter an ornate music-room. Windowless, with opposing doorways, it is the abode of a glass harmonica-automaton. The instrument is giving a solo concert. Its cogs and ratchets fly about, a group of tiny bellows is kept at work, their jets snapping back and forth at the immobile glass pipes. But evidently my arrival is during the closing stages of the performance. The final bars are succeeded by dying echoes and silence. After a short wait, and a certain amount of probing, it is clear the piece has ended.

2. Kubismus

At some distance through the remaining wide doorway, I become aware of an extraordinary enormity reaching far below this level. Parts of huge equipment or machinery can be seen. When professor Aza left the pair of us, a powerful, chord-like sound arose. Now this hallucination is repeated. But this time far from sounding like a circular saw, I hear the opening of the first movement of, yes, the first symphony by Anton Dvorak. This effect is induced by what I see on passing through and thence entering near the top. I am near the ceiling of a cubic room of appalling, breath-taking proportions. The entire room is filled by a single machine! The music is gone, leaving me conscious only of the awesome authority and stillness of this colossal device.

Where the passage opens it forms a junction with a wide, glass pavement of the type used in viewing platforms. To either side, facing the device are entrances to elevators. By following the polished, flat pavement, given time I could walk all the way around the top of the machine. Instead, I walk inwards towards it, the inner edge of the pavement is several metres away. To my shock, the edge is no more than that, there is no protective barrier. Falling to my hands and knees, I crawl then lie pointing at its edge, half poking my head over. At a glance I can see right down to the floor of the machine. After looking to either side, I inch back and return to the perimeter wall.

The whole is either suspended from or anchored to a colossal steel frame, enormously strong, yet gracefully architectured. Every metal, copper, cobalt, molybdenum, vanadium must be present, if not in its massive steel forgings, welded joists, bolts, rivets, then in its conduits, wiring, printed circuits and silicon wafers. I gaze downwards and towards the centre. Stanchions wide as a road can be glimpsed, rising from foundations many floors below.

I enter one of the elevators. It is very imposing, but offers only a single control, a jewelled button waiting to be depressed. Standing well inside, I oblige. From either side the doors slide noiselessy shut. With almost no delay, the car sinks, accelerating rapidly. The shaft is glass, I see the vast engine from an ever-changing angle as the elevator plummets to ground level.

Rapidly but uniformly the car decelerates, it comes to rest with doors open facing mechanisms near the foundations. This area is surrounded by a perimeter trench, several floors deep.

The machine is so vast that it reaches almost to the ornate cyan ceiling. And, aside from a generous gap for visitors to pass around the perimeter, almost to the far-spaced walls. Standing on the floor and grasping a handrail, I gaze far up into the vast assembly. Faint but distinctive machine oil odour fills the room. The whiff reaches me at the second of realising that although this is a fixed installation, more than half of the device was designed to move quite rapidly.

It is a great effort to wrench myself away from this place, I decide to walk the length of one wall in order to leave by a different exit.

Passing in front of the west wall, I walk north. Above the pavement are niches, each displaying a standing figure sculptured in translucent gypsum. These are taller than they would normally be, so as to reflect the scale of the room. The recesses happen also to be taller in proportion to the statues.

Approaching the corner I turn right, there is a considerable increase in overall brightness. Continuing, my path reaches the middle of the north wall.

The central niche is distinguished, bordered in gold braid, it is taller. Its alabaster statue is replaced by a form carved in agate chalcedony. Now, from the floor of the cube my gaze rakes the top of the machine: an array of parallel obliques near the ceiling is so interesting! But what if it starts up? Would I survive the noise? It may create deadly conditions. To run away would take too much time.

Intuition informed both myself and Roland, liberating each of us from fears about discharges from a monstrous chimney. Now that same intuition strikes again. Normally, only after it is made can a machine operate. But this device or engine gradually started operating, at first only conceptually, while it was being designed; and then ever more concretely during the long period while it was being fabricated and constructed. The ultimate, last stage of its assembly was completed at the instant at which it fell silent, having executing its final function. It has operated; now I am in the presence of a machine which will never again function.

As I withdraw from the unique cube, towards the far wall, the light level greatly increases. A window! The first I have seen since closing the door, at the oceanic corner. A large part of the east wall is window, it must contain tons of glass. It is dawn! In all its absoluteness, the Sun floods my eyes with light! Passing towards a decorative doorway, the final scene is of great orange shafts striking the silent engine.

Beyond the housing of the enormous, metallic device, a door-frame occupies the middle of a wall. Further away is an equal doorway, and beyond this, another, and again and again; light grazes the highly polished marble floor, it is reflected well, from afar. The marble resembles a continuous skating rink, interrupted now and then by walls and door-frames. The icy effect is exaggerated by the sharp-edged anti-silhouettes of the entrances ahead.

Should I venture into this seemingly endless succession? There is no choice! None of the rooms to either side has windows; all are in darkness, they rely on scant illumination reflected from the floor. But they are not empty, while pacing the tongue of marble, occasionally I pause and grope about in a room. Dim reflections seem to be pulled reluctantly from behind the furniture, the shadows vie for supremacy.

3. At the Edge of Colour

At last the distant succession resolves into evidence of a larger place. Indeed it leads into the atrium of an unimaginably vast library. In order to enter the great reading-hall, I pass various desks, at which are displayed lay-out plans. A hierarchy is thus revealed: surrounding the great reading-hall are lesser rooms, although still of staggering size. These are lined and stacked with books, parchments and incunabula. Circling the lesser rooms, on a much reduced scale and without books, are large vestibules. I approach the wide, ornate portal in the north wall: the passage into which it opens is itself decorated with tiers of books.

Even from within, it can be seen that the book-lined corridor leads into a vast reading-room: walking down the passage seems to make the room move away. Surely it holds more books than are contained in, could be crammed into all the libraries I've ever seen put together! Entering, I pace forwards, but without the feeling of advancing much. Then catch my breath on looking upwards: the galleries of stacks are on a scale normally only seen outside, out of doors!

Above the entrance, itself now behind, a smooth vertical wall rises to many times the height of the entrance. But the wall is no more than the front face of a marble plinth. The plinth of a first, colossal column! This slender, fluted pillar merely begins a leftward progression of equal columns, each surmounted by its capital. Upon these rests at great height a marble entablature. This is therefore perpendicular to the corridor.

Across the abyss before the colonnade is a clear view into the distant reaches of the great reading-hall. I have entered somewhere near one corner, the remaining three walls are similarly appointed with colossal, recessed colonnades. All the columns support architrave, frieze and cornice in the classic way. This room is an incomparable aftershock, worthy of the impact of the oceanic corner.

I walk in for some time, passing along to a reading-desk; then pull up a chair. The book-lined walls behind their spacious columns, seem to defy even mountains. And as with naked rock and sands in a certain light, a surface made of so many spines no more than touches the edge of colour. The ceiling is devoted to a compelling, writhing pattern. A modern airliner could do a full turn below it!

After a little exploration of the hall, I pull out a large reference packed with photos, taking the bulky and heavy volume to a table. As it sets down on the resilient surface, there is a flight of feathery echoes. In the perfect silence, they go on and on.

The encyclopaedia has an article on the ocean's corner! I study high-resolution pictures of decorations on its walls, some of which I remember. Further from the corner, carvings depict creatures from the deep. Along the pavement, the habitat of these oceanic creatures becomes less familiar, the creatures become weirder.

Absent-mindedly, I slam shut the weighty volume. The two halves thunder closed, there is a crack like dynamite, followed by an appalling echo, it fights all about, shows no sign of abating, just of getting bigger. The ceiling pattern with its marching perimeter, its turbulent interior, lowers darkly upon me. Not only horrified, I am pleased as well, the sound is magnificent! At last it falls away into the colonnaded walls. Had these been carved directly from a valley, then it would have had to have been a great valley. My own minuteness is counterbalanced by a feeling of having got away with the outrage. Hardly making a sound, I rise to replace the book.

In the course of walking across the middle of the great reading hall to the north entrance, at a steady pace, time has passed from early morning to nearly midday!

After very many passages out of the library, walking through the stately outer rooms, I pass between ponderous, vertical forms. Often behind glass, the stacks rise to within a few tens of metres of the ceilings. The outermost halls contain no books or manuscripts, they are museums for the display of vast paintings.

4. Fountains

Now I prepare to leave even the most unassuming rooms of the great, abandoned library. There's an unmistakable whiff of the external world. Yes! One of the halls contains stairs which lead out to ornamental gardens. Through doors fit for giants, doors which open automatically, and under a cloudless blue sky, I step out. Edged by flights of steps, the entrance piazza aprons onto lower terraces. After a long walk away from, and by now rather below the main entrance level, I am cut by the noonday Sun, high in the sky but behind the library.

The awesome cubic machine made a deep impression, impulsively I turn to look for it, or the place in the museum complex where it is housed. However, only the reading room and its surrounding halls are in evidence! Of course it's not possible to see behind, but somehow the library gives the strong impression of being the only building here. It is surrounded by breathtaking landscaping, then by uncultivated, increasingly wild terrain. Besides the library, no town, city, indeed building of any type is to be seen anywhere.

At last, after a considerable further walk, a wide and dizzying flight of steps unfolds. Broken by a series of lower ledges, this runs down to a polished floor far below, surrounded by grasses and forest. The scene is dominated, however, by twin landscaping ornaments.

Tending to stay to the left, I walk down the flight. The descent takes time. I am buffeted by, tugged at by a fresh, occasional wind. Not a third of the way down, indeed not a tenth, I pause to survey the gardens. Further out they include whole mountains and fantastic trees reaching to appalling altitude.

Gazing in a direction away from the library, across the surrounding landscaping far into the wildest, most distant terrain, as before I see no town, not a building. Only ever more chasmic features without parallel even amongst mountain ranges. These features seem to rise from a world, a corner is already familiar, that is flat!

And far before me tower the twin features: to either side of the steps play terrifying fountains. Very coherent, greenish jets rocket upwards for more than two thousand feet, before dismembering into ferns and nets of water which crash gracefully, almost motionlessly all the way down onto sculpted marble receptacles. Snow-white clouds of spray discharge and fold from these; an unceasing wash of sound reaches me from the basins.

There is of course no sign of the metropolis! It was clear from the moment of leaving the ocean behind me, by closing the irrevocable stone door: I'm no longer there! This is somewhere else, arbitrarily, infinitely far away. With not the slightest urge to depart so ethereal a place, I settle comfortably. Wind carries perfume from the terraced gardens by the ton.

***

Of all the characters I have met since encountering Row, could any have made a more indelible impression than Watts?

'What do you think of the arcade?'

Surely, he knew very well I was very impressed. So… instead I frowned with concentration then said, 'I regard it as a synthesis of past visions of the future, with those of the present!'

'A what…?' It looked as if he was going to get ugly, the overriding thought was: he can't take a joke. But:

'…you're just taking the piss aren't you…?… *Ha ha, Ha Ha, HA HA HA!*' He laughed outrageously, even once or twice after he'd turned away, evidently making an effort to stop.

***

Finally, I screw up the resolve to abandon this platform. At the top of the steps, my pace quickens on acknowledging that the Sun has passed its zenith: the bold shadow cast by the library is nearer than before the descent.

5. The Cusp

Re-entering the colossal reception-hall, I ascend the stairs, and still journeying for awhile reach a small, specialist wing. This is a place! How absurd! Everywhere is a place, of course. But... this discreetly proclaims itself as being a sovereign place, more than merely part of the library.

Now, with a hollowness and inner chill, comes acceptance that I must turn my back on a whole reality. The veneered, polished wood floor of a foyer is free of furniture and books, broken only by stairs. These lead down to a small reading-room. There, the wall display is packed with references: serials of uniform size, outsize books collected in special stacks. Scanning several titles, I seize an old volume, on decoration and interior design.

Its photographic plates are protected with leaves of thin rice paper. From the front of one, carefully I lift the translucent sheet. The early photo is of foliage, taken through glass doors left open. The protective paper in my hand glows with a cusp of greenish light. Putting back the book, I look up. Some metres away stands a pair of doors, the glazing is frosted; and through this filters a tell-tale green. Unlocked, the doors move easily. Sunshine. Gardens. Opening the doors fully, I go out... then turn to push them shut.

But before doing it I gaze there, for a last look into the library. Sight is fast adjusting to outdoors, the specialist wing appears dark. Huh! There's someone! The surprise is the absence of surprise. Not scared at all. Confidence in knowing who this is supersedes what can I can actually see. Row, isn't it? Come to bid me farewell! Yes! Roland! At the moment of certainty, he speaks, 'I must go now...' We shake hands. '...Till next time!' My pal turns to leave, or rather he is gone, there is no sign of him. It takes a moment for me to realise there are no books. The room now before me has long been in disuse, it has a mouldy smell. Shutting the doors slowly, firmly, I wander into the gardens.

Passing through the gardens, I walk up some sandstone steps towards another entrance to the building, then facing outwards sit on the top. Close by, a fluted porcelain urn stands above a little row of bottles. Picked up and rotated, an old vial becomes pierced with javelins of light. Absently replacing it, I take the entrance which leads along a stone-flagged facing passage of the building. There in the dim greenish light is the senary door of glass! It is open. My glance through is cut short, distracted as the wind briefly rises: an outside branch noisily brushes against the lichened window-glass.

Light streams in through the porch, someone has wedged open the front door. Walking out to bright sunshine, I sit on the steps. A steady breeze rustles the leaves, buffets the stonework. Blades of grass dance back and forth. The

Sun is alone in the hot sky. It takes only a few seconds to settle down, to fall asleep.

The long shadows of sunset awaken me. Digging through the lining of one pocket is the ignition key of the motorbike. On a small mouth-organ, I play quietly until long after the stars have appeared in ones, twos, thousands.

CODA TO *The Charmed Door*

FOREWORD

This supplement is intended for the use of readers of the book, who may well be familiar with the personalities and adventures therein. The work is based on and reaches beyond the remit of the book. The plan is to provide answers, answers liable to be eclipsed by bigger questions! Short additions or progressions for each chapter of the original build up to a new, detailed account of Chapter 10. And allowing for symmetry, observations of the closing episodes of the book are included.

CHAPTER 1

Before even the rain-drilled motorbike ride out of the city and into desolate countryside, prior to this was a call to a second-hand furniture repository, part of a half-hearted search for an old, working radiogram. One with stations like Hilversum, Athlone, Motala marked; and a magic eye.

Rising to several floors, the shop extends far behind its unimposing frontage. While peering at cut-glass vases and coloured bottles arranged in a cabinet, my attention is jogged. A silver-plate sleeve on one of the objects reflects a grey carrot-shape that swells and swings along the silver, in this direction. A man in overalls offers help, we discuss the radiogram. He leads the way upstairs lined with mirrors and framed paintings. I pause by a large plate-glass mirror from a demolished shop. Surprisingly expensive. We enter one of the upper showrooms, it is stacked in some places to the ceiling with electrical appliances.

The salesman slaps the top of a veneered cabinet. One side bears several concentric scratches. The lid is opened, all is in order. While trying the even resistance of the controls, he fetches a junction box and plugs the set into the mains. The magic eye brightens, as surely it has for many generations to an artificial green. The apex of a sharp-edged, twitching sector gazes out from the eye's centre. Turning up the volume of the radio causes the sector to jump as a stretched, over-stretched fan. Pencilling the item number in a battered notebook, he says, 'Show you some of the stuff at the back if you like!'

'Great!'

Piled furniture forms an avenue of wardrobes, chests, desks, divans. Ahead the assistant reaches awkwardly to draw a curtain back, his loose overall seems to almost slip off. Adrenaline! On the man's chest is an area of colourless, dull metal. He appears unsure if he's been noticed, keen to divert attention.

'You won't have seen round the back yet. Customers aren't expected to go there!'

'You've got so much stuff in here…' Picking our way around. '…The place is enormous!'

'There's floor space in the building even staff haven't visited for a long time. Especially in the large room.' Abruptly, it becomes unclear what he is saying.

'Right away, I'll be over!'

'Pardon?'

'Just coming, Mr Hawke…' Then to me, '…Don't spend too long up here!'

'Sure! See you in a minute in the downstairs office.'

***

The fact is, as the reader will recall, after blundering into one another, or to be honest after Roland saved my life, we have put adventure first, with caution tossed to the wind. After crawling our way past a vertiginous stone shaft, and receiving unambiguous instructions to take a certain passage, we are lead to a junk-room: all is clean, odourless. But the lumber has been heaped in desperation, awaiting sorting out in the future, and thence finding use in the next future.

Text-books on upholstery, picture books on mountaineering, bound encyclopaedias with volumes missing fill overflowing bookshelves.

'Look at this…!' My pal is suddenly excited. '…this book does not belong with the others, even in this place… this is an ancient guide waiting for us!'

'No, it isn't…' I brag. '…I know this book. It's a text-book on, er… geomancy.'

With the greatest respect, we painstakingly dust it; the book is very old, parts of it fall to the floor as we try to open it. Pages that have not been parted for decades make a dry complaint, as it turns out neither of us is right. Just an old book! Frustrated, we browse a few other volumes.

'*Interpretation of Dreams*, there's a silly book for you!'

'Give it a chance…' Roland grabs it. '…Oh yes, full of them. Let's see, what do you say to this careful account?' He reads it aloud:

"This dream is about the quality of light in a place called the Depression of Turfan. This is a region in the Sinh Kiang province of China, under the high walls of the Tien Shan mountains, and a thousand miles from the nearest sea. And yet it is itself seven hundred feet below sea level. The dream reveals that, much as light entering a polished shaft illuminates it to all depths, so a traveller riding across the plain of Turfan will notice this effect on his surroundings. Of course, in the bright sunshine all he sees will be clearly lit. But if a heavy blanket of cloud rolls over the region, carrying with it dark mists that press down to the ground, and all around the traveller, whether on foot or on horseback, he may yet find his way illuminated. For in this place, the light is reflected rather than immediately absorbed, being thrown back from the lush green grass up into the mist. While all is dark above, the traveller may find the ground below him throws off a strong emerald light. Movement in the mist may cause sudden changes in the appearance of the ground; and the journeying of the Sun through clouds of varying depths and qualities will cause the brightness of the mist about him to alter suddenly."

'That doesn't sound like a dream. Actually, I can't abide dreams, you know, dreams while you're asleep. Better deleted!'

'Hang on...' Row shuffles through the book. '...Yes, I thought so. The interpretation is missing!'

This pleasant, irregular jumble-room is obstructing us, we may never get past it! An antique television rests on a sofa, music scores are coiled up in a lidless pressure cooker. There are hand-written diaries, unused packages of stationery, piles of plates. On the top of a filing cabinet, on its superior black malacca case which is lined with dark blue velvet, and as always larger than expected, rests a violin. Under the guise of searching for a way out, each of us clambers and rummages independently, too engrossed to notice that bends in the shape of the room mean we no longer have direct line of sight to one another.

Half wondering where Roland is, I probe a dismantled harp, scan a pile of photo albums. One of the albums pokes out, it creaks open. Wait a moment! What? Check album after album. Not quite the right age. Here, getting warmer. These people, this book. This is the page, no, next... over here, one of these pictures. This one, where? Top row? Row? There he is in the third row! It's him!

'It's me!' The bastard! He's stolen up behind me!

'You bugger! Where have you been?'

'Look, I'm so sorry! No sign of a hatch in the floor, with steps leading down...' There's a half-humorous, half-conspiratorial expression in his eye. '...Look what I've found!' Row holds a portrait-photo in a plain frame, the glass is stained in one corner.

'Wait a sec... that's... it's me!' I exclaim.

'Yes...!' The black-and-white depicts myself with several people, all smiling. None of them do I recognise. '...Coincidence, isn't it? One thing I do know: there's a photo of the two of us together somewhere in here!'

'Impossible! Well... let's find it!'

'We can't, I shouldn't have said that. Searching would take too long. We've got to find a way out of here!'

'Sure... You know Roland... this is not the only building.'

'Well, from where your came, it would appear as only one.'

'Actually, I could see others from the gardens.'

'Could you? Wait a moment... that would have been only after you'd entered the outer passage...' With a wry expression, he divulges some bizarre information.

'...We are in an intermediate zone outside containment and giving consular access to anti-containment.'

Truly paradoxical is the lighting; there is little sign of darkness further away from the main body of the room. On the contrary, here and there, in many places it is easier to see things. Realisation! My hair stands on end! All along we've taken unexplained light for granted, just as one does diffuse daylight.

A short passage ahead is finished in veneered-wood panelling. As my companion looks on, by using the drawers I clamber up to the top of a wardrobe. This is a place where the wainscotting rises to the ceiling, and continues actually across the ceiling itself.

It is not unpleasant up here. So many obsolete effects are now visible, from a slightly different elevation. All look clean, nothing broken. In one direction there is a patch of slightly brighter light, made up of endless faded colours, yellowish, whitish, it is possible to see very far... Waayy-oooh...! This closet is rather tall... steadying myself, I move to climb down. But he insists that this is the only way out, that we must both take it, take it now!

Noticing an escutcheon surrounding a key, I give it a twist. There's a metallic click, and a panel swings down giving us access to a dark, velvet-lined opening.

Entering, we are lost in inky blackness.

CHAPTER 2

The heroes emerge to an appalling, shocking vastness, first taking time to struggle to apprehend what unfolds before them. There is pyramidal marble, granite, glass, it feels like gazing down an endless gradient. For several seconds, for minutes, our voices have fallen to all but whispers. But competition soon rears its ugly head, there is rivalry as to who recovers more quickly.

'How do we get down from this gigantic sofa?'

'I've never seen such architecture!'

The enormous amphitheatre supports us, unfolds below us. The whole lies before a double colonnade, enclosing on either side water-courses, rivers cascade over sculpted granite slabs. Up the middle of this runs a polished, marble avenue whose banks rise to flint and bronze walls.

'That's modern styling, Row!' He is looking in the same direction.

'I agree! Look at those sharp-edged indents.'

Still vast, there are many lesser columns, standing in progressions, circlets, fours, in pairs and alone. Throughout, the vertical forms are noticeably slender. Gardens abound, often with decorative fountains. Central to the vast room is the presentation of a marble or glass pyramid. While well-offset from the four corners, the walls bear immense vitrines.

The whole room has overall symmetry: were it to be rotated by a right angle about an axis through the pyramid, hardly anything would change. Here, generous comfortable accommodation is offered to titans, to giants. These figures may take a seat, may relax and view the extraordinary scene. Crescent-shaped, this amphitheatre is a petrifaction of classical forms on an unfathomable scale, for an unknown purpose. And indeed, simultaneously, on a range of lesser scales. But this interpretation obscures the possibility of a more interesting *total absence of purpose*.

The amphitheatre.

There is no way of knowing whether beyond this room lies an outside world, whether there lie other chambers, perhaps no less vast; or whether the region beyond is solid; or even some other possibility.

'This... is a social desert!'

To his companion, Row retorts, 'Is that what you're after: pavements jammed with people, trains too packed to get into, pubs overflowing into the road?'

'No!'

'Are you sure? It can easily be arranged.'

'Sure, I'm sure!'

'These buildings stand guard at the gate to greater scale: if what we see is possible, then why not buildings a million miles high? Because... because, to go any further in scale, one has go further than this in inventiveness, uniqueness, originality!'

A spontaneous question can be as deep as it is vague, devoid of definite meaning. Abruptly, I ask, 'Row, are you on leave or anything?' My companion speaks, yet the reply seems to come from someone else, it is affable, rational, hurried, distant, difficult to catch. Indeed, it apparently comes from several people.

'Sorry, what was that? Our encounter is an opportunity to join coincidence and applicability.'

'Right, got you! *Ha-ha*!' After getting down, pacing perfect marble floors, we gaze about in silence.

Roland speaks, 'You know, the city is dead, you may find this baffling, but evidence establishes it has always been dead.'

'How could that be possible? Impossible!'

'For cities such as this life is a mere after-touch, a luxury it has never enjoyed. It has never lived...' Left with no choice, I go along with this idea.

'Yet it is not devoid of life. Especially as to patterns... see... they are everywhere: halting, reversing, jerking, shunting, climbing, side-stepping, some are shaking!'

'The law of patterns is very strict.'

'Yes, that's true... Look!' There's a glint of what appears to be natural light at the apex of the central edifice.

First only glancing at the square-based pyramid, I then gaze intently at it. Soon, extraordinary visual acuity returns: just below the apex the copper appears lighter in colour. Resting in a channel cut into the pyramidion is a mirror mounted on trunnions. Staring into the mirror, I resolve still more detail: the silvered plane glints with light reflected from the Sun. This discovery springs into mind an extraordinary notion: that of an "abundance of faint light"!

The Sun is always at a certain distance, eight or nine light-minutes, a long way to be sure: but always scarcely nearer nor further. My skin crawls with rising hairs... in this place, it feels it is further from the Sun than usual. A great deal further! As if we have fallen into a place where the Sun is many, many times further away.

***

The Prime Senator, the Principal Executrix has not only received the two of us alone; she has been willing to pass a short time taking questions, mainly from me, especially about the pyramid.

'The very tip, the final metre is not copper. It's solid gold...!' The Lady continues, '...One of the functions is as a musical instrument. The device can focus on any event in the world, say the performance of a symphony. It synthesises orchestral sounds and natural effects. The instrument merges famous music with natural phenomena, distant thunder-storms, volcanic eruptions. The result is discharged into the void of the room. Whole concertos travel at the speed of sound like invisible jellies, elongating, turning inside out. The echoes are re-absorbed and re-discharged as the pyramid bounces them around the acoustic chamber!'

My gaze falls on a faraway glass citadel of glinting columns and pediments.

'Can we hear it?'

'We do not have time to sparc, it will have to be brief. Let's see... here's a short composition. It was played when another er, visitor like yourself, was received in this room. Interesting... that was long ago, many centuries.' Almost imperceptibly, Aza touches a key: silence! Then we are elevated, crushed by sounds and overtones at all wavelengths. To my enduring regret, the performance soon draws to a close, it is back to business: Aza gives the impression our questions are only the introductory stage, quite natural, but to be siphoned off to make way for something deadly serious.

While the Senator-General has been addressing us, I've become acutely conscious of her immense, unrivalled seniority, appearing now as she does in her vast auditorium.

While we take glasses of fruit juice, by some unexplained faculty, it is as if I overhear Aza telling Roland something *before* I met him... well in the past.

'I have a surprise for you, principal administrator. He is to travel through there without guidance. Yes... Alone!' Through where? They are talking about me...! Without guidance!

CHAPTER 3

The loco approaches an ornate, dirty arch. What! Just before the sky is blotted out, surely... again... I see the Moon amongst clouds. How could it appear in two quite different places? In the blackness of the tunnel, light flickers on either side through brick cloisters. Glimpses are much too brief to study the sky. At the far end... there's nothing to be seen... it was not the Moon, just a freak cloud formation!

CHAPTER 4

Fumes from the spiny nucleus of a cactus are released. These contain a powerful hypnotic substance, capable of altering both mind and world, resulting in an appalling, protected free-fall. The fall is so shocking; hardly do I notice that the drug's effects have worn off.

CHAPTER 5

During our long sojourn through the non-incandescent and the incandescent underworlds, Zircon describes some of his visits to extraordinary, far-futuristic cities.

'Of especial interest is the cubic city, which contains all its buildings within a single structure. The distinction between rooms and buildings becomes much less definite. Just one area of the structure may contain a million apartments!

'So everything is neatly contained in a box... the remainder of the world becomes an open park. How big is the actual cube?'

'Seldom less than three kilometres on a side. I've seen cubes more than ten kilometres in every direction!'

'New York, New Paris... A question of greater scale... here, the quality of life for everyone must be excellent!'

'All right...' the grandmaster continues, his sash pulled very tight. '...But the building I'm thinking of now, well, as you approach it by air, from above, you can see a spectacular formation at the corner of the roof. There's a gaping crater, where the building was struck by a meteorite! In the vicinity of the impact, the damage can be seen going down a hundred and fifty floors!'

'Ahhh!'

'Some of the destruction has been ameliorated in the course of time. Quite large trees grow in the zone. Some of the inner terraces of the crater have themselves been architectured! There are legendary accounts of older cubes having been struck twice!'

Not every discourse with Zircon has been recalled, revisited, divulged. A place he calls the castle nestles in rocks which fall to chasmic depths. A road along the top of the castle supports a balustered parapet. On the drop side, the parapet is decorated with equally spaced, empty stone urns. As we lean over, Zircon mentions that the drop beyond the parapet is 1000 feet straight down. But he carelessly lets slip some worthless trinket. It bounces and rolls very near the far edge. Another inch or two and it would have been lost to the abyss.

'Get it for me, you are nearer.'

'That's just an excuse!'

'Kindly step over and get it.' To humour him, I clamber over the parapet. The trinket has come to rest by the base of an urn; there is very little space. Lying flat on the outer paving, I make one or two attempts to reach it. Finally, I bump into the urn while doing this. It teeters on its base, rocking back and forth. Holding onto it is impossible; my efforts to stop the urn from toppling only help propel it over the edge. The two of us watch as the stone amphora falls over, taking the trinket with it!

The heavy object lazily turns bowl-down. From the parapet, we lean over to watch: what did he say? A drop of over a thousand feet! Zircon appears to be drinking in every detail and listening hard. The piece glances against the wall about halfway, some fragments fly off, the bulk gently rebounds outwards. Then a fan of white powder stabs in all directions, as the ornament detonates. It takes a second or so for the bang to reach us... Different branches of the echo come, trailing curious rattlings and whispers for long after.

CHAPTER 6

The town of Greyscar has few if any charms. We finish the last stage of the approach on foot. Stark brick buildings about the industrial complex ahead. A bird settles on a blackened television aerial. It is large, feathers slowly clamp tighter as it sways on the old fitting.

'Look!' A hair-dryer in a coiffeur's facility has been gutted: coloured insulation on some wire twitches. After a moment's stillness there are fibrillations, whiskers twitching. These belong to a rat, which stares out of the dome. Sniffing, it jumps out of the dryer, running to the window. I stare into its dark, liquid eyes. It lifts itself up against the glass, then scurries off!

The wind increases as we progress. Whistling noises are accompanied by sounds of tearing and objects falling. It is possible an unusual storm is not over. The clouds seem very near, just above us. An orderly tramp down a pavement is disturbed, as wind swoops in the direction of the street. It howls, overturning dustbins, yanking rubbish into the air. Shop fittings, advertisement panels, awnings become detached, flapping against the walls, dropping to the ground.

After a short lull, the wind returns with greater force: vortices form as paper, refuse, sections of discarded furniture are lifted and twisted. There are many noises. Now the wind has found how to rip open a larger prize: an unkempt warehouse ahead, to one side. The roof is already in visibly poor condition. But as we watch slates are being torn and sucked off. The old building has street frontage, and here two windows suddenly blow out, frames as well as the glass.

Quantities of waste industrial packing material, which evidently has been dumped in the warehouse, tip out of the gaps left by the exploded windows. The wind must be passing straight through the building: streaming funnels of the whitish waste rush out, without settling. The two billowing off-white intestines of waste twist and snatch spectacularly ahead of us, in the street and over the buildings. With great suddenness the wind drops to nothing, the airborne rubbish falls and the fibrous motes of waste disperse and settle like snow. We hurry on.

CHAPTER 7

When playfully challenged about his robotic nature, Roland skilfully moves the enquiry to the nature of the popular perception of the government. What matters is that Row is descended from the future, not founded on the past, as in such notions as "the development of robotics".

CHAPTER 8

Powerful, reconditioned second-hand motorbikes are made available to the rascals, who set off in search of the ruined city of Tenatis.

Half a kilometre from a ridge, there's the unmistakable glint of water. We head down to what is a small stream. At this altitude, the fast waters course noisily over bare rock. Where the stream widens, it is possible to kneel down on its stones and drink. At this suitable place we take turns. To rinse face and body in the clear water, to look into the reflection as it settles. From the twisting mirror, several faces stare up at me!

CHAPTER 9

The bikers have now returned their machines to take seats at the front of a bulldozing engine so bulky that it requires a complement of about a hundred operatives to keep it running. Presently the system, via its fast-moving hydraulic legs is passing over rivers and then arid tundra.

Suddenly…! Pandemonium…! Our conversation is wrenched apart…! Shrill alarms sound nearby, a very loud klaxon can be heard far below, accompanied by powerful electric bells:

'FIRE! FIRE!' We unbuckle and join the exit rush. Roland glances back at me, several men hold a door open. There is an acrid smell. Three blackened figures, one a woman, stagger into the control suite.

'It's out! We just had a huge blow-back in the main engine room. Everyone is accounted for, minimal damage. What a mess though!' We move towards a hatch leading below to get a look for ourselves; by asking the others he finds out a few things. But it is obvious we are in the way, we steal back to our seats.

How the mind works! Talking to him… from near panic, I swivel to calculating how we can get out of helping to clean up. In fact, as it turns out we are left alone while the conversation rights itself.

Subsequently, near the crater of a volcano, the pair find pyroclastic minerals and a grey, glassy stone. The obsidian seems to move by itself, filled with stirring, elastic reflections of the sky.

CHAPTER 10

Before he encounters and picks up his total stranger, Watts is in conference with the doctor. This total stranger is you, the adventurer, the protagonist, the narrator. Outside, people of all ages stroll past, in odd places there is broken masonry, weeds grow. But as he gazes down at the street through the blind, for once the scene is a blank to Watts. The expert addresses him, 'You should not be too worried about your brother. Particularly if you manage to find this bloke, concentrate on doing that. We'll get your brother and his pal back!'

'Yeh!'

'Will you be all right driving?'

'Sure, I'll be OK.'

'Really, I have to stay here. Do you want someone to come with you?'

'No. No way. Thanks...! Right! I'll be off then.' They go over the plan once again. There is an old, shiny map on the wall. The doctor pokes it with a forefinger.

'Here. Right here!'

'It's all right. Miles away, but I know this part of town. We own some machines in the local centre.'

'Remember, get over there nice and quick, but don't rush things, there's no rush.'

***

The kernel of this coda resides in the present chapter. You have been Shanghaied, emotionally blackmailed into jumping into Watts' powerful sedan for a gripping ride to his amusement arcade. But before resuming this account, you the reader might wish to be offered certain details. The merging of the partners' leisure enterprise and the Telecommunications Administration affords insight into a minor branch of a greater entity. This branch leads down into the deepest reaches of the government. The task at hand is to attempt to apprehend the constitution of this abstract higher directorate.

To do this, we'll concentrate on just one "quarter" of the evidence, while taking for granted many remaining quarters. This consists of lines of telecommunication, made possible by inventions from ancient to comparatively recent times.

For the purposes of this account, from the various cases (including telegraphy, heliology or solar telegraphy, typically using signals flashed by mirror or arc lamp, and for that matter, semaphoring) it is easiest to take as representative telephony. And the various cases mentioned above are merely representatives of hosts of discarded choices which might have been made. So, for "telephony" read "all kinds of things".

Wild advances in telephony occur on an almost daily basis. Not only can sound and pictures be transmitted by pocket-sized mobile phones; applications are available which permit the user to monitor what someone else sees and hears on their handset, simply by pointing the user's phone at the target, and switching to surveillance mode. Such advances are highly misleading. The only question of substance is the constitution of the single entity through which is drawn the connection, or line of communication between users. In this detailed study, these may be taken to be users of desk or hand-held terminals on the telephone network.

Here it will be argued that the only viewpoint capable of offering a glimpse of the intrinsic nature of the permanent higher directorate, the only viewpoint of technical irrefutability, is that founded on lines of telecommunication. The object of study, therefore is the unified world telephone network, which is the aggregate of all lesser networks. In the pleural, governments as they occur in one-to-one correspondence with nations, are essentially a misleading venture into concepts, much as individual volcanoes are mere testaments to the fires of the underworld.

It goes without saying that the greater is the syllogistic, analytical, cerebral, rational, deductive, articulate penetration of the cortex of the government, well, the greater is the likelihood of becoming lost. The wealth of avenues which may be taken at any juncture, some of them indeed interesting, this wealth invariably destabilises and debilitates the most hardened explorers. The individual falls into the grip of what is a pattern of crystallographic interfaces, leading only inwards, yet getting nowhere. Strenuous withdrawal all the way back to familiarity is effectively the only course, the researcher may have difficulty in rendering an account of his discoveries, even to himself.

***

After a successful pick-up, and en route to his arcade, the curvature of our path fleetingly gives direct line-of-sight to the lower corner of an apartment block, tall but square. Just long enough to notice that by it lies a huge tunnel. The ornate, ground-level entrance is fed by sheaves of roads, all swarming with traffic. For a third of a second, it is possible to see far into it, before our path curves violently away.

So, where does Watts dwell? No less proud of his ignorance than of his knowledge, his is territory more real than either. In my imagination he smiles with roguish pride at this. How the faculty of perception plays tricks! Now it feels as if there is no hurry, that there is plenty of time to do many things on the way from the entrance of his arcade to the rear door. We inspect a machine installed at the front.

'Put your hand in there, at the back. Hey! Don't get too close!' I try, and feel a strong draught of hot air.

He says, 'That machine has been producing amounts of heat since we had it installed long ago. Recently, if anything the output has increased. Wind from the street helps carry away the heat pouring out of the works. That is why we've got it near this entrance! That little panel there covers the plug to the mains. The cable is as wide as your finger. But… no chance we'd take this one out. Much too popular. River of cash. But, that connection… seeing to the wiring was dodgy. By-passes the fuses. *Ha, ha*! I doubt that we could disconnect it if we wanted to!'

On the point of showing me another machine further into the arcade, Watts is briefly called aside.

Momentarily alone, I catch a voice. 'Hiya! You all right?' It's someone talking to me.

'Yeah, thanks!' A slightly patronising tone fades from my voice, on realising the guy is familiar. No use turning to let Watts know, he's busy with a problem. I turn back and bluntly stare at the fellow: it is a salesman, a man in overalls, the very person who reserved a radiogram for me in the furniture depository. That was before a long, rain-lashed bike ride... Way back at the start of it all...

'Don't freak out! I work here as well, some of the time!'

'Uh! How are you? We're going over to the office. Will you be there?'

'Fine! OK! No... Er, I'll be off!'

On his return, Watts ignores the departing figure, still keen to draw my attention to a prized machine further inside. It seems a lost cause to even mention to him that I have already met one of his staff, and I remain silent. But... our eyes meet: he knows something has just been going on. I don't think I know that he knows. I know. But how? How do I know? Or why? But the real question is: who? Who cares? A smile spills into a laugh. Watts just wasn't interested in any of the complications, only in a triumph for anarchy.

Soon my gaze is caught in the middle distance; we have a quick exchange.

'Oh! Wow! I'd no idea the arcade was so...'

'No! It isn't!' What? How... how does he know what I am going to say...? And he is wrong!

'Eh? Really, Watts...' I gaze into the colour-filled glare. '...the room is huge, it goes on and on!' Ceiling lighting panels seem to recede in perspective patterns. It is as if I can hear the sounds of activity, laughter, scuffles even from ever further into the arcade, from hosts of preoccupied players, from crowds.

'It doesn't! This is just a small, local arcade!'

Even stranger! I think to myself with astonishment. *He's not wrong... he's right!* Must have been an illusion which built up, possibly from past epochs. It is vanishing as he speaks...

Watts draws my attention to another unit further into the arcade.

'Look! There's still time. I must show you this machine!' His pride cannot be contained. Snap! The host plugs in and switches on a new unit. Very soon a violet light bathes his face. 'Have a go! To get to the winning square, well, you see these people you meet on the way... you've got to work out which are regular people and which have been teamed!'

'Teamed?'

'Come on! Don't you know what teamed means? It means someone who's had a small circle removed from the top of their skull, and a germanium chip put in; to make sure, how shall I put it, they don't come out with anything too unexpected!' I playfully feel the top of my skull.

'You can't tell if someone has been teamed of course! *Ha, ha!*' He laughs and laughs.

The unsubtle colours and basic shapes give the impression of kids' stuff. But hardly aimed at youth, these pastimes are directed at adults. The game is to stay entertained into late adulthood. Surrounding us are deadly serious electrical amusements. This is a dangerous world of heavy smokers, aged arcade kings. Still the industry strives to beat the demands of the human anatomy, strives to proves there is yet an un-tried amusement. All you need is cash: after that in theory you could bring down a whole sector of the electronics industry for failing to provide recreation. The spoiler of course is government regulations which prohibit games which are too daring or hazardous. There is even an unspoken code of conduct among manufacturers which says that any firm hiding behind the regulations is a lame competitor. The purpose of life itself is to remain sufficiently amused.

'Come and have a look at this new enjoyment appliance!'

A player stands over the main glass panel, the field of light from under it illuminating his face and clothes with primary colours. Beneath the glass panel, some of the mechanism can be seen; but the containing box is unusually deep, and I move closer to look over its edge. Nearer the bottom, as more of the wheels and pulleys are revealed, the pool of electric light gets fiercer, I look up to accustom the eyes slowly. Thus my gaze catches the turquoise sleeve of the player. He has a white metal bracelet on his wrist, and from out of the cuff I see a filament of cotton against the dark skin. The player looks up, licks his lips, and walks away from the machine.

Quite apart from Watts' apparent delaying tactics, there is the disconcerting dilation of time: my watch agrees to the minute with the one or two clocks we happen to pass, there's no difficult keeping tabs on the time; yet within just few minutes, at most within a little snatch of an hour, long conversations seem to have passed, it feels as if we have been doing things, accomplishing things even, on our way to the seat of the crisis. It becomes an effort to let go of watching the time, and allow various bizarre circumstances to take over. Time has somehow come to meander like an intestine, two moments close together mask unexplained interludes of memories and events. This of course is a quite separate matter, and yet apparently it proliferates whenever intimations of telepathy lurk near.

Only now do I realise how much time Watts has wasted getting me to the site of the emergency. We're in the warehouse, when he suddenly remarks, 'Some of them are pretty rough!'

'Who?'

'The customers! That's why the games are surrounded by metal!'

'This one's not! It's plastic…!' I rap the casing with my knuckle. '…Anyway, how else could you see through it?' The remark seems to leave him aghast.

'What? That's not plastic. Feel it with the flat of your hand!'

'Yes! You're right! That's not plastic! It's metal! Transparent… metal!'

'Well, of course it is. You must have seen that before? Look! This is an old rig… got a few dents in it already. Let's see…' He looks around. '…Here! This'll do!' With a spanner in his hand, he clouts the case. The wood figures within jolt sideways, as excited as offended by the shock. He strikes a couple more times, then brushes it down. '…Feel that!'

Sure enough, while the stuff takes the blows without cracking, there is now a slight dent. I ask him, 'Hadn't we better be getting on?'

'There's still time. Look! I must show you this vibrational pleasure centre!' His pride cannot be contained...

It is no less my fault for egging him on, but at long last we take a step, but no more than a step, towards the place of the doctor, and of those waiting with him. My host is keen to explain the working relationship which his business has with the Telephone Administration.

'The building here and its many basements are used to store every available piece of antique or even merely obsolete telephone network equipment, domestic, commercial, industrial; and of course the apparatus seen by no one but technicians and engineers with the Administration. *The Fax Museum*, we call it!'

'Yeuchh!' I shudder.

'Furthermore, press photos of telephony equipment, collected from many places, some of pieces of which there is no known existing example, are archived with particular care. Other photos, films and videos include still and motion pictures of all the main stages of manufacture...'

We have stopped walking, he hasn't finished. '...Every used directory, regardless of condition, is considered a collectors' piece; every memo sent from one department to another, no matter how trivial, no matter how many copies happen to be available, all are boxed, some even stored in humidity-controlled warehouse rooms. I don't mean to disturb you, you would be if you knew just how much material is kept!'

The route we must take is via a door which happens to be obstructed by a leisure appliance. After several wrenches and a few scratches on the vinyl floor, the machine is hauled out of the way. Watts adopts a confidential tone. 'Our side of the franchise actually occupies more rooms than you might think. It's not that we need all of these to run the arcade; it's that the arcade is, well, just the visible part of the franchise.'

He seems to enjoy allowing the eyes to get used to the faintest light, relying on only the vaguest cues. Suddenly, I exclaim, 'How do you keep track in here?'

'It is difficult. I've lost a number of guests over the years!'

'*Ha, ha*!'

'Let me know if you notice any dried-up remains!'

Now his demeanour rapidly changes from apologetic to proud, to reflective.

'We are never going to get to help those two!'

'I haven't, er, disclosed everything to you, there's still more time… I was actually asked to delay you a bit…' With some alarm, I listen to his words. '…You'll figure it all out when you meet the doctor! Trust me!'

I interject, 'I trust no-one. Not even someone I've known as long as you!' Watts' brief smile fades as he listens engrossed, while I relate some personal incident or other.

Following a baffling, very interesting and personal route, at last we enter the operations room, dominated by the presence of Doctor Chandrasekharan. A number of police stand behind him, showing bulky hand guns. The doctor speaks so lucidly his words are almost no effort to listen to. So lucid is what he has already said, he produces the feeling that taking in what he is currently saying could scarcely be necessary.

Thus am I fitted with a psychic dome and sent to chase after Watts' brother Ramon. This first foray is to no avail, even though he is sitting there before me.

Looking away from Ramon, lifting the dome from my head, I return to the operations room and the doctor. Then tell him we still have the problem. Again there is the feeling that everyone in the room is staring at me. Everyone? After a quick look around, I find this comprises only Watts, his sibling, the other psychonaut and... the doctor.

'Where are the police...?'

'It's OK. We don't need them any more!'

My subsequent foray, quite an adventure, has already been covered, but one series of encounters might be mentioned:

Passing the glass-cased barometer, I pause for another look. The wheels appear so delicate, in a device surrounded by the noisy arcade games. Idly, I try training my hearing on the minute sounds it may make. To my surprise, the acuity of hearing increases until there is the impression of detecting remote, tiny sounds. Unexpectedly, the metal bellows expand slightly. Despite the music and clicking of pin-balls, sounds of the intricate device operating can now be distinctly heard and followed.

Watts' warehouse and office has been portrayed, so has my pursuit of and catching up with his brother. Now there's an opportunity to recount something else. Something that has nothing whatever to do with the outcome of the foray. It occurs in the archive.

Time is my own, for the simple reason of wearing the psychic dome. Ramon will be OK, his time-frame and mine are independent, unless we meet. This is a chance to find out a few things about the huge registry, although as it turns out I will learn nothing.

From the outset, it is and it will be necessary to cope with interpenetrating narratives. This usually means choosing the more interesting narrative and holding on to it. Evidently, a visit to the discreet archive tucked away behind Watts' electronic palace stimulates awareness of a grander access-place. In particular, this will be the downtown concourse of the telephone administration, colloquially known as the porch. Firstly, considerable, unrequited curiosity about this place has to be satisfied.

Returning to the guide-book after checking a catalogue room, it looks as if someone has touched it while my back was turned. There's no dust to give away handling marks; but it was not as I'd seen it shortly before, it appears to have rotated a little. Before picking it up, I look round for any other changes.

Two more things show up. To my great surprise, the carpet has moved nearer to one wall! A most plain carpet, hard, woven hessian, it has been milled so as to look shiny with use, but in fact could well be new. Without any patterns, its only features are slight widening of the material due to the hem at each edge. And as well the whole carpet has moved down the corridor. I crouch down to look closely at it. Yes! I can see it has moved by the position of a slight crease.

Now for the third change: the light bulbs produce only a dim illumination; but some of these bulbs can be seen quite clearly to have started lowering from the ceiling! Their cords are lengthening from the sockets above! Some bulbs and their flat shades are now as low as my head.

Others are visibly moving down. I can see one or two approaching the floor... Whatever is going to happen next? This question I ignore, actually as it arises, if not sooner. In the desolation of the featureless corridors of the telephone archive, there is an almost sexual liberation from normality. Recalling the oppressive, drab colours and poor lighting makes my hair stand on end even now. I recall the unique smell of the place. Faint, not offensive and... not at all interesting or attractive.

Soon it will become clear that the archive and its extraordinary manifold of corridors is the place of culmination, the objective of the adventurers exploration, and the location of the secret of the Telephone Administration.

But to begin, note that users naturally think of telephony as handsets. Smart mother-of-pearl hand-sized units that project a holographic image on top of a table in a bar or the chunky executive-type desktop-terminals. Or the early black Bakelite telephones that were connected to the few other telephones in the locale. But in every case their lines converge on exchanges.

At one time of course, all telephone exchanges were government property, everyone knows this. But even today, there are extensive, undisclosed government exchanges. This is not for any secret police-work, anything like that. It is in the nature of telephony. The pioneers encountered unexpected areas of instability, undercurrents in their efforts to close all required links. The phenomenal ballooning of demand meant that far from being able to get rid of them, they had to be brushed under the carpet. You may have inadvertently been switched to a government line, when there's the impression the subscriber who you're talking to, no matter how familiar this co-respondent may be, one's lover, life partner, intimate family member is replying while underwater. One of the main tasks of the engineers is to prevent this happening and rapidly becoming worse. All the time, efforts are underway to concentrate these regions into orderly cortices, but the truth is they outweigh many times over the normal network.

Despite their blank, windowless exteriors, massive, unmarked government telephone nerve-centres can look very imposing, gleaming even from the outside, but this is indeed misleading. There are administrators in the directorate who are facing retirement and yet are still only in the early stages of their training; so daunting is the work.

To say the advance, the enlargement of telephony has created this unpredictable, accidentalist uncontrollability would be false; better to say that all along it has been hiding round the corner, waiting to pounce.

To give an instance of the vertiginousness faced by government engineers, there have been, there are priority projects where massive trunk connections are made, the most sophisticated optical channels buried in concrete shafts making them near-indestructible; yet there are administrators further up the hierarchy who know, not expect, *know* these lines will never be used. But without this activity, given telephony as understood by highly qualified experts, uncontrollable randomisation would gain the upper hand.

Really, I don't think the doctor knows what I've been up to. Top man in his field, no argument there. But I have travelled further into the archive than the sojourn related to him. He never asked about this or seemed to suspect it. Well before letting him know I'd lost the trail of Ramon, I decided to walk at length into the warren of corridors and staircases. There was a carefree feeling that there was no chance of getting lost as a result of moving outwards: to get back, all I had to do was head towards the little table supporting the *Guide*.

While I learn that in the first place the layout is chosen to satisfy the fire regulations, otherwise the justification remains obscure. In the dim, spooky setting, the structure gives the impression of orderliness. A false, outwardly impression: no tidy system has ever been devised to organise records detailed enough for the requirements of this quarter of the directorate.

Rooms further in generally become more interesting, but correspondingly more difficult to leave. University-level expeditions have been mounted, striving to reach and survey the mysterious boundary which divides full rooms from the unending empty rooms yet ahead. Of course as time passes, corridor space further from the entrance becomes filled. Therefore these forays become more challenging and exhausting for the expeditioners.

A record consists of two things: the medium upon which information is impressed, and the information itself. The articles of medium are neither robust nor fragile, but are always stored with care, and so aside from a very few cases, are stored intact awaiting organisation; breakages are rare. However, the last remnants of the morass of information-bearing articles in the vicinity of the boundary is as unstructured as if it had been deliberately stirred.

Every deposition into the archive only contributes to an information burden in excess, well in excess of the technical capabilities of the current system. Yet every time a new source of information arises, so follows official backing for capturing what it produces. In a conversation between two subscribers, for example, if it can be proved the timbre of one (or, discounting the highly unlikely event of both) alters because he or she wants to go to the lavatory, then this fact would need to be recorded and highlighted in an appropriate way.

Ramshackle means are resorted to, to expedite the sequestration of data. Carefully reprocessed photographs containing almost no information are linked together in order to capture and hold information. Full clinical sterilisation is applied where potential information is contained in hospital waste. Failed or unconsummated efforts to hold back the burgeoning mounds of records simply have to be accepted.

Enforcement of strictly correct archiving procedures has, of course, no bearing on the impasse. Evidently the hope is to return and reorganise and compactify the records. But this is a forlorn hope; piles of new matter are being added to rooms far further in, new material is being pushed into rooms already full.

It should be pointed out that doors occur in neat, rows, equally spaced. This is indeed misleading, they do not correspond to the space beyond. Possibly a closet sharing adjacent doors may be found; or at the other extreme, a long, dimly-lit room going back indefinitely far into which all the nearby doors open.

A near room reaches far, far back, who knows, perhaps all the way back to the entrance. Skipping a door, I find a far side room which reaches ahead into the distance. Therefore the room sandwiched between them must have its own, and just its own door. This looks like the perfect opportunity or me, what more could a man ask for, this is tailor made to my requirements I joke to myself, I almost burst out laughing, nearly every entrance is virtually identical to all the others. Boom! Brazenly I bang open the door. Oh no! I am confused, I am doubly confused. It's occupied! Against all odds, I've disturbed someone else. And worse than that, it appears to be a husband and wife team. We engage in conversation, I apologise for barging in. All right they are not married, Priscilla is his girlfriend, now he pushes her into the corridor.

'Fred's the name. Yes. Look, you've got the place to yourself, we are just leaving.'

'Are you sure?'

'For sure. As a matter of fact, we've got to deal with a small domestic emergency… immediately.'

'Well, Fred, er, can I help?' This notion causes him great amusement.

'Thanks. No need.' He is at the door, now even closing it for me. Raised voices, footsteps soon fall to nothing. Silence clamps around me.

What! The seedy light reveals that the two of them have left behind their notes. Without touching the papers, I approach slowly, closely to get a clear view. It's just possible to read what they have been jotting down. Incredible! How could they too have been seeking almost the very definition of my own enquiries? It is a duty to myself to determine exactly what they happen to have found. Once more, how the mind flashes into action. This is tantamount to a crime scene. Don't touch. Somehow accusations of eavesdropping have to be circumvented. Hardly able to cope with this new complication, I hear voices, footsteps, getting louder. There's a polite but panicky knocking on the dull brown door. Without waiting, the door bangs open.

'Oh! There's the stuff...!' Fred pounces. '...I'm so sorry...' He has snatched the notes, stuffing them into a bag. '...please don't report us for intruding.'

'All right, sir. This time I won't...' Hardly able to hold back more laughter, I add, '...But don't let it happen again.'

'Thanks, mate!' They shut the door and vanish in almost a single action.

In utter protest I jump up at the unendurable frustration of having Fred's notes, certainly the critical documents, ripped from under my nose. With one foot I stamp thunderously on the floorboards, gather my things, leave by the door and forget all about, completely write off my own personal enquiry.

Even with the dome on, there is the sense that this place will be difficult to get out of. Then it occurs to me that, this far into the archive, it won't make much difference if I take it off. So, after removing the headset things look much the same and I soon forget about it.

Insufficient lighting is hardly a drawback, it is almost an encouragement to investigate further. The search for reinforcement of the developing, forming picture among the traces of evidence which happen to be available becomes obsessive. After all, there is neither rhyme nor reason to what it is that is chosen by the authorities for preservation. To find just a hint of what one is after is a great victory.

In one of the larger rooms, at the early stages near to the central corridor and other entrances, repeated inroads have been made to tidy up the contents. But further in these are swamped by mountains of unsorted detail, which obviously presents the wardens of the archive with a confusing choice. To get on with coarse tidying, or to cover up earlier, failed attempts? Thus do I discover evidence of far-fetched, abandoned government schemes for dealing with what its colossal but limited resources were up against: regional incineration command, office of testing recruit performance, bureau of automated jettisoning, department of mechanised compactification. Such designations give a false impression of there being order, design, pattern within the Administration. The projects under each heading have been scrapped, while there are others that have been only partly got rid of.

Being placed in a world of corridors is itself interesting; this is an archive built of intersections of corridors, staircases, junctions, right angles. A world to myself by the way. But thinking it is getting time to find my way back, a notebook falls into my hands, written by an archivist who has travelled much further into the finer galleries. I become alarmed because it looks as if the author may have gone missing, and that this journal has been found and brought back by someone else. It is prefaced with a warning not to attempt to get to a particular area by the route described.

**

On the one hand there is the organic, metabolic, living being, the person. While on the other there is the inorganic, preemptive, invincible rampart. The latter entity precedes, and is therefore out of reach, of all analysis. Driven by intolerable curiosity, the explorer strives to bring these two into close proximity, if not to actually slam them together.

Such research is not to be classed with for example rock-climbing, dirt-track racing, boxing, stuntman-work. In every such case, skill may prove inadequate, luck may run out, resulting in permanent injury or death. And if a healthy outcome is excluded, if the intention is to commit suicide, it would surely be easier to swallow a tea-pot full of aspirins.

No. Danger is to be avoided, yet these investigations should be viewed as prospecting on the far side of mere danger. The findings are liable to imprint on the consciousness an irremovable, indestructible certainty as to the constitution of the world.

So where does the law, the mysterious law, fit in to all this? Backed by prisons and in some places by barbaric executions, the law is capable of sustaining heinous injustices, all within its massive, ubiquitous dispensation in all walks of life. This can be accounted for in only one possible way: in the course of time, over years, generations, centuries, millennia the ruling authority has been caught off guard, in its incessant battle with the relatively feeble forces of democracy, sexuality, intoxication. This is how the law has become incremented, while at every step, worldwide legislatures, assemblies, senates boast and exult at the mightiness of their accomplishment.

Bear in mind this is not an exposition; it is a warning: in light of the above, the first axiom of the law is the enforcement of the law. To "get on the wrong side of the law" is folly. That is, excepting legal professionals, within or without the courts, professionals whose job it is to dispense justice, thereby allaying the suffering of victims of injustice or crime. Making these clear, explicit exceptions, no sane person would ever wish to be even touched by the law. However, the invincible barrier of privacy is untraversable even by the long arm of the law. Privacy can be so effectively assured that an individual may plot, chart and conspire to bring about the downfall of an entire national government, taking the law with it.

So how does telephony enter into the discussion? Let us briefly branch onto the question of the stars of uranology. Only establishment physics disputes that the cosmos is infinite, while within this infinitude there are discovered and extensively documented "exo-planets" in orbit about many, if not all, of the staggeringly distant and numerous stars. Veering away now from astrometry and back to the land-line and the radiotelegraph, the key of course is infinity. The aggregate of all conceivable interstellar telecommunications may be understood by taking to the limit the presently well-understood world telephone network.

Every activation of every terminal on this grandiose network has to be recorded. The records are then stored, awaiting the day which may be long in coming, the day when they are given files containing every detail the authorities have been able to uncover, which in some way relates to the connection.

Provided that no part of the archive is damaged by annotation or vandalism, the researcher is free to enter and investigate at will. However, this individual will have to accept that the further in, the weaker will be the hegemony of his or her metabolism. The archives contain no toilets, no chocolate bar dispensers. The individual will have to keep careful track of his world line, as this has to be followed in reverse, in order to turn around and get out of the structure holding the annals and ledgers.

To have gained access is to be regarded as an achievement, there are many cases of pushing and shoving to get in. But this is only near the start. As already discussed, soon it becomes a rarity to encounter anyone else attempting to locate a record. And further in, virtually out of the question. Always each individual is aware that no matter how many stages of the great manifold of corridors he may have passed through, what lies ahead exceeds all of these stages put together.

Visitors have to get past well-practiced scrutineers before gaining access. The justifications for entering the vaults often become embarrassing, some prospective researchers even suddenly turn away, not to be seen again, rather than divulge the purpose of their research.

There have been instances of manic rages or of ecstatic outbursts from investigators who have failed, or who have at last succeeded. The electrical alarms are of dubious reliability, but should an alert find its way back to the front desk, then action has to be taken. Uniformed anti-sabotage personnel are faced with the task of flash lighting their way to the location of the disturbance, and if necessary arresting the incontinent researcher. In this case the offender, after being dragged to the main entrance might well be handed over to the bizarre Nanny-State Correction Service.

Such arrests are comparatively rare, but a morbid lust for excitement is prevalent among both uniformed and plain-clothes entrance staff. After hours, while relaxing in a nearby tavern, commissionaires will vie for being the one who relates the most memorable anecdote, particularly those cases where the offender has to be subdued. Some even complain that these days vandalism is not what it used to be. There is a general murmuring of agreement (although detailed logs kept by officers up to the rank of superintendent contradict this).

To highly-motivated students of the telephone termitary, the actual connections between terminals (or, in other words, the pair of connected telephone numbers) are of scant interest. And similarly in the case of the precise times of starts and the ends. No prizes are to be handed out for guessing the true motive: it is the actual content of the communication that is invariably of exclusive, paramount, even maniacal interest. Interception, eavesdropping – there are many terms for this activity.

There have been cases, many such, of users who have given convincing reasons for deserving entry but where the draughty, unfathomable reaches of the manifolds have provided almost impenetrable privacy, to be used to hide some other activity. Instances where the user has no intention of deriving something of value from examining the records. Cases where the user gets overwhelming sexual gratification from listening to two (or perhaps more than two) subscribers discussing intimate matters. Examples where the user is compelled to indulge in masturbation, followed by disgusting ejaculation over fittings owned and controlled by the authority.

It is the incongruous, vibrating activity of this kind of user which trips the detectors. Zealous guards have been known to reach the location in the manifold so quickly that they have to awaken the user, who is to be found fast asleep and slumped over the carrel desk. After the name is recorded, it is a sight to behold: the so-called researcher is physically ejected from the main porch. Thus it is that the cleaners are directed to the site of the slimy mess. Usually no more than absorbent paper rolls, rubber gardening gloves and bulky anti-bacterial trigger-siphons are sufficient to restore the carrel to freshness.

But is this the only deviation from normal behaviour to be encountered by those who have to enforce the law? Of course not. From time to time alcoholics, even meth drinkers find their way in. After successfully presenting a bogus route map request, a drinker will arrive with a concealed bottle and a glass tumbler, set down the items on the study cell table and proceed to get very drunk. The bottle could even contain schnapps, Polish white spirit, containing more alcohol than water. Very far into the archive, the "user" will get away with making loud, insulting noises. Every time his moods show signs of abating, he will take another sip, indeed another larger sip, it is the beverage which shields him from sword-swallowing sensations.

The bottle could run out. Or before that he might simply collapse, loudly snoring. However the illicit, one-man party ends, hours must pass. Eventually, he will come round, grappling with the chair, the desk, the door. The dull pinkish-brown décor forcefully asserts itself. At first he tries violence, only bruising his knuckles. All around is total, utter confusion. The student of cyber-space has to spend a whole day wandering, re-orienting himself before finding the correct route back to the front desk. Somehow he slips out to the street without anyone smelling his breath.

CHAPTER 11

The oceanic room, the climax of Ch11, has a dual. Namely a corner at which the ocean occupies three parts, instead of only one as just encountered.

Perfectly transparent, the water shows blue-green increasingly with depth, and colour is somehow trapped or made visible within the waves. Saline, ozonic – the air is startlingly fresh. Inhaling it deeply is like holding on to a handrail for dear life. There are hydra, jellyfish, sea anemones, corals.

Furthermore, occasionally there are flights of steps that hug the marble sea-wall, descending into the water. Chained to one of these flights, and riding on the swell, is a small boat. It contains an oar, and is large enough for me. It appears to have been inlaid with mother-of-pearl, and lacquered. Carefully descending by the waterside staircase, I climb in and release the boat. I row it around, passing far enough away from the colonnaded wall to view the inlaid gilt metal work of the sea-wall beneath the plinths. By now there is an awesome view of the wall through which... I... entered, of its ever increasing colonnade, of its vaulting canopies. Some shells rest on the keel. They remind me of the pebbles. Unhurriedly rowing, I return, hitching the bronze chain of the boat to its mooring. Shaking water off the oar, I replace it.

Preoccupied with the decoration of the columns to my left, it is only after they have become sizeable that I notice flights of cormorants sweeping between them. A dark, long-necked form retro-thrusts onto a ledge. Wind, stronger this far out, snatches at the feathers, at the neck, on one wing. The bird remains impassive, contemplating the ocean.

There is a definite blueing of the overall blue-green transparency. Now there are accesses of deep colour, pure blue, almost black. Rising against the ocean shelf are banks of coral.

CHAPTER 12

Through a wide doorway can be seen an illuminated passage. From this, via a central staircase, I descend into a gallery filled with oil paintings. A few are very large, all in magnificent ormolu frames. My faint shadow hovers over as the canvasses reveal a common subject: each depicts a machine. Who are the artists? One is a careful study of a huge marine engine, as dynamic as a murder scene, executed by Picasso's double. Another canvas is entitled Franz Kafka on a Touring Motorbike. The large, battered machine appears to have been specially braced for rough terrain. Kafka sits astride the bike, the velvet blackness of space around his countenance. A series of canvases entitled *Reality Exceeded* depicts texture and movement in rudimentary, virile scenes; one scene portrays a distant combine harvester. Each bears the name Vincent.

Tearing myself away from the exhibits, and taking the far entrance to the gallery, I become aware of an extraordinary enormity reaching far below this level. Here, the reader will recall an encounter with a single machine as big as a city.

***

Prior to taking a passage to the library of the closure of all knowledge, a vestibule largely in darkness has to be entered. A shadowy form at the centre of the hall is noticeable, inescapable; brick-shaped, it rises to several times my own height. After catching the outline, I reckon it some kind of occasional piece or flourish in the hall. Mounted transversely, this is perhaps an early computer. Just inside the hand-rail, is a row of switches. I push each of these, at first they snap without effect: but very soon there is the staccato chaos of strip lights warming up. Thus are revealed in the four directions brightly-lit corridors, leading away from what is indeed a dinosaur, a huge valve computer. After completing a circuit then leaving the diode mountain, I walk to the library passage. Books are now in evidence.

***

In order to enter the great reading-hall of the unimaginably vast library, I follow a passage straight ahead. Here I pass shelves containing various bound volumes. These are not in locked glass cabinets, the books are removable, free to be taken out and used or examined. It is here that a trial of strength between vying mysteries, profound mysteries, is to be conducted, with as it turns out, a laughably inconclusive climax.

The question of coincidence is no less unplumbable than that of ambiguity. Coincidences can be camouflaged as ambiguities; ambiguities can be interpreted as coincidences. In either case, one may be used to cause the other to vanish. In cases where all warnings have been ignored, incautious dependence on analysis can bring about an unstoppable fall into a bottomless well of mirrors, where endlessly back and forth one is reflected into the other.

Occupying a lower shelf in the passage is a sequence of tomes, uniform in size and binding. Owing to the curvature of the spines, on them I can see embossed gilt lettering. But the book or manuscript at the end of the sequence is damaged: the spine, correctly in place in the upper and middle parts, is detached from the covers of the book near the base. There, the spine has risen by a few millimetres so that a needle-chink of background is enclosed by it. The chink guides the eye up to the irregular tip, to the apex of disappearance. Now I notice a small tear in the middle of the binding. At once the spine detaches itself further from the hard covers: the detached part jumps outwards slightly. A particle of dried gum, embedding several woven threads, drops to the ground, trailing gently settling dust.

I set out towards the rack containing the damaged volume. Between banks of shelves are statues in polished onyx chalcedony; the females wear jewellery, affected by gems set in the stone. Nearer the ceiling are various framed paintings. One shows a figure holding in the right hand an open book, yet staring over it into a mantelpiece mirror. The figure all but obscures the book, holding it between himself and the mirror. But in the reflection, the image can be seen clasping the book, the volume supported behind by three middle fingers and therefore wedged open with the thumb and little finger around the base of the spine. The eyes of the part-turned head of the image gaze into those of the figure.

Limpid brushstroke furrows, set long ago in the paint, become visible within a gleaming area of reflected light.

The gleam is brighter than the remainder of the painting. At one place, as I walk past, it moves over the head and shoulders of the figure, causing this area to become an enamel diagram set opposite the still-detailed and coloured region depicting the reflection.

Moving up to the worn volume, I pull it out. The binding creaks as it opens. What a predictable coincidence! It could not be on a more engrossing subject. How could such a text have fallen into my hands by chance? And at a time when other business has priority. After a nominal shuffle through, I firmly shut the book and dutifully return it to the end of the shelf.

For me, reality is tilted downhill. It's over; the visitor is inexorably slipping away from it all. My encounter with this world has passed its climax, is drawing to its end. Beyond the hill, now I am taking the easy downslope, a process over which I have not the least control. This is the final opportunity to savour a different reality; there is room for no more than one thought: may I return!

People here have moved close, even very close, in different ways. Memories, imageries, reveries flood forth. So real it is hard to disbelieve they are no more than that. It is as if, for one more time, the conscious figures join me:

***

…Again Aza's countenance shines, as from a medallion or banknote. In her presence, there was a feeling of being entrusted with the fragile embodiment of irreplaceable knowledge, ancient juridical authority. Surely by shouting loud enough you could kill her! Frail fingers close repeatedly around a jewel at her neck.

'It is possible you may come... here... again!'

'Certainly hope so. As perhaps you know, this isn't the first time. Well, anyway, I was planning to sort of come on a regular basis!'

'You are right; I know you've been here before.'

Uhh! Stifling the urge to enquire how, instead I ask, 'If I do come back, will we meet again?'

But all she says is, 'If you do, that will imply many things... You may come with others... But in any case, it is possible you may be unable to return!'

***

During our long descent the sculptor pressed me for details about an empty room, into which the Sun shone from below. But later on the way up from the maze, Zirco returned to this. He touched his head absently, as if pausing before rendering a drawing.

'I know the room you mentioned. In fact, it is possible to get up onto the roof. This gives an unobstructed view of the upper sky, actually opposite the Sun!'

'It was amazing enough from where I was! Can you see anything different from up there?'

'It is much as you described. As you look upwards, there is, of course, the gradual change in colour, from pale to deep blue tinged with mauve and purple. But around the region of sky opposed to the disc of the Sun...' He draws in his belly, tightens his sash. '...There you'll find a dark, unfathomable pool of violet!'